National Institute of Economic and Social
  Research
Policy Studies Institute
Royal Institute of International Affairs

Joint Studies in Public Policy 6

Slower Growth in the Western World

National Institute of Economic and Social
   Research
Policy Studies Institute
Royal Institute of International Affairs

Joint Studies in Public Policy

STEERING COMMITTEE

National Institute of Economic and Social
   Research
Policy Studies Institute
Royal Institute of International Affairs

Joint Studies in Public Policy 6

Slower Growth in the Western World

Edited by
R. C. O. Matthews

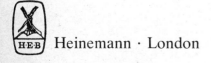 Heinemann · London

Heinemann Educational Books Ltd
22 Bedford Square, London WC1B 3HH
LONDON   EDINBURGH   MELBOURNE   AUCKLAND
HONG KONG   SINGAPORE   KUALA LUMPUR   NEW DELHI
IBADAN   NAIROBI   JOHANNESBURG
EXETER (NH)   KINGSTON   PORT OF SPAIN

ISBN 0-435-84515 2 (cased)
ISBN 0-435-84516 0 (paper)

Acknowledgement

The Steering Committee gratefully acknowledge the support of the Social Science Research Council which financed the conference and the research and editorial work involved in the preparation of this book.

Typeset by Inforum Ltd, Portsmouth
and printed by Biddles Ltd, Guildford, Surrey

Contents

Contributors and Participants

Contributors

Professor A.J. Brown, Consultant, National Institute of Economic
and Social Research

Professor M. Bruno, The Hebrew University of Jerusalem

Dr Victoria Curzon Price, International Management Institute,
Geneva and Chargée de Cours, Graduate Institute of European
Studies, University of Geneva

W.A. Eltis, Exeter College, Oxford

Charles Feinstein, Professor of Economic History, University of
York

J.S. Flemming, Bank of England

Andrew Glyn, Institute of Economics and Statistics, Oxford

Richard Jackman, London School of Economics and Political
Science

Robin Marris, Professor of Economics, Birkbeck College, London

Professor R.C.O. Matthews, Master, Clare College, Cambridge
(Chairman)

Mrs A.D. Morgan, Senior Research Officer, National Institute of
Economic and Social Research

David A. Peel, University of Liverpool

Professor S.J. Prais, Senior Research Fellow, National Institute of
Economic and Social Research

J.R. Sargent, Group Economic Adviser, Midland Bank plc

Maurice Scott, Nuffield College, Oxford

G.D.N. Worswick, Director, National Institute of Economic and
Social Research

Other Participants

A. Britton	A. Kilpatrick
T. Burns	D.E. Lea
D. Glynn	A.N. Ridley
Professor C.M. Kennedy	D. Stanton
Professor K.A. Kennedy	Mrs G. Wenban-Smith

1 Introduction: A Summary View
R.C.O. Matthews*

This book deals with a major feature of slow growth in the west: the slow-down since 1973 in the rate of growth of labour productivity. The chief features of that slow-down were these:

(i) It was common to almost all advanced countries. It was most severe in Japan, where there was a slow-down of 5–6 percentage points in the rate of growth of productivity in 1973–9 compared with 1960–73. On most measures the slow-down was rather less severe in the US (1–2 per cent) than in Europe (upwards of 2 per cent). In some European countries, notably Sweden and Italy and also the UK if North Sea oil is excluded, it was significantly greater than the European average, though not as great as in Japan.

(ii) There was no general tendency to a productivity slow-down before 1973. In 1974 and 1975 the rate of productivity growth fell steeply, down to near zero or below in many countries. It was this that was responsible for the slowness of productivity growth over the peak-to-peak period 1973–9 as a whole. Between 1975 and 1979, productivity growth was fair, but it was not sufficient to make good the ground lost between 1973 and 1975. However any thought that the slow-down might have been no more than a once-for-all downward step in output, possibly reflecting measurement bias in the abnormal years 1974 and 1975, was dispelled by a renewed retardation after 1979. The UK was alone in showing a rise in productivity growth in the year 1981.

(iii) A productivity slow-down of such magnitude and duration has few if any precedents in earlier history, except for periods involving major wars. However, in most though not all European countries, the rate of growth of productivity after the slow-down still compared fairly well with the period before the Second

* In this review I have drawn freely, and usually without acknowledgement, on points made during discussion at the conference. I also had the benefit of seeing advance copies of three substantial papers, by Edward Denison [2], Herbert Giersch and Frank Wolter [4], and Assar Lindbeck [6], prepared for the Royal Economic Society's annual conference in July 1982 and forthcoming in the *Economic Journal*, March 1983.

World War. This was not true in the US, where productivity growth virtually stopped; though the slow-down there was of less than average severity, the speed-up after the Second World War had been much less than elsewhere.

(iv) The slow-down was not dominated by a few sectors, nor did it owe much to shifts in weights between sectors. It occurred in most sectors. Countries differed in the sectors worst affected. In general the slow-down was at least as marked in non-manufacturing as in manufacturing.

(v) In all countries the slow-down in productivity was due to a slow-down in output rather than to a speed-up in numbers employed. The US was unusual in having *some* speed-up in employment. In the great majority of other countries, there was a slow-down in employment as well as in productivity.

The problem of the slow-down is quite different from the much studied problem of why countries differed from one another in their growth rates in the 1950s and 1960s (and earlier). The slow-down affected all countries, while leaving largely unchanged their ranking both in the growth rate of productivity and in its level. Moreover the slow-down coincided with stagflation, that is, rising unemployment and rising inflation, in a way that is most unlikely to have been accidental, whereas the long-standing problem of international differences in growth rates did not have much to do with unemployment or inflation. Ideally, we need an explanation that embraces all the aspects of stagflation, including the productivity slow-down, doubtless with multi-directional causation. There exists an enormous literature about stagflation, but most of it does not help much, because it is usually written within a theoretical framework (whether Keynesian or monetarist) that does not purport to deal with what determines the rate of growth in the long run.

Measurement Bias?
Before seeking possible explanations, it is wise to ask whether the whole thing was just a statistical illusion. Possible sources of bias include: index-number problems of the Laspeyres-Paasche type associated with the change in the movement of import prices relative to ths price of value-added; increased shading of list prices on account of the recession; growth of the black economy (which affects the measurement of inputs as well as output, but not necessarily to the same extent, hence perhaps causing bias in measures of productivity as well as of output); variations in quality; and straight statistical error, particularly in years of violent inflation. Some tendency for the

slow-down to be exaggerated by index number bias is generally acknowledged. Certainly there is, too, reason to be suspicious of margins of a few per cent in statistics for a period when inflation sometimes exceeded 25 per cent and when unrecorded output was thought to constitute a quarter or more of GDP in some countries. The consensus is, however, that the greater part of the slow-down survives even the maximum possible allowance for statistical bias.

Demand

The role of demand-side causes, as opposed to supply-side causes, is a central issue in the explanation of the slow-down in productivity, just as it is in the explanation of the accompanying trend rise in unemployment. It also leads on to most of the other issues.

There was fairly general consensus at the conference that demand deficiency bore an important part of the responsibility for the slow-down, and a good many participants held that its responsibility was the paramount one. This was notwithstanding Denison's well known contrary view in regard to the US. Denison's chosen measure of demand intensity, based on factor shares, is debatable, as he would himself admit, and it does not encompass all that other economists have meant by that concept.

Belief that demand was, as a matter of history, a major cause of the slow-down, does not necessarily imply that crude injection of demand now would cure all the problems. Demand deficiency did not occur just as a random shock: there were reasons for it, and those reasons – inflationary or structural or whatever – might just reassert themselves.

'Demand' in the present context is not unambiguous. It may refer to the level of demand relative to productive potential ($q/\bar{q}$), which raises an obvious difficulty about defining productive potential. Or it may refer to the rate of growth of demand, as measured by the rate of growth of output ($\dot{q}$), of absorption or similar measures – which raises identification problems, since an *exogenous* slow-down in productivity could lead to a slow-down in output and absorption. These two concepts ($q/\bar{q}$ and $\dot{q}$) are very different. Moreover reference to the *volume* of demand seems to imply vertical demand curves – how does it accommodate the case of products for which there *is* a demand but only at a price that makes a loss?

Despite these theoretical difficulties, it is undeniable that firms after 1973 in general felt demand to be more of a constraint on output than it had formerly been. Moreover, whatever else may have affected demand and output, it is also undeniable that governments, to a greater extent after 1973 than before, consciously restricted demand in order to restrain inflation and that this adversely affected output not only in their own countries but also in countries linked to them through international trade.

Granted that output was affected by lack of demand, why should productivity have been affected?

As far as the short run is concerned, the reason is familiar: Okun's Law. I shall use that term in a broad sense, to mean the proposition that the short-term output-elasticity of employment is substantially less than unity. (As originally stated by Arthur Okun, it was a more specific rule of thumb about the relationship between output and *un*employment in the US during a particular period). The length, in years, of the short run in this connection is an important question which I shall take up in the next section.

In the longer run, the reasons are those commonly described under the heading Verdoorn's Law, and mainly relate to $\dot{q}$ rather than $q/\bar{q}$: slow-growing demand discourages investment, innovation and structural change. How demand affects the rate of structural change is a matter that has been debated. This is not surprising, because structural change has two components, a relative decline of activity A and a relative expansion of activity B. Low demand stimulates the (absolute) decline of A but it discourages the (absolute) expansion of B; so there is an ambivalence. Worswick, however, quotes evidence that the slow-growing 1970s exhibited less structural change than the fast-growing 1960s, and this is the usual view about the net direction of the outcome (see Chapter 3).

Significance attaches to the variability of demand as well as to its level and growth rate. It is easy to see why productivity should have been adversely affected by the increase that occurred after 1973 in the size of fluctuations in demand and by the uncertainties and disappointments that resulted.

Okun's Law, Shake-out, and Rigidities

A fall in demand relative to the level for which a firm's capital stock and labour force are appropriate would not depress productivity if labour were immediately laid off to a fully corresponding extent. Indeed, it might well raise productivity, as the least efficient firms and plants bore the brunt of the cut-back (vintage-based diminishing returns). The reasons why this does not normally happen in cyclical recessions are partly that, with a given organisation of production, some labour has an overhead character and partly that costs of hiring and firing make it worthwhile for a firm to hold on to underemployed labour so long as there is a prospect of a recovery. The strength and duration of these influences, and the consequent effects on productivity, depend on a complicated set of considerations: the magnitude of the fall in demand; the extent to which it is concentrated on particular industries and firms; the scope for cutting down overtime or shift-working; the size of the hiring-and-firing costs; the financial strength of the firms affected; the degree of optimism or pessimism about the prospects of recovery. It is therefore not surprising that the output–employment relationship turns out to vary between countries and periods. It is interesting to note in this connection that, in manufacturing, differences between European countries in the extent of the productivity slow-down owed much more to differences in the extent of employment slow-down than to differences in the extent of output slow-down (see Chapter 6, table 6.1). Thus the slow-down in employment was relatively great in Germany, with its particular flexibility in employment of guest workers, and relatively small in Sweden and Italy, with their particularly tight employment protection arrangements.

It is to be expected that as time goes on, more of the effect of a fall in demand will be felt in employment and less in productivity. Big reductions in employment – shake-outs – will occur when production has been rearranged, when firms run out of money, or 'when hope dies' (Arthur Brown's expression). The fall in employment and the belated rise in productivity in the UK in 1981 are no doubt largely to be explained in these terms – a phenomenon unique, so far, to the UK, perhaps because other countries have not experienced such a prolonged absolute fall in output.

Can the productivity slow-down be explained mainly in terms of the unexpectedly long persistence of Okun's Law in face of depressed demand? The output–employment relationships observed earlier in the post-war period would not have predicted such a prolonged slow-down in productivity. This may not be too significant, however, since relationships estimated from earlier postwar data may not have very much of use to tell us about the consequences of such an unprecedently deep and prolonged slow-down in output. Linearity and constant lag patterns can certainly not be assumed, and it must remain open to doubt whether or not the *underlying* output–employment relationships have changed compared with, say, twenty years ago. However, there is little doubt that they have changed compared with the days before the Second World War, when, at least in the UK, there was little sign of Okun's Law ([8], pp. 295–6, 322). This is one part of the often mentioned argument about increasing rigidities. Job protection legislation and protection and subsidies to industries and firms in the greatest difficulties may well have diminished and delayed the adjustment of employment to output and so contributed to bringing about a greater slow-down in productivity than in earlier severe recessions.

However, it is difficult to explain the whole of the productivity slow-down in this way, especially since it was by no means confined to countries and sectors where output fell absolutely. Okun's Law (or its equivalent) is admittedly not confined to absolute falls in output; it can apply wherever demand falls below the level that the firm is capable of producing, and that level may well go on rising during a recession, as a result of technical progress or earlier investment. None the less, one would expect Okun's Law to be less relevant to a mere slow-down in the rate of growth of output than to an absolute fall. Hence the effects of demand on productivity found in such econometric estimates as Bruno's are likely to have become increasingly of the Verdoorn variety, rather than the Okun variety, as the 1970s advanced. Renewed Okun-effects will, however, have been brought about by the further recession after 1979.

Profitability
Low demand and low profitability are closely related and difficult to separate, both in their causes and in their effects. On the side of causes, slumps have always been associated with a fall in profits' share: complaints that wages are too high have been a regular refrain in every major slump in the last 150 years. On the side of effects, low demand and low profitability alike depress output and investment and discourage growth of new innovatory firms. However, it has often been argued that the downward trend in profitability – already apparent in many, though not all, countries before 1973 – had causes other than low demand and therefore ranks as an independent element in the situation [7]. Possible such causes are: (i) exhaustion of labour surplus; (ii) increased labour militancy, supported *de facto* in its effects on profitability by governments through price controls; (iii) increased international competition, impinging disproportionately on profits, partly because they are quasi-rents and partly because of real wage resistance; (iv) the oil price rise, which, again largely because of real wage resistance, was in effect a tax on profits; (v) previous overshooting in capital accumulation; (vi) inflation, either through inadequate indexation of taxes on profits [3] or through a combination of monetary accommodation and money illusion, which temporarily, but only temporarily, lowered real interest rates [4].

The effects of most of these are discussed separately below. The most important way in which the fall in profitability may have impinged on productivity growth is through capital investment, to which I now turn.

Capital Investment
Any slow-down in output, whatever its cause, is likely to lead to a

slow-down in capital accumulation. The latter will then serve as a reinforcer. Its role may become more central if there are other forces, independent of the slow-down in output, tending to inhibit its amount or reduce its yield.

One possible such cause is a decline in the propensity to save. This was a good deal discussed at the conference, as it has been elsewhere. There is dispute about the right way to characterise savings trends in the 1970s. However, as the supply of finance was manifestly not the main obstacle to investment in most countries during that period, this dispute does not seem to me worth pursuing.

More interesting, in my opinion, is the line of argument advanced, in somewhat different language, by Sargent in Chapter 5 and by Glyn in Chapter 9. It runs as follows. The 1950s and 1960s were characterised, like earlier booms, by an unusually rapid rise in investment, more rapid than the rise in GDP. This was artificially prolonged by the tendency of governments to grant increasingly large subsidies to investment. The result was exhaustion of the best investment opportunities, a decline in the marginal efficiency of investment and a fall off in the rate at which the capital stock was increased. Evidence of declining marginal efficiency of capital can be found in the widespread tendency, especially from the late 1960s, for the capital–output ratio to rise and for profits' share and the profit rate to fall. The process affected the rate of growth of labour productivity in two ways: declining marginal efficiency reduced the benefit derived from a unit of investment; and the volume of investment was, presently, reduced. The downward pressure on the rate of profit in a given country arose not only from its own capital accumulation, but also from capital accumulation in its competitors, including newly industrialised countries (NICs).

I believe that there is something in this and that the 1950s and 1960s did have non-maintainable features on the side of capital accumulation. How much of the productivity slow-down this explains is another matter. Its contribution to the slow-down, according to conventional growth accounting, can be calculated for manufacturing from Sargent's table 5.1, taking into account both the change in the rate of growth of K/L and the change in profits' share (Bruno's table 6.6 takes into account only the former). On this reckoning capital's contribution accounted for over half of the slow-down in Japanese manufacturing productivity and it actually over-explained the small slow-down in Germany. It does not explain much of the UK slow-down and it has the wrong sign for France and the US.

This is a mixed score. It might be different if we had figures for the whole economy, not just manufacturing. Moreover the growth accounting measure of capital's accumulation can be criticised for many reasons. Scott makes some radical criticisms of it, based on a model analogous to Arrow's learning model, but there is plenty of room for questions even at a less fundamental level. The use of a vintage model does not, it is true, make as much difference as is often supposed [2]. But the marginal return from capital may have held up better (or worse) than its average return, as measured by the profit rate; the fall in the profit rate may have been partly or wholly due to forces, like some of those enumerated in the previous section, that reflected changes in the degree of monopoly or monopsony rather than changes in the marginal physical efficiency of investment; investment may have externalities; the existence of subsidies may lead to overstatement of the social return from investment and *increases* in subsidies may lead to understatement of the *decline* in its social return. Given such complications, an undisputed measure would be too much to expect.

However, the supply-side effect of the fall in the rate of gross investment itself was not quantitatively large enough to explain much of the slow-down, except in Germany and Japan. A decline in the quality of the investment has to be invoked, whether due to capital saturation or inappropriately allocated subsidies or to other causes. Insofar as there was such a decline, it took place notwithstanding a shift of investment away from long-lived buildings (capital-widening) towards less long-lived equipment (capital-deepening), which would by itself tend to increase the flow of capital services per unit of investment and so increase its measured effect on output.

The Sargent-Glyn hypothesis is interesting in that it views the slow-down as having an essentially *cyclical* character, rather than as the consequence of shocks. Some cyclical elements are also present in the hypothesis to be discussed next.

Oil and Other Raw Material Prices

Most economists agree that the oil price rises of 1973–4 and 1979–80 had important adverse effects on real demand, both directly and by strengthening inflation and so leading to restrictive actions by governments. Insofar as demand was responsible for the productivity slow-down, the oil price rise was thus an important constituent.

Bruno and Sachs have been prominent in drawing attention to the possible ill effects of the oil price rise through a different channel, on the supply side. This idea is further investigated by Bruno in Chapter 6, perhaps the most substantial one in the volume. Bruno is now inclined to give more weight to demand and its interaction with supply as explanations of the general productivity slow-down, though he still holds that straight supply-side effects were important especially in manufacturing, it being more material-intensive than other sectors. Oil and other raw material prices fell relatively to other prices in the 1950s and 1960s and rose in the 1970s. It is the difference between the two periods that is relevant to the slow-down.

The effect of a rise in a raw material price on labour productivity has several aspects, the relative importance of which will depend on the shape of the production function. First, a rise in the price of oil and a reduction in its supply may be analogous to an adverse change in the environment of production, lowering the production function for any given combination of labour and capital. Secondly, an increased oil price may call for substitution in favour of products and methods of production that use less energy but more capital or labour per unit of output. Until this substitution has been made, some lines of production may become absolutely unprofitable and cease. (This, it may be noted, will affect production rather than productivity, apart from demand feedbacks.) Substitution will be delayed by the non-malleability of the capital stock – some of the existing capital stock may be made obsolete (this argument, associated with the name of Baily, could have been referred to above in the last section since it implies that conventional measures overstate the rate of growth of the capital stock, but I have preferred to include it here, since it does not relate to gross investment but to retirements).

This broad line of argument has a long background – a case in point is the time-honoured attribution of fast growth in the US in the nineteenth century to the abundance of its natural resources. Its quantitative importance, as applied to the oil price, has been a good deal disputed in the econometric literature, and no consensus has been established. At the level of casual empiricism, it is sometimes argued that obvious examples of the supposed energy-saving substitutions of labour and capital are not as numerous in industry as might be expected if their overall effect were really major. In some cases, however, the energy-saving may be concealed, because it is of a kind that would show up only from a full input–output table. An interesting example quoted at the conference was in brewing, where plans for centralised production, bringing important economies of scale, were rendered uneconomic by the oil price rise because of the increase it brought about in the transport component of distribution costs.

What *is* generally agreed, by Bruno as well as others, is that oil by itself is not a large enough element in costs in most industries for the alleged effect to be other than small. Other raw material costs must also be brought into the reckoning. These too rose after 1973 and have not (so far) fallen back to their previous level.

This raises important questions about ultimate causes. The OPEC price rises can be more or less convincingly regarded as exogenous shocks. The rises in the prices of other materials were, however, the response to high demand in the years immediately before 1973. If they had a (deferred) effect on industrial productivity, the process had a cyclical character – retribution for the excessive boom. (Why material prices did not fall all the way back when the recession came is a further question.)

Bruno suggests that a main source of the troubles may have been that the low level of demand, itself largely due to big rises in oil and other material prices, hampered the structural adjustments made necessary by the changes in relative prices themselves. This brings us back to the question of rigidities, already several times mentioned. Structural changes, at more or less fine levels of disaggregation, are a necessary feature of economic growth at all times, as a result of technical progress, the emergence of new competitors, and so on. Large changes in relative prices, as brought about by OPEC, must tend to increase the need for structural change, though it is a fair question for debate whether this is a large or a small increase relative to the changes that would have been needed anyway. These changes, it is held, have become more difficult to bring about, for a variety of reasons which are assigned different emphasis by different authors: the low level of demand; alterations in personal responses to change, reflecting the high income-elasticity of demand for 'security' in face of the rise in incomes in the 1950s and 1960s; and government interventions, themselves largely an expression through the ballot box of the same preference for security, perhaps without full appreciation of its costs. The importance of such *allocative* effects of government actions is emphasised by Curzon Price in Chapter 7.

Inflation

Attempts to find cross-country correlations between the rate of inflation and the rates of growth of output or productivity have yielded some interesting results, but nothing at all conclusive, as Brown explains in Chapter 4. Straightforward regression of the one on the other is in any case unlikely to constitute a structural relationship: the effect of inflation depends on what caused the inflation, and moreover some degree of reverse causation from low productivity growth to high inflation is extremely likely. However the fact that no obvious correlation is to be found between inflation and productivity growth is worth mentioning, if only to dispose of naive hypotheses.

Leaving aside the causes of inflation, what effect on productivity growth can be traced from inflation as such?

By far the most important effect, it seems to me, was the most obvious one: inflation led governments to adopt restrictive demand management policies which in turn inhibited productivity growth. To say this does not, of course, *necessarily* imply that those policies were mistaken. It is, however, interesting to note Bruno's observation that middle-income countries, which in general chose to accept very high rates of inflation in the 1970s, did not experience nearly as much slow-down as did the advanced countries.

It is commonly argued that rapid inflation must introduce 'noise' into the signals transmitted by the price system and so prejudice allocative efficiency. This seems reasonable enough in a general way – if even the accountants cannot agree on the right way to treat inflation, surely businessmen must sometimes be led into wrong decisions, including wrong investment decisions? But evidence of its actual importance is hard to come by, and the consensus of the conference was against setting much store by it. (The organisers had tried before the conference to recruit some contributor prepared to assert its importance on the basis of empirical research, but had failed to find one.) It was mentioned that the very high rate of inflation in Israel had led Israeli economists to investigate the question, and the only form of misallocation they could clearly trace was excessive absorption of resources by the financial sector. Signs of this are certainly apparent in other countries as well. This diversion of re-sources towards financial services is not primarily of the equilibrium type represented by 'shoe-leather' costs. It is, rather, a disequilibrium phenomenon, due to slow and imperfect adaptation of financial instruments and tax regulations to an inflationary world. Such a situation increases the return from financial operations and diverts resources and energies from production. This is a genuine cost, but its effect on measured productivity is difficult to assess.

Governments, as well as businesses, may sometimes have been misled by inflation or failed to adapt to it quickly enough. As is well known, the tax treatment of inventories came near to causing a major financial crisis in the UK in 1974, and it was changed only just in time. The need, in measuring the PSBR, to calculate interest payments in real rather than nominal terms is not a complicated idea and it is, of course, well understood by government economic advisers. It is possible, however, that it has not always been perfectly clear to Ministers themselves and to the popular supporters whose views they must take into account. Nor is it entirely a notional matter. Imperfect adaptation of debt investments presents governments, as well as borrowers, with a front-loading problem, and although this may seem rather a far cry from productivity, there may be a connection through the amount and direction of investment.

Finally, what about *uncertainty* regarding inflation? In fact, the standard deviation of price increase has not been closely connected with its average level. But that does not mean that people did not *feel* more uncertain or, for that matter, did not entertain expectations about inflation that proved wrong. This may have affected the quality of the investment decisions already taken in the early 1970s, particularly in the property boom, and those investments may as a consequence have had a poor return in measured output in the period after 1973.

All these are possible ways in which inflation may have prejudiced productivity growth. Undoubtedly they amounted to something. But the onus of proof is on those who would attribute high importance to them.

Catch-up

Most of the matters considered so far are connected in one way or another with stagflation and stabilisation policy. Catch-up, by contrast, is a hypothesis concerned exclusively with the production function.

It is a familiar idea, studied by Marris in earlier writings, that the scope for productivity growth depends on how far you are below the frontier represented by best practice – usually measured by US practice. The exceptionally high growth rates exhibited during most of the postwar period by Japan and Italy, and latterly by the NICs, provide telling evidence in support. So does the exceptional largeness of the slow-down in Japan and the relative smallness of the slow-down in the US.

An important novelty in Chapter 8 is that Marris takes as his explanatory variable not the shortfall below the US but the level at the beginning of each period of real income per head in each country, as measured by Kravis and collaborators. This brings the US itself within the scope of the hypothesis: the higher the level of income at the beginning of each period, the more difficult growth is likely to be.

An obvious objection to this specification, made by Feinstein in his Comment, is that although it correctly predicts a large proportion of the slow-down since 1973, including the slow-down in the US, it implies a tendency to steady deceleration through time, a tendency which has not actually been observed. It would have raised false alarms about a slow-down at any time since growth began. Nevertheless, it raises some interesting points.

Straightforward catch-up theory would predict that the productivity gap between the US and other countries would close steadily but at a declining rate. This is not what happened. The gap was closing much more rapidly in the 1950s and 1960s than in previous periods. Some further consideration must therefore be introduced. Still within the conceptual framework of the catch-up model, one could postulate that after the Second World War the facilities for international transfer of technology suddenly increased, say because of the more rapid growth of world trade or because of the activities of multinational companies or because of the removal of obstacles to transfer, formerly created by xenophobic governments. The opening of the floodgates to technological transfer might then cause catch-up to follow a logistic path, slowing down not only because the absolute level of productivity elsewhere had come near to that in the US, but also because the special impulses that started the logistic had exhausted their effect.

What about the US itself? Despite Marris's suggestion, we should not, I imagine, wish to subscribe to a model of progressive exhaustion of technological possibilities such as misled the stagnationists in the 1930s. Catch-up notions may, however, have relevance, in two distinct ways. In the first place, the US is a continent, whose states and regions differ as much as do the countries of north-west Europe; there has been scope for interregional catch-up, which may now have been largely exhausted. In the second place, attention needs to be given to the effect of catch-up on the country caught up with, as well as on the catchers-up. The effects of increasing competition, as American producers found more foreign rivals near to their own standards of efficiency, may have had some of the same adverse effects on US performance as have been thought to have been suffered by the UK in similar circumstances in the last quarter of the nineteenth century [1].

Any catch-up model, whether applied to the US or to other countries, has an obvious difficulty about timing. By itself, catch-up is bound to be a gradual process. It clearly needs to be supplemented by reference to some tripwire to explain the abruptness of the change in 1973. But there were plenty of tripwires about.

The possibility cannot be ruled out that the catch-up explanation of the slow-down is completely wrong: it may be that after present macro troubles have been overcome, Japan (if not continental Europe) will forge ahead and take over the leadership from the US, even as the US took over the leadership from the UK at the end of the nineteenth century. The cross-country pattern of slow-down is, however, broadly consistent with catch-up having played a significant part in it. It seems to me that there is scope for more research to test its quantitative importance, along the lines pioneered by Marris.

Conclusions on Causes

The foregoing review has been mostly non-quantitative. With so many feedbacks in the system, it is not surprising that econometric measures of the influence of this cause and that differ widely between authors. If we added together everyone's econometric estimate of the consequences of his favourite cause, the slow-down would be many times over-explained, rather than under-explained as it seemed to Denison (who brought to his enquiry no preconceptions other than methodological ones). Nor has the above review exhausted all the possible causes that have been suggested in this book or elsewhere – such as the breakdown of Bretton Woods, and the exhaustion of surplus labour in advanced countries accompanied by increased reluctance, for social reasons, to go on absorbing immigrants.

There are, however, some alleged causes that the evidence does enable us to exclude from any major role. Among these are changes in the age–sex composition of the labour force and changes in government's share in GDP. More important, perhaps, there is little reason to suppose that there has been a permanent slow-down in technical progress in the strict sense (though troubles may have arisen from changes in its nature (see Prais's Comment on Chapter 9)). Popular pessimism on this score seems to have little foundation and is indeed itself often expressed in inconsistent terms – we are condemned to permanent slow growth because technical progress has slowed down and we are condemned to permanent high unemployment because technical progress has speeded up.

The answer to the question why the slow-down occurred must depend in large measure on the answers given to two other great questions: why growth was so much faster in the 1950s and 1960s than earlier, and why inflation and unemployment became so much worse in the 1970s. Since there is no consensus on either of these, any explanation of the slow-down is bound to be tentative. However, in the broadest possible terms, the slow-down in productivity may perhaps be described as having arisen mainly from two elements.

(1) The 1950s and 1960s had many of the characteristics of a long cyclical boom. This could not persist indefinitely, whether because it contained the seeds of its own dissolution (through wage-inflation, diminishing returns from investment, or whatever) or else because it was vulnerable to shocks. The ending of the boom was bound to bring some slow-down.

(2) In addition, attitudes and institutions had become geared to boom conditions and continued to be after they had ceased. They were not such as to foster even the more moderate productivity growth that might otherwise have been continued in non-boom conditions. Inflation persisted, and governments found no way of dealing with it that did not make matters worse for the real economy; expectations had been generated of job stability, rapidly rising living standards, amenities and social provisions; and many businesses, having become accustomed to growth through general expansion, interrupted by no more than short and mild recessions, could think of only defensive ways of responding to the changed conditions.

To these were added two purely supply-side elements of an un-avoidable character, which were of more importance for some countries and some sectors than others: catch-up, and worse terms of access to raw material supplies.

All this is, of course, tremendously general. The qualifications to it are implicit in what I have said earlier. One further point may be made, however. Most of the research that has been done on the slow-down has related to the US. But the experience of the US was untypical in a number of ways: employment rose faster in 1973–9 than before; slow-down in the measured rate of growth of the capital stock was relatively small; profitability had not fallen off much in the years before 1973; the country was on the opposite end of the catch-up process from most; it had not experienced so much speed-up in the 1950s and 1960s; and the productivity slow-down itself was smaller than in most other countries, particularly, so it seems, in manufacturing, though it had already become perceptible before 1973. It may well be, therefore, that the relative importance of the various contributory causes of the slow-down was rather different in the US from elsewhere. Generalisations from its experience therefore require caution.

Prospects and Policies

Only an extreme optimist would expect the growth rates of the 1950s and 1960s to be regained in OECD countries as a whole in the foreseeable future. But there is nothing in this volume that would justify a belief that we have to go on doing as badly as we have done since 1973. The difficulties are mainly of our own making and should be capable of being overcome. The balance of evidence seems to me to point to the restoration, ultimately (in the late 1980s? in the 1990s?), of a growth rate nearer to that of the 1950s and 1960s than to that of the 1970s.

What can governments do to help bring that about? What was said in the last section points to two alternative directions for policy: to hurry up and bring about another boom, or to improve adaptation to a slump. Choice between them depends on one's views about stabilisation policy. The adoption of some micro measures (for example on the side of training) and the avoidance of some other micro measures may conduce to either end and are relatively uncontroversial. Macro measures are at the centre of debates reflected in this volume but peripheral to its main subject. The persistence of inflation during a slump does undoubtedly present a dilemma without historical precedent and the increased openness of the world economy does limit what can be done by individual national governments. It is difficult to believe, however, that the macro policies so far adopted represent the ultimate in wisdom.

The dangers of expecting too much or too little from the system have been well put by Arthur Lewis. One group of economists, he says, 'expect every recession to be over in eighteen months . . . The unfortunate consequence of this over-optimism is that measures to end the recession are underplayed . . . The other group are the children of the Apocalypse. Starting with Marx in 1848, every time there has been a recession critics have predicted the imminent arrival of Judgement Day. Capitalism will certainly pass away; all social and economic systems do. But its capacity to survive great shocks has been thoroughly demonstrated and has to be taken seriously by friend and foe alike' ([5], p. 233).

References
[1] Abramovitz, M., 'Welfare quandaries and productivity concerns', *American Economic Review*, March 1981.
[2] Denison, E.F., 'The interruption of productivity growth in the United States', forthcoming in *Economic Journal*, March 1983.
[3] Feldstein, M., 'Inflation and the stock market', *American Economic Review*, December 1980.
[4] Giersch, H. and Wolter, F., 'On the recent slowdown in productivity growth in advanced countries', forthcoming in *Economic Journal*, March 1983.
[5] Lewis, W.A., *Growth and Fluctuations 1870–1913*, London, Allen and Unwin, 1978.
[6] Lindbeck, A. 'The recent slowdown of productivity growth', forthcoming in *Economic Journal*, March 1983.
[7] Martin, W.E. (ed.), *The Economics of the Profits Crisis*, London, HMSO, 1981.
[8] Matthews, R.C.O., Feinstein, C.H., and Odling-Smee, J.C., *British Economic Growth 1856–1973*, Stanford, Calif., Stanford University Press, 1982.

2 Productivity in the 1960s and 1970s
Ann D. Morgan

In 1974, after twenty years or more of almost uninterrupted and unprecedentedly rapid expansion, there was a marked slow-down in the growth of the western industrial economies. Following the quadrupling of oil prices at the end of 1973, which in its effect coincided with a cyclical downturn, output stagnated or fell in most industrial countries and, though it rebounded in 1976, growth remained slow in comparison with the rate achieved in the 1960s. In 1979-80 there was a second massive rise in oil prices and once again growth in the industrial west slowed almost to a standstill. This unhappy experience has been accompanied by sharply rising unemployment, particularly in the last few years, and by a further acceleration in the rate of inflation. There has also been a fall in the average rate of increase in 'productivity' or, more precisely, of output per person employed. So much is common knowledge. But as to the essential origins of the decline in the rate of productivity growth and its nature – whether it is a comparatively short-term reaction to changes in the world economy or involves a clear break in the long-term trend of postwar productivity growth – there is no agreement.

Most of this book is concerned with possible explanations of the slow-down. This chapter, however, is intended simply to describe what has happened to output and labour productivity in five major industrial countries – France, Germany, Japan, the UK and the US. It examines the growth of output and of output per head from 1960 to 1981, in total and by broad economic sectors insofar as the data permit.

Some Problems in the Measurement of Productivity
Productivity is measured as a ratio of output to the inputs used in production. For the economy as a whole, productivity is calculated in relation to net output or value-added, that is the gross value of output less inputs of materials and services, and to the primary factors of production – labour, capital and, occasionally, land. Total output is thus usually represented by GDP. In sectoral analyses of producti-

vity, value-added may be a less appropriate measure since labour and/or capital may be substituted for materials and other inputs purchased from the rest of the economy and *vice versa*, particularly in periods of changing relative prices such as the 1970s. Instead productivity may be calculated in relation to gross output with material inputs specified as a factor of production. Clearly, the different measures will produce different results unless relative prices, of labour and capital as well as of material inputs, are stable.

Ideally, net output at constant prices is measured by the value of gross output deflated by an appropriate price index less the value of intermediate inputs deflated by their appropriate price index – hence the term double deflation. Few countries begin to approach this ideal in calculating GDP, because the necessary data are lacking, or are believed to be so unreliable that other, simpler, methods produce a more trustworthy result. Instead they use a variety of methods – deflated gross or net output values, physical output indicators and in extreme cases employment or deflated earnings. Provided that intermediate inputs are small in relation to gross output, as in many service industries, or that the ratio of net to gross output remains roughly constant, the use of deflated values is an adequate measure. If changes in the relative price of intermediate inputs induce changes in the ratio of net to gross output, as may have been the case during the 1970s, then it becomes increasingly inadequate.

Further, and this applies also to double deflation, during the 1970s the price indices used to deflate current output values may have become less reliable. In periods of rapid inflation, large and frequent price changes may not be fully reflected in price indices that cover a limited sample of goods. On the other hand, in periods of slack demand, firms may resort to price-cutting and discounts which are not fully reflected in indices based largely on list prices. There has been both rapid inflation and slack demand in the later 1970s. Measures of the value of investment at constant prices may also have become less reliable, involving as they do similar but more acute problems to the measurement of output. It is much more difficult to construct an adequate price index for disparate capital goods and to allow for quality changes that may be reflected in output prices than is the case with other goods.

It is also suspected that, because of the growth of the 'black economy', output is being less accurately measured now than was formerly the case. Theoretically, this does not affect the measurement of productivity, since inputs as well as outputs in the black economy are excluded from the calculation, but in practice it may have some significance. If, for example, a trader does not record his sales (and purchases) in full in order to reduce his tax liability but does give a true report of the numbers employed in his operation, output per head will be understated. Thus it is possible that errors of measurement have increased during recent years. Add to this the fact that initial estimates of GDP are based on incomplete information and may be substantially revised over a period of years, and it is plain that we cannot be confident that we are as well informed about the course of output in the 1970s as in the 1960s.

The use of physical indicators of output also increases uncertainty about the rate of growth. It has been argued that, for goods industries at least, estimates of changes in output based on physical quantities may be biased downwards, possibly because this method gives poorer coverage than does price deflation for goods where physical indicators of output are not available, and makes inadequate allowance for quality improvements. In international comparisons of growth rates, this is a matter of importance because some countries, notably the UK, rely much more heavily on physical indicators in calculating sectoral output than do others. Certainly a comparison of UK estimates of GDP growth made by different methods supports the view that the output measure tends to be biased downwards, and that the bias is becoming increasingly serious. From 1960 to 1973, GDP at factor cost grew by 3.1 per cent annually when measured by the expenditure method but by 2.8 per cent annually when measured by the output method, based largely on physical indicators. From 1973 to 1980 the corresponding figures were 1.0 and 0.6 per cent.

Comparisons of rates of growth over long periods of time and between countries where deflated values or physical indicators are used to measure output are at best imprecise; where employment is used as an indicator of output they may be entirely misleading and for purposes of productivity measurement meaningless. Our five representative countries use some measure of output for all the goods producing sectors and for two major service sectors – distribution and transport. For financial and related services, public administration, education, health and other personal services they rely heavily on employment indicators, supplemented by a ragbag of other methods. The rate of 'output' growth as calculated depends largely on the method employed to measure it; hence growth rates are not comparable between countries. They are in general low, particularly where a pure employment index has been used as the indicator. As these sectors have increased in importance in all countries, they have increasingly influenced the measured rate of GDP (and productivity) growth. Many recent productivity studies, and all American ones, sidestep this problem by considering growth in the business economy, rather than in GDP, though even this involves including some activities where output is not properly measured. It seems preferable to show estimates both for total output and for measured goods and services (all goods producing sectors, commerce and transport) so that the effect of the shift to these pure service sectors on the measurement of output and productivity can be shown.

There are at least as many problems in measuring labour inputs as in measuring output. In the present context two are perhaps particularly important. What definition of 'employment' should be used, and is the proper measure persons employed or the sum of hours worked by persons employed? I have used the most comprehensive definition of employment, that is total civilian employment including employers, self-employed, family workers and employees, since the ratio of the first three to employees varies over time and place. Employees alone, particularly in some sectors such as agriculture, do not measure changes in employment adequately. It would have been desirable to use labour hours rather than persons employed as the measure of labour input, especially since hours worked fluctuate cyclically, but since data on hours worked generally relate to some much smaller segment of the labour force than civilian employment, there is an awkward choice between comprehensiveness and precision. Outside manufacturing the effects of changes in working hours and in part-time employment are largely a matter of guesswork, at least over relatively short periods.

The existence of these difficulties should not be forgotten: the measurement of productivity is neither simple nor precise.

The Growth of Total Output and Labour Productivity

Table 2.1 shows annual average rates of growth in GDP and GDP per person employed for the high growth years 1960-73, for 1973-9 and for 1979-81. It also includes figures for 1967-73 which are probably more reliable than those covering 1960-73, and for two sub-periods during the 1970s – 1973-5, the years of recession, and 1975-9, the years of recovery. It should be noted that there is a cyclical movement in productivity growth which tends to rise rapidly in the early stages of an upswing and to grow progressively less rapidly (or even fall) in the downswing. The periods in table 2.1 do not coincide with cycles in the different countries. Measurement from peak to peak would show rather different rates of increase, but they would still show a similar pattern – a fall in the rate of growth of output and productivity during the 1970s.

The fall in the growth of output per person employed between 1960-73 and 1973-9 was most marked in Japan, where it was 5.5 percentage points. Elsewhere the slow-down ranged from 1.8 percentage points in France and the US to 1.6 in the UK and 1.2 in Germany. (If North Sea oil is excluded the fall in the UK was larger –

Table 2.1   Changes in GDP (Q) and GDP per person employed (Q/N)*: annual average increase per cent

	1960–73	of which: 1967–73	1973–9	of which: 1973–5	of which: 1975–9	1979–81
France						
Q	5.6	5.6	3.1	1.7	3.9	0.8[a]
Q/N	4.7[a]	4.7	2.9	1.9	3.4	1.1[a]
Germany						
Q	4.5	5.3	2.4	−0.6	4.0	0.8[a]
Q/N	4.4	4.8	3.2	2.1	3.7	0.8[a]
Japan						
Q	9.9	9.5	3.7	0.7	5.3	3.7[a]
Q/N	8.5	8.3	3.0	0.9	4.0	2.8[a]
UK						
Q	3.1	3.4	1.3[b]	−0.8	2.4	−1.5[b]
Q/N	2.8[a]	3.3	1.2	−0.7	2.2	2.1
US						
Q	4.1	3.6	2.7	−0.8	4.5	1.0
Q/N	2.2	1.4	0.4	−1.0	1.1	0.3

Sources: OECD National Accounts Statistics, OECD Labour Force Statistics, CSO National Income and Expenditure, CSO Economic Trends, US Dept of Commerce Survey of Current Business, NIESR estimates.

[a] Estimated or partly estimated.

[b] If oil and natural gas are excluded, it is estimated that GDP grew by 0.8 per cent annually from 1973 to 1979 and fell by 1.8 per cent annually from 1979 to 1981.

* GDP refers to GDP at constant market prices, employment to civilian employment.

more than 2 percentage points between 1960-73 and 1973-9.) It is apparent that in every case the slow-down was particularly severe in 1973-5 and that productivity growth recovered during the next four years though not to the rates previously achieved. During 1980 and 1981 productivity growth decelerated again, sharply in France and Germany where the rate fell below that achieved in the 1974-5 recession, but less markedly in Japan and the US. In the UK the average rate of productivity growth in 1979-81 was higher not only than in 1973-5 but also than for the whole of 1973-9. The average is, however, deceptive, masking a slight fall in 1980 and a rise of almost 5 per cent in 1981 when firms shed labour and productivity surged. In sum, the countries with most to lose – Japan, France and Germany, with the highest rates of productivity growth prior to 1973 – have lost most ground since then, the US, where productivity growth was already slowing down in the late 1960s and early 1970s, and Britain least.

Part of the explanation of the exceptionally large fall in the growth rate of Japanese productivity may arise from the nature of the Japanese labour market and the government's employment protection policies. Unemployment has risen, but only from 1.3 per cent of the labour force in 1973 to 2.1 per cent in 1979 and 2.2 per cent in 1981. Elsewhere the rise in unemployment has been greater, both absolutely and proportionately. By 1981 it ranged from 4.3 per cent in Germany to 11.4 per cent in Britain, where the growth of unemployment has accelerated particularly sharply since 1979. Trends in unemployment and in employment (implicit in the differences between the rows for Q and Q/N in table 2.1) need also to be viewed in relation to trends in the labour force, which differed substantially among countries (also shown in table 2.2).

Table 2.2   The labour force and unemployment

	France	Germany	Japan	UK	US
Annual average increase per cent in labour force					
1967–73	1.0	0.4	1.1	0.0	2.0
1973–9	0.8	−0.3	0.9	0.5	2.4
1979–81	0.5[a]	0.7	1.0	−0.7	1.7
Standardised unemployment rates: unemployment as per cent of labour force					
1967	1.9	1.3	1.3	3.4	3.7
1973	2.6	0.9	1.3	3.0	4.7
1979	5.9	3.2	2.1	5.7	5.7
1981	7.6	4.3	2.2	11.4	7.4

Source: OECD Labour Force Statistics
[a] 1979–80.

Sectoral Changes

Table 2.3 shows the growth of output and output per person employed in broad economic sectors – manufacturing, other goods and measured services (that is agriculture, mining, utilities, construction, distribution, transport and communications) and in those service sectors where output is not adequately measured and where, therefore, productivity cannot be measured. Since what is reported for these latter sectors will influence the apparent growth of GDP per person employed, they are included here in order that the extent of their influence can be assessed.

In the 1960s and early 1970s, manufacturing was everywhere the leading sector in terms both of the growth of output and of output per head. In some industries, notably utilities, both grew even more rapidly, but on average other goods and measured services showed a lower rate of output and productivity growth. There was considerable variation in the recorded rate of increase in 'output' in non-measured

Table 2.3   *Sectoral changes in output (Q) and output per person employed (Q/N)*: annual average increase per cent*

	Manufacturing[a]		Other goods and measured services		Other[b]	
	Q	Q/N	Q	Q/N	Q	Q/N
France						
1962–73	7.6	6.5	4.3	4.7	5.1	1.4
1967–73	7.7	6.5	3.9	4.7	5.7	1.7
1973–9	2.9	4.1	2.2	3.0	4.1	1.1
Germany						
1962–73	5.2	5.3	3.6	4.9	4.6	2.6
1967–73	6.5	5.4	4.2	5.3	5.0	2.6
1973–9	1.9	3.2	1.9	4.0	3.9	2.0
Japan						
1962–73	13.2	10.1	9.2	9.4	7.5	4.0
1967–73	13.4	10.8	9.4	9.7	6.0	3.0
1973–9	5.0	6.4	2.3	1.5	4.0	1.3
UK[c]						
1960–73	3.0	3.6	2.9	3.5	2.6	0.0
1967–73	3.6	4.6	2.9	3.7	2.7	0.4
1973–9	−0.7	0.8	1.6	1.8[d]	1.9	0.1
US[e]						
1960–73	4.7	3.5	3.9	2.6	3.7	0.4
1967–73	3.6	3.4	3.8	1.5	3.1	−0.3
1973–9	2.0	1.1	2.4	0.1	3.0	−0.4

Sources: As table 2.1.
[a] These figures differ from estimates prepared by the US Bureau of Labor Statistics used in other chapters, because the BLS uses a different definition of employment in most countries and relates output to all hours worked by employees rather than to total civilian employment. The slow-down in productivity growth after 1973 thus tends to be smaller than that shown here, notably so for France and Germany.
[b] Financial and related services, community and personal services including government.
[c] At factor cost. The figures are therefore not consistent with the UK figures in table 2.1.
[d] Excluding mining, where output and productivity rose very sharply because of the development of North Sea oil production, output per person employed rose by only 0.3 per cent annually.
[e] Based on unrevised output data which slightly understate growth since 1973.
* Output data are derived from GDP, employment refers to civilian employment. Employment data, particularly in years prior to 1967, are in many cases estimated or partly estimated.

services, but invariably a lower rate of increase, in the US after 1967 a decline, in recorded output per head.

After 1973, the rate of increase in output and output per person employed in manufacturing fell sharply in all five countries. If allowance is made for shorter hours of work and longer holidays, then the slow-down in productivity (output per hour) was less marked. In Germany, shorter hours may have accounted for anything up to 1 percentage point of the 2.2 per cent fall in the rate of growth of output per person employed but elsewhere for, probably, less than half of 1 percentage point. (These figures are based on estimates of hours worked in manufacturing prepared by the US Bureau of Labor Statistics.) Generally speaking, the slow-down in other goods industries and measured services was smaller than in manufacturing, but in Japan productivity growth in these sectors fell more rapidly than in manufacturing. The fall in the rate of increase in manufacturing output per person employed between 1967-73 and 1973-9 was 4.4 percentage points on average, in other goods and measured services 8.2 percentage points. In the UK also 'other goods and measured services' excluding North Sea oil and gas showed a big decline – 3.4 percentage points – in productivity growth from 1967-73 to 1973-9, though it was even so somewhat smaller than the fall in the growth of output per head in manufacturing. In the remaining service sectors the fall in the growth rate of output and output per person employed after 1973 was comparatively small in all five countries, but the growth of output per person employed was generally very low or negative.

The rise in output in the residual service sectors during 1973-9 reflected, for the most part, a continuing rise in employment which invariably grew faster than in the rest of the economy. The result was to increase the share of the non-measured services in both GDP and employment, thus depressing the measured rate of growth of GDP per person employed. The share of non-measured services in employment had already been rising during the 1960s, but after 1973 the rise was faster in France, Germany and Japan, though not in the UK and the US. The effect of this shift and of sectoral changes in the rate of productivity growth between 1967-73 and 1973-9 on the measured growth of GDP per person employed is illustrated in table 2.4.

Employment shifted from sectors with a higher to sectors with a lower rate of productivity growth. The effect of this shift was calculated by multiplying the inter-sectoral difference in rates of productivity growth during 1967-73 by the change in employment from 1973-9. (This weighting maximises the effect of changes in the structure of employment; if inter-sectoral differences in productivity

Table 2.4   Percentage contribution to reduction in the rate of growth of output per person employed 1967–73 to 1973–9

	France	Germany	Japan	UK	US
Shift in employment	13	10	4[a]	6	5
Fall in output per person employed					
Manufacturing	36	49	18	55	45
Other goods and measured services	40	30	71	34	47
Other	11	11	7	5	3

Sources: As table 2.1
[a] Including an increase of 0.4 per cent in employment in other goods and measured services.

growth rates during 1973-9 were used, the effect would be slightly smaller.) The employment shift itself accounted for 10 per cent or less of the fall in the measured growth of GDP per head, save in France where it reached 13 per cent. Even adding in the effect of the fall in the rate of increase in output per person employed, the non-measured services accounted for only about a quarter of the slow-down in GDP per person employed in France, around one-fifth in Germany and 10 per cent or so elsewhere.

In every case, the greater part of the slow-down was attributable to slower productivity growth in manufacturing and in other measured goods and service industries. But whereas manufacturing accounted for the greater part of the fall in Britain and Germany, in the three remaining countries, especially Japan, a larger part of the fall in the rate of growth of GDP per person employed originated in other goods and measured services. The fall in the rate of growth of productivity in manufacturing was, of course, important in these countries; in Japan the fall in productivity growth in other goods and measured services had a greater effect on GDP per person employed because of the larger than average share of this sector in output and employment. Even so, had that share been the same as in the UK, where it is lower than in any of the other four countries, other goods and measured services would still have accounted for a half or more of the fall in the rate of growth of GDP per person employed between 1967-73 and 1973-9. The pattern as well as the magnitude of the slow-down has been exceptional in Japan.

Table 2.5 shows changes in the rate of growth of output and of output per person employed in other goods and measured services, distinguishing six different sectors. The data are less reliable than for

Table 2.5   *Changes in annual percentage rates of growth of output (Q) and output per person employed (Q/N) 1967–73 to 1973–9*

	Agri-culture	Mining	Utilities	Const-ruction	Com-merce	Trans-port
France						
Employment share 1973	11.4	1.0	0.8	9.6	15.5	5.9
Change in growth rate						
Q	−1.1	0.0	−3.1	−3.4	−2.0	−1.0
Q/N	−2.7	−1.7	−4.0	−1.2	−0.7	−1.7
Germany						
Employment share 1973	7.5	1.6	0.9	8.7	14.7	5.9
Change in growth rate						
Q	−2.0	−7.0[a]	−4.2[a]	−3.9	−1.6[a]	−0.9
Q/N	−3.4	−6.3[a]	−7.1[a]	−0.3	−0.4[a]	+0.6
Japan						
Employment share 1973	13.4	0.2	0.6	8.9	20.6	6.4
Change in growth rate						
Q	−3.3	−4.5	−4.3	−10.8	−7.9	−7.1
Q/N	−7.8	−16.0	+0.3[a]	−8.3	−7.5	−5.0
UK						
Employment share 1973	2.9	1.4	1.4	7.4	16.7	6.5
Change in growth rate						
Q	−2.2	+20.9[b]	−2.6	−3.5	−3.0	−3.0
Q/N	−3.8	+15.7[b]	−7.2	−1.9	−3.5	−3.4
US						
Employment share 1973	4.2	0.8[a]	1.1	6.5	21.0	5.8
Change in growth rate						
Q	−0.2	+0.2	−3.9	+0.9	−2.4	−0.8
Q/N	−1.6	−5.3[a]	−3.7[a]	+1.9	−1.8	−1.2

Sources: As table 2.1.
[a] Estimated or partly estimated.
[b] Excluding oil and gas the growth rate of output rose by 0.9 per cent but that of productivity fell by an estimated 4.3 per cent.

the group as a whole, particularly for sectors with a small share in employment and output, and should only be taken as rough indicators of what has happened.

All countries show a fall in the rate of growth of agricultural output and output per head. At least two factors involved are readily identifiable. First, the long postwar decline in numbers employed in agriculture slowed after 1973, save in Germany. The deceleration was particularly marked in Japan, where from 1973–9 agricultural employment fell at only about a third of the rate of the previous six years. Secondly, oil is an important agricultural input, both directly as fuel and indirectly as fertiliser raw material, so that agricultural costs rose sharply in consequence of the oil price rise.

Two other energy-related sectors, mining and utilities, also experienced falling productivity growth in almost every instance. The exceptions were mining in Britain, because of the coming into production of North Sea oil, and utilities in Japan, but the latter exception is derived from a rather unreliable estimate and may be disregarded. Both sectors, but more particularly mining, may have been affected by relatively higher demand for low-grade coal and by the depletion of natural resources.

The productivity slow-down in construction, commerce and transport was generally smaller, outside Japan, but given the relative size of the sectors it was also more important. In Japan the fall in the rate of growth of both output and output per head was very large in all three, and it was sizeable in commerce and transport in the UK. Otherwise the decline in the growth of output per head was modest – less than 2 percentage points between 1967-73 and 1973-9 – while productivity in German transport and communications industries and in construction in the US actually seems to have risen faster after 1973 than before. The figure for construction in the US, and indeed elsewhere, is suspect because of the high proportion of casual and self-employed labour in the industry which exacerbates the difficulties of productivity measurement. Over a similar period, the rate of growth in US output per hour in the construction industry showed a very much smaller rise, or rather the rate of decline in output per hour diminished only slightly.

US estimates of changes in output per hour outside the construction industry show that the effect of shorter working hours on output per head was, as in manufacturing, comparatively small, reducing the fall in productivity between 1967-73 and 1973-9 by, usually, around 0.5 per cent and at most by under 1 per cent. Data on hours worked in non-manufacturing industries outside the US are scrappy but they suggest that the fall in hours after 1973 was as great, if not greater, than the fall in manufacturing hours. Hence a fall in the rate of growth of output per person employed of less than 0.5 per cent annually could certainly, and a fall of anything up to 1 per cent could very probably, be almost wholly explained in terms of shorter working hours.

On this interpretation the growth of German labour productivity (measured as output per hour) was no slower after than before 1973 outside agriculture, mining and the utilities, while the growth rate of French labour productivity slipped very little until 1979. Thereafter, judging by the fall in GDP per employed person, it probably did fall sharply in these countries. Elsewhere the growth rate of labour productivity in the sectors included in 'other goods and measured services' did fall, but it is noticeable that the fall in the rate of growth of output per head was less than the fall in output which was also largely true of France and Germany. It is only in the UK that the growth of output per head fell more than the growth of output (or rose less) in almost every sector. Perhaps the most surprising development here is the rise in employment in commerce, despite the very small increase in output – 0.2 per cent annually – between 1973 and 1979.

Conclusion
The fall in the average rate of growth of GDP per person employed since 1973 shows major differences from country to country in size, in pattern and in timing, as do changes in the labour market and in investment. The post-1973 productivity slow-down was most pronounced in Japan, where the greater part occurred outside manufacturing, but, to set against this, the rise in unemployment was by far the smallest.

In the US also, the slow-down in non-manufacturing industries was more pronounced than in manufacturing but the distinguishing features of American experience were that the productivity slow-down pre-dated 1973 and that output, though not productivity, recovered unusually sharply after 1975. Until 1979 the slow-down was much less serious in France and Germany than elsewhere; measured in terms of output per hour rather than per person employed it may have been comparatively slight. In Germany it was concentrated in manufacturing, but it was rather more widespread in France. Since 1979, the slow-down in these two countries, and particularly in Germany, has been more pronounced than in Japan or the US.

Britain, as usual, was at the heel of the hunt in Europe. The fall in GDP both after 1973 and 1979 was larger and more prolonged than in France or Germany; manufacturing output has never recovered to the record level of 1973; the rate of productivity growth, especially in manufacturing, fell off sharply during 1973-4. Since then unemployment has risen more sharply than in any of the other countries surveyed here. And yet, over the last two years, the UK's productivity performance compares favourably with that of France and Germany.

3 The Relationship between Pressure of Demand and Productivity
G.D.N. Worswick

The concept of the 'pressure of demand' became prominent in British economic discussion during the later 1950s and early 1960s. There was concern that the pressure of demand in the economy was too great. Other expressions were used such as 'excess demand' or 'overheating'. In 1958 the Council on Prices, Productivity and Incomes issued its first Report and began its analysis with the question: 'What has been the cause of the rising trend of prices and incomes since the end of the War?'. The answer given was that: 'Viewing the period as a whole, we incline to believe that the main cause has been an abnormally high level of demand for goods and services in general, maintained for an abnormally long stretch of time.'

In the same year as the Council's first Report there appeared A.W. Phillips' famous paper in which he fitted a curve to wage rate changes and unemployment in the UK for the whole period 1861-1957 and concluded that '. . . it seems from the relation fitted to the data that if aggregate demand were kept at a value which would maintain a stable level of product prices, the associated level of unemployment would be a little under $2\frac{1}{2}$ per cent.' During the 1950s actual unemployment had ranged between 1 and 2 per cent. Thus it appeared that if the government would engineer an unemployment rate on average about 1 per cent higher than what it had been, price stability could be ensured. This is the most widely remembered claim for the benefit to be derived from $2\frac{1}{2}$ per cent unemployment. But there was another claim; F.W. Paish argued that a somewhat greater average gap between output and capacity would have a favourable effect on the rate of growth of capacity [5]. In conditions of excess demand there could, he argued, be no effective competition. 'Only if at least a few firms in every industry are short of orders and urgently seeking new business does competition become a reality. In its absence, there is no compulsion on the least efficient firms to improve efficiency or to go out of business.' Paish did not go much further than qualitative arguments of this kind any more than did those, like myself[9], who thought that on balance the high pressure of demand was favourable to the growth of capacity and output because in a climate of labour shortage managements would be able to pursue labour-saving investments and to reduce restrictive practices.

The economic circumstances of the 1980s seem light years away from a time when it could be seriously, and heatedly, debated whether engineering the average level of unemployment up to 2½ per cent would be enough to secure price stability and faster growth. Unemployment has been over 5 per cent for six years now and well over 10 per cent for recent years and we have both inflation and slower growth. On the other hand, if it is suggested that some of the unemployment may be the consequence of the pressure of demand being too low, some people say this is absurd since the aggregate of money expenditure has been rising from year to year. The government claim that the elimination of inflation is the only way to secure faster growth in the long run, even if there is no longer any suggestion that a small reduction in the average pressure of demand would suffice to secure both objectives. It seems worthwhile to examine more closely the concept of pressure of demand, to consider whether it was helpful in interpreting economic movements at the time it was developed, and to go on to ask whether it is still a useful concept in what, on the surface at least, appear to be very changed circumstances.

The Pressure of Demand
The concept of the pressure of demand is closely associated with inflation, and in particular the notions of cost inflation and demand inflation. The first question is this: if there is a spontaneous increase in aggregate monetary demand, arising, say, from an increase in demand for exports, how is it that demand split between increases in output and increases in prices? The textbook Keynesian answer is that it depends where we start from. If initially there is considerable unemployment and under-utilised capacity then a rise in demand will elicit a rise in output in sectors of the economy where prices are administered and where it is supposed that 'supply curves' are fairly elastic. As the expansion continues, under-utilised capacity will be drawn into use and as the economy approaches full employment so there will be a tendency for prices to rise. In this model it is not required that the prices of administered goods remain indefinitely fixed. What happens is that the higher 'derived' demand for inputs may push up wages (Phillips Curve) and raw materials in inelastic supply. This rise in costs is then 'marked up' into higher prices. A 'demand inflationist' supposes that in the main an increase in aggregate monetary demand will raise final product prices directly while a 'cost inflationist' will expect most of the gap between aggre-

gate demand and aggregate supply to be closed by output increases although there may be some price increases, not so much brought about by the direct pull of demand but because the derived demand for inputs puts up their costs which are then passed on into product prices. There is a suggestion here that in a dynamic world, if there were demand inflation the price rises would come at once, whereas with cost inflation cost rises and hence marked up price rises might lag behind. There is the further suggestion that if there are fluctuations in demand, demand inflationists would expect to find mostly corresponding fluctuations in price while a cost inflationist would expect output fluctuations, followed, after some time lag, by price fluctuations, probably on a smaller scale. The ideas of demand inflation and cost inflation do not seem to be mutually exclusive and there seems no obvious reason why actual inflation might not consist of an admixture of both.

The other key notion of cost inflation is that wages and prices can rise indefinitely without there being, in any very visible sense of the term, 'excess demand' or a 'high pressure of demand'. Consider a very simple model of a wage-price spiral in a closed economy, with no intervention of government and no technical progress to raise productivity. When prices rise, workers demand increases in their nominal wages sufficient to restore *real* wages. When costs rise, employers raise prices in proportion so as to maintain profit margins. If there are discrete intervals between successive wage adjustments and price adjustments there seems to be no reason why they should not chase one another's tails for ever. In real life there are many factors which could damp down such a spiral, such as foreign trade, or a rise in productivity. On the other hand, if workers succeed always in (momentarily) raising real wages, they would make the vicious spiral turn ever more widely, and, of course, more quickly if the interval between wage and price adjustments becomes shorter.

A piece left out of the above story was money. In most economists' books, be they Keynesian or monetarist, if the quantity of money is fixed and there are pressures to increase nominal incomes, a genuine gap of 'excess supply' will emerge, and either prices will not after all rise, or output will have to be reduced. Thus the everlasting inflation spiral presupposes 'monetary accommodation' which could occur either because the banking system is very elastic or because the authorities choose to make it so. In the case where there is accommodation, then both aggregate demand and aggregate supply, expressed in monetary terms, will rise each year, but there need be no change in the balance between the two.

Two alternative approaches have been adopted to measure the pressure of demand. In his successive studies of economic growth in the US, Denison talks of the 'intensity of demand'. The main reasons he puts forward to explain fluctuations in the use of inputs are fluctuations in demand: the minor reasons include work stoppages of one kind or another. Denison reckons that the percentage share of non-labour income in actual corporate national income (share of profits) is a good measure of 'intensity of demand' [1]. To the annual data of the non-labour share he fitted a trend line over the period 1947-69 and used N, the deviation from trend, as his measure of intensity of demand or intensity of utilisation. British economists in the early 1960s tended to follow Dow and Dicks-Mireaux [2] in using labour statistics. They pointed out that however high the level of demand, unemployment could never fall to zero. As demand pressure increases therefore, unemployment becomes a decreasingly sensitive index of the pressure of demand and beyond a certain point it is better to use the vacancy statistics. The index of demand for labour which Dow and Dicks-Mireaux constructed is based on the idea that at some point net excess demand is zero: above the zero point the index is based on the vacancy statistics and below it on the unemployment series, both vacancies and unemployment being expressed as percentages of total employees.

The Movement of Prices and Output

The sketch of cost inflation suggests that fluctuations in the pressure of demand will show up as much or more in fluctuations around some trend in output as in prices. Chart 3.1 shows the annual percentage changes in real GDP and the GDP deflator in the UK in the period 1922-39 and again in 1952-80 (the figure marked against any one year is the change since the previous year). In the inter-war period, once the rapid fall in the price level, following the postwar boom, was over, by 1924 annual price changes, which were mostly falls, rarely exceeded 2 per cent in the next 12 years, whereas annual output changes were less than 2 per cent on only three occasions and exceeded it in the other nine.

In the postwar years, the period from 1952 to 1969 shows price changes still comparatively steady, only now instead of showing a tendency to fall for much of the time they range around annual increases of 3 or 4 per cent while the deviations from trend of output appear to be a little larger. In this period an interesting pattern, not very noticeable in the inter-war years, emerges in which the output and price changes appear to be inversely related. A possible interpretation of this phenomenon would be that there are quite long transmission lags between the successive stages from changes in demand to changes in output to changes in employment to changes in costs and hence prices. The evidence so far gives little cause to dissent

Chart 3.1   UK annual percentage changes in GDP and home costs

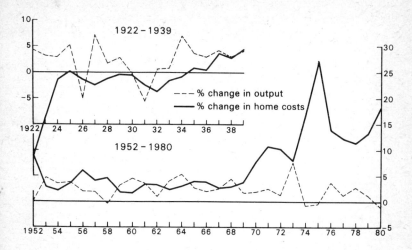

Notes: The figures for 1922–39 are defived from C.H. Feinstein *National Income, Expenditure and Output of the United Kingdom 1855–1965* C.U.P. 1972. The output measure used was the index of the compromise estimate of GDP at constant factor cost (Feinstein Table 6, col. 4). This was divided by the total employed labour force (Table 57) to obtain output per worker. Expenditure is derived from GDP at constant factor cost (Feinstein Table 5) and the GDP Deflator is derived from Feinstein Table 61 Col. 7.

The figures for 1952-80 are derived from *Economic Trends: Annual Supplement* CSO 1982 Edition. GDP output is derived from the constant price output estimate (page 5) and productivity is the Index of Output Per Person Employed (page 97). The figures for 1952-60 were obtained from *British Labour Statistics: Historical Abstract*, 1971 Table 204. The GDP figures are derived from the Expenditure Estimate (Trend Supplement page 5) and price changes from the Implied Index of Total Home Costs (Trend Supplement page 5). The various measures of GDP in both periods are not exactly the same and correspondingly the year-to-year changes can differ.

from the idea that changes in output are, in the main, responses to changes in the pressure of demand. This is not to say that some changes in output were not responses to shocks on the supply side – 1926 is an obvious instance from the inter-war period – but the 'demand variation' explanation of the pattern of price and output variations seems altogether more plausible than the story of a succession of unexpected shocks on the supply side.

After 1969 the story changes; output becomes more erratic. There is a huge jump in 1972 to 1973 followed by two small negative figures in succession. After a not too convincing recovery we are back in negative figures at the end of the period. With prices the story is quite different; the gentle slopes of the 1950s and 1960s are replaced by a roller-coaster. Increases of 10 per cent are encountered first in 1971 and 1972; after a dip in 1973 we are up to well over 25 per cent in 1975; a sustained deceleration until 1979 is followed yet again by a big jump. If we were to try to explain the post-1969 behaviour of prices and output in terms of the model we found acceptable up to 1969 we would have to say that variations in the pressure of demand now show up mainly in large price changes and to a comparatively lesser extent in output changes. One can see at once that that is stretching things a lot. Something is now going on which appears not to have been going on in the earlier periods; the most obvious candidates are the two oil price 'supply shocks' of 1973 and 1979. Whether the pressure of demand concept retains any of its usefulness remains to be seen, but it is already clear that it cannot be applied in any mechanical way.

Output and Productivity

Chart 3.2 shows the annual changes in output and productivity (output per person employed) in the UK for the two periods 1922-39 and 1952-80. It is immediately apparent that there is a close association between annual output and annual productivity changes throughout both periods which together constitute nearly half a century. It is noticeable that in the recovery after the slump of the early 1930s, the rapid cyclical spurt in the growth of productivity was not sustained. Between 1922 and 1929 output rose by 22 per cent and productivity by 12 per cent, whereas between 1932 and 1939 output rose by 26 per cent and productivity by only 6 per cent. In the 20 years from 1960 to 1980 output rose by 59 per cent and productivity by 47 per cent. In the main what these figures tell us is that total employment was growing much more slowly in the postwar period and that short-term

Chart 3.2   UK annual percentage changes in GDP and productivity

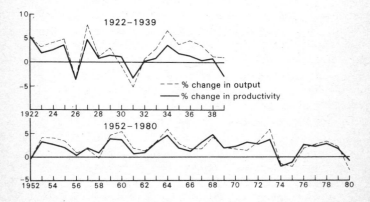

Notes: see chart 3.1

fluctuations in output were accompanied by larger variations in employment before the war than since.

To the extent that we use deviations of output from trend as our measure of 'intensity of demand' then it is perfectly plain that in the short run there is a close association between changes in the intensity of demand and changes in productivity. We remind ourselves, though, that while the association between output and productivity changes remains close, we had earlier expressed doubts about the association between pressure of demand and output changes in the 1970s.

In the American case Denison gives us a direct link between pressure of demand and productivity. His concept of the latter is not labour productivity but total input per unit of output. However, he does indicate that labour productivity fluctuations are closely associated with fluctuations in total inputs per unit of output. We have already mentioned his measure of intensity of demand, N, which is the deviation from trend of the non-labour share in corporate income.

He defines a further variable, U, which is the ratio of actual productivity to trend line productivity, that is, what productivity would have been if intensity of utilisation had been the average for the period of estimation. He then estimates a simple regression between log U and N over the period 1948-69. Both the UK figures and the Denison analysis demonstrate a short period relationship between pressure of demand and productivity changes. Similar relationships can be observed in other countries, as well as for the manufacturing sector of industry (See *Bank of England Quarterly Bulletin*, March 1982, p. 10).

The question arises whether Denison's measure of changes in the intensity of demand can contribute anything to the explanation of the slow-down of growth since 1973. Between 1973 and 1976 his particular indicator is of no help from this point of view, standing as it does at 99.63 in the former year and 99.99 in the latter (See [1], table 5.1 page 65). In the intermediate year of 1974 the index had dropped to 95.7. There are, however, some reasons for doubting whether Denison's indicator would be a good measure of a persistent tendency of demand to be deficient. Consider how it is constructed. His primary measure of year-to-year changes is the share of non-labour in the corporate national income, or the 'share of profits' for short. When the share of profits rises above trend, productivity may be expected to be above trend and vice versa. But what are these trends? They are simply linear or exponential trends fitted throughout quite long periods. Inspection of the data shows that there may be 'bends in the trend' of the share of profit when fitted over sub-periods;

similarly there may be 'bends in the trend' of productivity change. The association between the two variables is sensitive to the choice of trends, and a different choice might show demand contributing something to the slow-down in the US. There is, however, a more serious worry, namely that the association between demand changes and productivity changes in short period fluctuations, while telling us something about the dynamics of a fluctuating economy, cannot be used to tell us what would happen to the trend of productivity if pressure of demand were to remain persistently above, or more pertinently below, the previous trend. In that case we are obliged to look for other approaches to our original question.

Productivity in the Long Run
If short period relationships, however well established, cannot be safely extended to the case of sustained high, or low, pressure of demand, we must try something else. Both the alternatives considered in the next two sections are concerned with pressure of demand, but they are designed to answer somewhat different questions. In the first example the question is whether there is something in the structure of advanced economies which constrains the growth of demand below some otherwise achievable potential, with the corollary that if this constraint were removed growth of output could be higher. If one adds a further corollary that in general fast growth of output is associated with fast growth of productivity, then we have shown a way in which restriction of the pressure of demand is unfavourable to productivity growth. In the second example the question is: given that we have a period in which output and productivity growth have fallen below that of some earlier period, can we detect any change in the structure of the economy which might account for the slow-down? The implication is that if no such 'supply-side' change can be detected, then there is a presumption that the slow-down in productivity comes from a reduction in the pressure of demand.

The Balance of Payments Constraint
The first type of approach is well represented in an article by A.P. Thirlwall in 1979 [7], which is an extension of a simpler model put forward ten years earlier by Houthakker and Magee [4]. The kernel of the argument is as follows. A country's exports are postulated to be a function of the volume of world trade, or of world economic activity, and of the relative prices of its own goods against competing goods. Its imports are a function of its own national product and the relative prices of its own goods as compared with competing imports. Setting aside for the moment the question of relative prices, we

assume that we have, (which of course we do not) unambiguous measures w of the volume of world trade or of economic activity, a country's own national product y, and its exports x, and imports, m. It is postulated that there is an unchanging export elasticity with respect to world trade, b, such that $\Delta x/x = b\Delta w/w$. Similarly $\Delta m/m = a\Delta y/y$ where a is the income elasticity of demand for imports. If, initially, exports balance imports and if subsequently balance between them is continuously maintained, then $\Delta m/m = \Delta x/x$ from which it follows that $\Delta y/y = b/a \, \Delta w/w$. If a and b can be estimated for individual countries from observations of their statistics of output and trade and we have a suitable series for w, then different countries' growth rates would be proportional to the ratio of the two trade elasticities.

Thirlwall starts off with a more sophisticated analysis than the stripped-down model just described. He stresses the importance of relative prices for exports and imports, and thus for the current balance. But he argues that while an effective devaluation could alter the level of exports and imports, it would not alter the long-run rate of change of either so that in the end the permissible GDP growth rate will be back to the constraint imposed by the ratio b/a. He also sees the 'balance of payments constrained growth rates' as an upper limit to what will actually occur, as the authorities restrain demand to make sure of the current balance. In fact the estimates he provides of what growth rates the balance of payments would permit are in all cases, though in different degrees, greater than the actual growth rates found in different countries.

The Thirlwall type argument is well known among modellers of the British economy and anyone familiar with the detailed history of postwar British economic policy, confronted with this type of analysis of the evidence, is bound to think that there is, or was, something in it. The only question I would venture at this point, without attempting to answer it, is whether it is right to treat a devaluation change as entirely a static phenomenon changing levels but not influencing rates of change in the manner of the export propelled growth theories which flourished in the 1960s.

The Pressure of Demand and the Structure of Production

Using the results of an ECE study of structural change in Western European manufacturing industries, in the 1970s compared with the 1960s [8], Saunders considers the implications of the consequences of slower growth on the rate of structural change in manufacturing industry [6]. He notes that many people hoped that policies of restraint exercised in the 1970s would have as one consequence the acceleration of structural adjustments of Western economies through changing international circumstances. Slower growth of demand, it

Table 3.1   *Structural change and growth in manufacturing: nine industrial countries*

	Rates of structural change[a]						Growth rate of output		
	Output (constant prices)			Employment			% a year		
	1960s[b]	1970s[c]	1970s as % 1960s	1960s[b]	1970s[c]	1970s as % 1960s	1960s[b]	1970s[c]	1970s as % 1960s
Belgium	10.7	10.2	95	6.5	7.8	122	6.5	3.4	52
Finland	10.4	8.7	84	7.9	6.3	80	6.9	3.1	45
France	9.4	13.2	140	7.9	6.8	86	6.3	4.4	70
Germany	10.2	7.7	75	7.8	5.8	74	6.3	2.0	32
Italy	9.4	6.6	70	6.7	5.3	79	8.3	2.9	35
Netherlands	13.6	7.9	58	7.8	7.4	95	6.8	2.9	43
Norway	9.3	9.0	97	7.8	7.6	97	5.3	1.5	28
Sweden	11.2	6.8	61	6.7	7.4	110	6.9	0.7	10
UK	7.7	7.3	95	5.5	3.5	64	3.3	0.7	21
Weighted average[d]	10.2	8.6	85	7.2	6.4	90	6.3	2.4	37

Source: Derived from ECE, Economic Survey of Europe in 1980, Tables 4.1.1 and 4.2.4.
[a] As defined in text.
[b] 1958–60 to 1968–70.
[c] 1970 to 1978 (for columns (2) and (5) expressed as equivalent 10-year rates).
[d] Taken from figures above, not from Table 4.2.1.

was thought, would pick out the strong enterprises from the weak through the creation of a more intensive competitive environment. This line of thought is in the same vein as that of Paish in the early 1960s. The ECE report proceeds to ask whether there has in fact been any acceleration of the process of industrial adjustment whereby some sectors expand output and employment and others contract during the 1970s as compared with the 1960s and earlier. In particular, has there been any acceleration in the shift to high value-added branches of manufacturing? We note that the ECE study took it for granted that the pressure of demand in the 1970s in Western European countries and the US was lower than earlier, a matter to which we will return in the final section. The broad conclusion they drew from the evidence available was that in West European countries the degree of structural change in the 1970s was on balance no greater, indeed slightly less, than in the 1960s.

The measure of structural change adopted was based on summarising changes between the beginning and the end of any chosen period in the share of eighteen branches in total manufacturing output or employment in each of nine countries. That is to say we take the share of industry i in total output in year 1, measured in percentage points and a similar share in year 2; the sum of the differences is the desired index of structural change. The results of this analysis are given in table 3.1. It will be seen that in every country the rate of structural change in output declined, if only slightly, between the 1960s and the 1970s, with the exception of France where change accelerated in the 1970s. The main reason given for this exception was a particularly fast expansion in the shares of both electrical and non-electrical machinery. Countries with more than average declines in the rate of change between the 1960s and the 1970s were Germany, the Netherlands and Sweden. Britain, it will be seen, slowed down rather less than the average. It has been argued by Forsyth and Kay [3] that North Sea oil called for a decline in the share of manufacturing in total UK output; such an adjustment might possibly also speed up the rate of structural change within manufacturing itself. We thus have a candidate to explain why the slow-down of change in Britain was less than elsewhere. However, it must be added that the Forsyth and Kay proposition is not uncontentious.

On balance, what this analysis suggests is that structural change slowed down in the 1970s and this slowing-down was associated with the slowing-down of growth of output. Thus, to the extent that the slower growth of output was a function of a reduction in the pressure of demand, the conclusion is that reduction in the pressure was more often a deterrent than a stimulus to structural change.

The Interpretation of the 1970s

The ECE report takes for granted that there *was* a reduction in demand pressure since 1973 in OECD countries and that there *was* a slowing-down of productivity growth. As regards the former, there are, as we noticed above, some people who have argued that the persistence of inflation is sufficient evidence that demand cannot have been deficient. We gave our reasons for rejecting this view. If we think of aggregate demand in real terms, the evidence that in Britain and in most other countries there has been a lower pressure of demand in the last decade than in the decades before seems very strong indeed. One interpretation is that since the first OPEC oil price rise the stance of monetary and fiscal policy in most industrial countries has been more restrictive than previously and that during this period we have witnessed a prolonged, partially policy-induced recession on which there have been superimposed two shorter additional recessions in 1974-5 and 1980-1. On this interpretation, a revival of real demand could take the economy back on to the trend of growth experienced before 1973, albeit that the consequences of such policies would be a higher rate of inflation than has been actually experienced. Another interpretation is that while part of the slowing-down of output and productivity growth can be attributed to demand, hidden beneath the recession is a slowing-down in the long-term growth of productivity such that if real demand were to recover, whether spontaneously or induced by policy, the ceiling of productive capacity would be reached sooner and would be found to be less steeply sloping than previously. We are doubtful whether the evidence to date can enable us to distinguish between these alternative hypotheses. Either way we take the view that the 'pressure of demand' in the 1970s was lower than in the 1960s. In the last twelve months an apparently contrary hypothesis has been put forward in Britain, to the effect that productivity change, at any rate in manufacturing, has shifted into a permanently higher gear. The evidence is that there has been a sharp increase in productivity in UK manufacturing in the past year or so (10.7 per cent between the fourth quarter of 1980 and the fourth quarter of 1981). Since manufacturing output, which had sustained a very sharp fall, had not yet started to rise, this increase in productivity was contrary to the 'normal' relationship with output. Whether or not this rise in productivity will be sustained if the demand for and output of UK manufactured goods begins to rise once more for any length of time, remains to be seen. It should be added that this exceptional behaviour has not been repeated in other major industrial countries, although none have so far encountered in the current recession large falls in manufacturing output of the kind experienced in Britain. It is also worth noting that for any finite period a rise in the average rate of growth of productivity over that period is not sufficient to indicate superiority of performance. Starting from 100, a 3 per cent annual growth brings us to 134.4 in ten years. If initially there had been a short period fall of 10 per cent, it would require an annual growth rate of over 4 per cent over the ten years to reach 134.4. Thus, from a welfare point of view, faster productivity growth, but with always higher unemployment, may be worse than slower productivity growth with full employment over quite a long period.

Conclusion

Does the pressure of demand influence productivity growth? Although we only examined at all closely the cases of the US and the UK, there is a good deal of evidence for many countries, in the years after the Second World War, that variations in the pressure of demand led to variations in the short-term rate of change of productivity, for output as a whole as well as for manufacturing industry.

However, such evidence may simply be telling us about the short-term consequences of fluctuations in demand, and we are not entitled to deduce that the same relationships would persist between sustained high pressure of demand and sustained faster productivity growth.

We looked at two alternative approaches. The balance of payments constraint argument suggests that growth rates of imports and exports are tied to the growth of domestic output and of world output, or trade, respectively. As the figures worked out, the 'balance of payments constrained' growth rate for the UK turned out to be lower than in other countries, as indeed the actual rate of growth in postwar years was lower. This approach is bound to get a sympathetic response from anyone familiar with the stop-go history of Britain in the 1950s and 1960s. Nevertheless, one is obliged to add two cautionary observations. First of all, by contemporary standards the stops of those decades were very mild. Secondly, there is a line of argument that altering the effective exchange rate might bring about not merely a once-for-all change in the level of the trade balance, but also faster output and productivity growth in the long run (export propelled growth). However recent history has not been altogether kind to this latter argument. First of all devaluation, and later on the abandonment of a fixed exchange rate, implied, so at any rate some economists assured us, that the shackles of the balance of payments constraint had been broken. Unfortunately if there has been a slow-down in productivity growth, it occurs in the later, and not in the earlier period. In my view there has been constraint of demand in recent years but the primary reason has been more the desire to restrain inflation than to escape from a balance of payments strait-jacket.

The second long-run type of argument postulated that there has been a slow-down in productivity growth which calls for explanation. The Economic Commission for Europe provided interesting evidence concerning the process of structural adjustment. Their tentative conclusion was that lower pressure of demand was not helpful to productivity growth, but this is a line of investigation which might be pursued further. However, in Britain there is recent evidence which might seem to point the other way, namely that large reductions in demand have brought forward an acceleration of productivity growth. It is too early to say, however, whether such exceptional increases in productivity will be sustained when employment recovers.

My own conclusion at this stage is that there is a fair amount of circumstantial evidence that in general lowered pressure of demand is likely to be unfavourable to productivity growth. The transmission is from reduced demand to slower output growth to slower productivity growth. On the other hand there is little evidence that a revival of employment, whether it occurs spontaneously, or is induced by policy measures, would be harmful to 'normal' productivity growth. The question still remains, however, whether a sustained recovery in employment would not re-kindle inflation.

References

[1]   Denison, E.F., *Accounting for Slower Economic Growth*, Brookings Institution 1979, Appendix I.

[2]   Dow, J.C.R., and Dicks-Mireaux, L.A., 'The Excess Demand for Labour', *Oxford Economic Papers*, February 1958.

[3]   Forsyth, P.J., and Kay, J.A., *Fiscal Studies*, July 1980.

[4]   Houthakker, H., and Magee, S., 'Income and Price Elasticities in World Trade', *Review of Economics and Statistics*, May 1969.

[5]   Paish, F.W., 'Output, Inflation and Growth' in *Studies in an Inflationary Economy*, Macmillan, 1962.

[6]   Saunders, C.T., (Consultant). *Draft Note for Senior Economic Advisers to E.C.E. Governments*, August 1981 (EC.AD. (XVIII)/AC.1/R.1).

[7]   Thirlwall, A.P., 'The Balance of Payments Constraint as an Explanation of Growth Rate Differences', *Banca Nazionale de Lavoro, Quarterly Review*, March 1979.

[8]   *UN/ECE Economic Survey of Europe in 1980*, UN, 1981.

[9]   Worswick, G.D.N., 'Prices, Productivity and Incomes', *Oxford Economic Papers*, June 1958.

Comment on Chapter 3
J.S. Flemming

The issue addressed in Chapter 3 is notoriously intractable. It is therefore no criticism of David Worswick's characteristically lucid and honest contribution that it does more to clarify the issues than to resolve the problems. His conclusion that there is clearly a link in the short run but more confusion about the long run is unobjectionable. I do, however, have some differences of emphasis and some perhaps more fundamental criticism.

Perhaps the most surprising omission is the absence of any discussion of the determinants, other than the pressure of demand, of the long-term growth of productivity. Where the latter is taken to be labour productivity, investment in knowledge and machinery must have a role. It is hard to assess the significance of the pressure of demand without knowing the other determinants which may account for the time series. Indeed, it is particularly plausible that there should be a complex interaction of demand pressure, investment and productivity.

In this connection it would be natural to think of the pressure of demand in terms of the utilisation of physical capacity. This is, of course, a slippery concept but attempts have been made to measure it in ways which are not reflected in Worswick's list of three indicators.

These are: (i) the deviation of output from trend; (ii) a labour market indicator based on unemployment and/or vacancies; and (iii) capital's share in income. Of none of these is it true that shifts – especially in the long run – can safely be identified with demand changes. The first must average zero over a long period. Even in the short run not all output variations are necessarily attributable to demand. The second indicator would shift, independently of demand, if the natural rate of either unemployment or vacancies were to change with unemployment benefit changes, redundancy payments, computerised job placements or other factors. Finally, capital's share in income would change, independently of demand, if technical change were non-neutral, or factor proportions changed and the elasticity of substitution was not unity or with changes in the composition of output. Moreover, on this basis, an autonomous 1968-style rise in labour's share would be interpreted as a fall in demand, although any fall in output in this case would more plausibly be a supply response.

These comments suggest that each representation of the pressure of demand requires consideration of other factors before one can hope to isolate the effect on productivity change. Rather than address these issues, Worswick's section on the balance of payments constraint devotes more space to Thirlwall's version of the thesis that there is an external constraint on the growth rate of demand.

I agree very strongly with his criticism of this approach as involving too static a view of relative prices. Even if 'dynamics' does not involve any mysterious self-reinforcing synergistic process, the introduction of relative prices into the supply and demand function for tradeable goods means that any relative growth rates of demand at home and abroad can be reconciled by an appropriate rate of change of relative prices. These prices are our terms of trade rather than a nominal exchange rate with only transitory effects. There may, of course, be some domestic (real) price rigidities which interfere with this process – but that is not an external constraint.

The next section refers to work on the association between the rate of industrial structural change and the growth of output. A problem here is with the hypothesis that with a low pressure of demand intense competition will induce structural change. Saunders did not, however, measure the level of demand but the rate of change of output. If the income elasticities of demand for the products of sectors differ, one might expect a positive correlation between growth and structural change which could mask the Paish competitive pressure effect which might work the other way – though whether it could operate over a long period of consistently low demand pressure must be questionable.

In fact, the relationship between competition and demand pressure is complex. Paish is cited as having argued that there cannot be effective competition if there is excess demand. Uzawa has argued that competition cannot be perfect if there is excess supply. Excess demand and supply both mean that some agent cannot buy, or sell, all that he wants at going prices. That is, markets do not clear as competitive ones should. One needs to know a lot about how and why they do not clear before one can say much about a link to productivity.

In these remarks, I have made no comment on David Worswick's comments on history and policy because their common sense – again so characteristic – leaves me nothing to add.

4 Accelerating Inflation and the Growth of Productivity
A.J. Brown

It is easy to think of a number of channels through which inflation might affect the rate of growth of productivity, which I take to mean real output per person-hour of work. In the medium or long run, the rate at which productivity grows may be expected to depend largely on the rate of accumulation of capital, not only for the reasons implicit in the static production functions of the various industries, as they are usually visualised, but also because faster investment means faster adaptation of the economy to changes in patterns of demand and in economic circumstances generally, and because either a faster growing or a more rapidly renewed capital stock confers the once-for-all benefit of a fall in the average age of the technology which the stock embodies.

Whether inflation increases or decreases capital growth in the medium and long run depends on what sort of inflation it is, and on the mechanisms of price formation that operate. If entrepreneurs or public authorities are ambitious in their plans for capital formation, and finance them in part by injections of money which enable total nominal expenditure to increase faster than real product, then, *ex hypothesi* we have high capital formation (and, unless the capital is unproductive, probably high productivity growth) going with inflation. It is true that one might say that the high investment plans came first – that they caused the inflation rather than that it caused them in the first place – but so long as wages are in some degree sticky, and prices of goods fairly sensitive to demand, such a situation will lead to windfall profits and windfall tax receipts, which may encourage the investment planners and push the boom along. Indeed, given sticky wages and a degree of market flexibility in product prices, any injection or series of injections of effective demand may cause a shift to profits conducive to high capital formation and fast productivity growth. The latter enables real wages to rise absolutely, as well as real profits. So long as a higher proportion of profits than of wages finds its way, either directly or via public revenues, into productive investment, a rise in the profit share means faster growth. Inflation, which keeps prices (or rather, prices multiplied by productivity) a step

ahead of wages, will effect such a rise. Wages lagging a step behind
productivity, in the absence of price inflation, will also, of course,
give a shift to profits, but price inflation will give an extra one, with,
on the assumptions we have just stated, an extra push to productivity
growth. In these circumstances, therefore, inflation will help a secular
growth boom along.

The immediate pressures leading to inflation may, however, be of a
different kind. They may operate on import prices, or in the labour
market. In the former case, the outcome depends on the elasticity of
substitution between the imports in question and domestic substi-
tutes. If it is low, then the effect is to raise cost curves and at the same
time to deflate aggregate purchasing power, so that, in the absence
of adequate counter measures, the profit share, investment, and
productivity growth, as well as real wages, are depressed. If for any
reason inflation of money wage rates sets in, profit margins will again
be squeezed, unless the authorities take steps to expand aggregate
demand sufficiently to restore them. In practice, reduction of real
wages through inflation of import prices is very likely to be closely
followed by money wage inflation, so that these two types of cost
inflation often go together; though the latter not infrequently happens without the former. Whether together or singly, they seem likely
to reduce the rate of growth of productivity, both in the short run,
following single episodes of import price or wage inflation, or in the
medium or long run, if such episodes recur. Concerning the medium
or long term, therefore, these arguments suggest that, if continuous
or recurring pressures come mainly from the demand side, it is likely
that high profit ratios, high investment ratios, and rapid growth of
productivity will be promoted, whereas, if they come mainly from the
cost side, via import prices or wages, there will be a tendency towards
low profit ratios, low investment ratios, and slow growth of productivity.

The most obvious qualification to this suggestion arises from the
existence of choice between more and less labour saving forms of
investment. Dear labour, *ceteris paribus*, is likely to make what
investment there is more labour saving than it would otherwise be,
thus making for higher growth of productivity, though for slower
growth of employment. What matters in this connection, however, is
the relation between the expected price of labour and that of the use
of capital goods. The latter depends on the *current* price of capital
goods (which, if they are home produced, we can take as being
related to the current wage level) and the current rate of interest at
which long-term borrowing can be done. What effect inflation has on
this relation will therefore depend on whether current interest rates
fully reflect the relation between present and expected wages. If they

do, then it is not clear that inflation will directly affect this particular matter; if they fall short, some bias in favour of labour saving is, indeed, likely. But there seems little reason to assume that interest falls short of reflecting inflationary expectations; that it mostly seems to have fallen short of reflecting *subsequently realised* inflation is not strictly relevant evidence, though it presumably means that entrepreneurs have enjoyed some windfall profits at the expense of rentiers. It seems much clearer that a low realised profit ratio, consequent upon wage inflation running ahead of final purchasing power, will tend to reduce the amount available for investment, and that apprehension of this state of affairs will reduce the inducement to invest.

Another qualification we have already foreshadowed. If the elasticity of substitution between imports and home products is high, then inflation of import prices, even though it stimulates domestic wage inflation, may have an encouraging, protectionist, effect on home investment and the growth of physical productivity.

The existence and the kind of inflation can thus affect investment and growth through its influence on factor shares; it can, however, presumably do so by influencing the propensity to save, independently of income distribution. It used to be assumed (perhaps from experience in the hyper-inflations of the 1920s) that expected inflation was unfavourable to saving. Recent experience has pointed the other way, and numerous reasons for this have been put forward. It is suggested that inflation makes for insecurity and thus increases the size of the reserves of wealth that people wish to keep, that it makes people 'shop around' more, and so increase their average balances by delaying their spending, and (smelling rather less of the lamp) that it erodes reserves of assets denominated in money, and thus creates an urge to replenish them. For the moment, our chief concern is that, if it does indeed increase the propensity to save, it can have important effects on the growth of productivity in either direction.

If capital markets worked perfectly, an increase in propensity to save would, of course, increase the rate of growth of the economy. It would increase the Harrodian 'warranted rate of growth' and, even though the marginal product of capital was eventually lowered by the extra investment and the propensity to save thus pushed down again, the net effect would still be faster growth, at any rate for some time. But the capital market does not work perfectly. A Keynesian 'liquidity trap' may prevent interest from falling far enough for full employment savings, after the increase in saving propensity, to be absorbed. Physical and administrative constraints of many kinds may prevent the higher warranted rate of growth from being realised, and if it is not realised, multiplier and accelerator forces will push the level of activity further below what should be its equilibrium trend. More saving is a double-edged weapon. It may reduce growth by keeping activity, and investment, further below the full employment level on average.

So far, we have been supposing that changes in the productivity of labour depend only on the rate of *per capita* investment and the embodied technical progress which goes with it. There is, however, a very considerable variation in the average intensity of work, even as measured in person-hours actually paid for. It is most obvious in the short run, going with the variations in demand over the trade cycle, but the extent and pattern of these variations can affect estimates of the average rate of growth of productivity over longer periods, comprising a number of cycles. They can do so in at least two ways; in the first place because the amplitude of short-term fluctuations affects the average intensity of work, and through that the level of output, the rate of investment, and so the rate of growth of capacity; in the second place because variations in the amplitude and timing of cycles can distort measurements of the trend slope of output or productivity. Perhaps we should look more closely at these complications.

Some labour – perhaps clerical and administrative more than manual, though it is true of some manual labour as well – has an 'overhead' quality; it is retained, and probably works standard hours, so long as the establishment in question is functioning. It may be busier at some times than at others, though not necessarily in proportion to variations in the establishment's physical output. Other sections of the workforce may be more susceptible to short-term variations either in total numbers employed or in average hours worked per week, but it is by no means the case that total hours worked by them are fine tuned to the level of physical output. Some surges or dips in the flow of orders are thought (rightly or wrongly) to be likely to be short-lived, so that hiring and firing to accommodate them would be too wasteful of effort and goodwill, or too slow in producing effects, to be practicable. There is probably a good deal of spontaneous variation of effort to take advantage of the more leisurely pace made possible by times of slack workload, to 'spin the work out', or, on the other hand, to cope with heavy workloads by speeding up, especially where the payment system makes that worth while.

The extent to which output per person-hour, rather than average hours worked, or numbers on the books, takes the strain of fluctuation in total workload varies a good deal from one country to another. In manufacturing industry, in the period 1973-9, year-to-year changes in output were coped with in the US mostly by employment changes, to only an insignificant extent by changes in hours, and to the extent of a quarter or a third by variations in hourly productivity. In Italy, it was the other way round; productivity took more than half the strain and hours most of the rest, with employment nearly constant. Germany managed to keep the growth of productivity nearly constant (though it fell in the next year, 1979-80) when growth of output again ceased and varied hours and employment to nearly equal extents (not always in the same direction). In the UK employment and productivity seem to have contributed to the adjustment about equally, with hours making a once-for-all contribution in the recession of 1973–4. And so on. But one can make the generalisation that sudden falls in the growth of output are usually accompanied by falls in productivity growth; productivity spurts nearly always accompany spurts in total output, but also sometimes happen after a sharp recession, with output still declining, apparently as firms abandon hopes of a speedy recovery or, in some cases, go out of business – the phenomenon of 'labour shake-out', as in the UK, US and Germany in 1980-1.

Over a period in which there are a number of cycles of roughly similar amplitude, with efforts always forced up to about the same peak level in the boom, a fitted trend line will, of course, show a slope similar to that of the line through the peaks, but will lie below it. Productivity will be less on average, but will grow as fast as if the employed workforce had worked continuously at full tilt with the equipment actually in place. But if there had been no recessions, there would presumably have been more investment, so that the line of full tilt productivity would have risen more steeply than that through the actual peaks. More generally, a period of wider fluctuations, with efforts at the peak as great as those in a period of narrower fluctuations, may be expected to show a slower rate of productivity growth, whether this is measured by a line fitted to all annual (or quarterly) readings, or only to the peaks. This is the penalty for the person-hours of capital formation lost in the deeper fallings-off from peak levels.

The second of the points mentioned above is that if the period under discussion is one *within* which fluctuations tend to increase in amplitude, still coming to peaks at which the employed workforce is fully stretched, the average productivity will not, of course, rise as fast as that in peak years. Even more clearly, there will be a distortion if, for instance, the period in question starts with a peak and ends with a trough. Account must also be taken of *weak* peaks of productivity, in which the workload fails to rise to match, or at least to stretch, the workforce assembled to meet it, though after one or more such episodes, and perhaps a recession or two, it is likely that expectations of boom conditions will become more sceptical and shake-outs of labour will help to restore productivity to the highest level which the technical progress actually embodied in equipment permits. In one way or another, however, recessions of demand can affect the medium-term or long-term growth of productivity through reduced intensity of person-hours worked, as well as through the size and modernity of the capital stock. Greater severity of frequency of demand recession is, of course, not a direct consequence of inflation as such (in the usual sense or rise in the price of final output), but it can certainly be a consequence, directly or through effects on policy, of cost-push, whether from imports or from domestic factor prices.

Another way in which it has been suggested that higher inflation may produce lower growth of productivity is through its effect on business calculations. Two kinds of effect seem to be possible here. First, the increase in uncertainty introduced by varying and unpredictable inflation may lower the propensity to invest. Growth of productivity is inhibited because investment is inhibited. The second possible effect of this kind of uncertainty is that mistakes in the direction of investment are more frequent, so that the incremental capital output ratio is raised (see Friedman[3]). This latter effect, but not the first, can help in explaining a fall in productivity growth which is not accounted for by changes in factor inputs. Both effects, however, are seen as consequences of unpredictability, essentially in relative rather than absolute prices, rather than as consequences of inflation itself. It is assumed that this unpredictability and the general rate of inflation are positively associated.

So much for general reflections on the possible effects of inflation on productivity growth. It is clear that, separately, they are mostly not very easy to investigate empirically. Let us, however, start from the most general empirical question: what relations, if any, are to be found between our two variables, either over time or through a cross-section of countries? The most obvious fact is that, from 1960 to 1973, a period which, by any previous peacetime standards, was one of quite rapid inflation, productivity in all the main countries grew faster than in any previous period of anything like comparable length. In the US the superiority was not sensational (2.3 per cent a year, compared with about 2 per cent from 1870 to 1913 and between the wars), but in the UK the rate was nearly three times as great as in 1870–90, which in turn was better than the rates of 1890–1913 or 1929–38. In Germany and France, the 1960–73 rates were nearly twice as great as those from 1929–38, which in turn were better than those before the First World War, and Japan's rate from 1960 to 1973 was not far off three times her inter-war rate. If one looks back to the period from 1870 to 1913, and compares the generally deflationary first half of it with the generally inflationary second half, one finds that among the three biggest European industrial countries and the US there was not much change of performance; the UK did worse in the second half, France did better. On this record there is, to put it mildly, no evidence that sustained inflation, up to the level at which it was experienced in the main industrial countries in 1960–73, is bad for productivity growth.

The higher rates experienced since then are another matter, as are the rates previously experienced in certain other countries. There have been several investigations of the simple relation between inflation and growth across a number of countries, of which I shall refer here only to that by Thirlwall and Barton [6], who deal with 51 countries in the period 1958–67. Unfortunately for our purpose, they make use of growth rates of total real income, rather than of *per capita* income or hourly productivity, but that does not by any means totally destroy the relevance of their study.

Broadly, their main finding is that, for the seventeen countries in their sample with *per capita* incomes of more than $800, which experienced rates of inflation varying from 3 to 8 per cent, there was a significantly positive correlation between inflation and growth; that for the 34 remaining poorer countries as a whole there was no significant relation, but that if one selects from them those with inflation rates higher than 10 per cent, the seven countries in question show a *negative* correlation. They found, moreover, that the countries with the highest investment ratios were not those with the highest or lowest inflation rates, but those in the middle. Their general conclusion was, thus, that inflation at rates up to about 10 per cent a year seems to have stimulated growth, higher rates possibly to have inhibited it.

Insofar as this is relevant to rates of growth of hourly productivity, it would tend to reconcile the excellent growth performances of the main countries from 1969–73, at inflation rates of 3–7 per cent, with a deterioration in the period 1973–80, when average annual rates ran up to 17 per cent. We need, however, to look at the later period more closely.

First, we may look at the relation between inflation rate and growth of *per capita* real income for 28 countries between the years 1973 and 1979. The correlation turns out to be positive, but not significantly so. Moreover, if one removes the two countries with the highest inflation rates (Brazil and Turkey), the correlation falls to near zero. For the six big industrial countries included (US, Germany, Japan, France, UK and Italy) the correlation is negative, though not significant. What it amounts to is simply that the average growth rate for Italy and the UK is lower than the average for the other four big industrial countries (though Italy had faster *per capita*

Chart 4.1   *Average annual changes in manufacturing productivity and consumer price index*

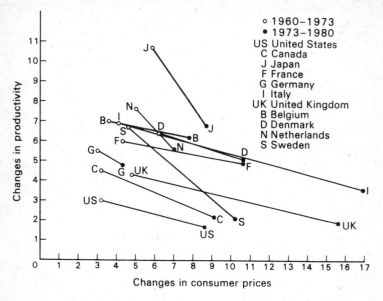

growth than the relatively low-inflation US). So, in a *per capita* version of something like a sequel to the Thirlwall and Barton investigation, one finds a hint of negative, instead of positive, relation of growth to inflation among the big developed countries, but, among the sample as a whole, no general relation except for that introduced by the fact that the two countries with by far the highest inflation rates still managed to be fast growers.

We are, however, still quite a long way from looking at productivity, properly defined; the above growth data are for income per head of the whole population, and include, for instance, a negative figure for Switzerland (the country with the lowest inflation rate in the sample) which takes no account of a substantial fall in manufacturing employment, and the departure of numerous foreign workers, which must have affected the active population total proportionately more than is reflected in total population figures. For statistics of hourly productivity in manufacturing in eleven countries we may turn to the US *Monthly Labor Review* (see Capdevielle and Alvarez, [1], where trend slopes are given for those data, and for the consumers' price index, for the periods 1960–73 and 1973–80. Chart 4.1 displays these data plotted against each other, for both periods (circles for the first, dots for the second, the pairs being joined to show how every country slipped to higher inflation and lower productivity growth).

The figure also shows how a positive correlation between inflation and productivity growth in the first period (significant at the 5 per cent level) turns into a negative, though less significant, one in the second. The rank order of productivity growth rates is little changed, apart from an especially big fall by Sweden. There is, however, some tendency for the countries with the most rapid productivity growth, both before and after 1973 (Japan, Belgium, The Netherlands) to show the smallest increases in inflation rate, while those with the lowest growth rates (US, Canada, UK) increased their inflation rates more.

It is hard to see any plausible causal mechanism indicated in this particular association of higher *absolute* growth with a lower *rise* of the inflation rate. If inflation is (say, above a certain level) bad for growth, we should look for a relation between the 1973 change of inflation rates and the 1973 change of growth rates. We can do this by either of two tests; plotting against each other either the absolute percentage point changes of the inflation and growth rates respectively, or the ratios of post-1973 to pre-1973 rates. Whichever we do, for these eleven countries, we get a negative correlation ($r = -0.47$ and -0.53 respectively), some way short of the 5 per cent significance level. We have, therefore, some (though not overwhelmingly strong) evidence that the higher *rise* of inflation from about 1973 is associated with the larger *fall* in productivity growth.

Perhaps this is the place to note that this association may arise from a causal connection in either direction – or, of course, in both, or from some third set of forces. Indeed, it is likely that productivity growth has a negative causal effect on price inflation, since it has such an effect on cost inflation. There is no reason why this should not be combined with a causal effect, either positive or negative, of price inflation on productivity growth. Using x to represent the percentage rate of growth of productivity, and p for the rate of price inflation, a two-way relation would give us:

$$p = p_o - a x \tag{1}$$

and $\quad x = x_o + b p \tag{2}$

where p_o is simply the inflation rate when there is no growth of productivity and x_o the productivity increase when there is no inflation, a is a positive constant which must normally be less than one, because domestic labour costs are not the whole of the cost of production, and b a constant which may be positive or negative, according to the direction of the effect of inflation on productivity growth, and, from the empirical evidence, is pretty certainly a good deal less than unity. We thus have: $x = (x_o + bp_o)/(1 + ab)$. If b is positive (inflation good for growth), then the actual growth of productivity when there is inflation will be greater than, or less than, it would be in the absence of inflation, according to whether p_o is greater or less than ax_o, the extent of the difference rising somewhat as b rises. This, clearly, does *not* help us to explain the fall of actual productivity growth after 1973, when it seems obvious that the zero-productivity growth rate of inflation, p_o, was higher in relation to the zero-inflation rate of productivity growth, x_o, than it had been before.

If b is negative, (inflation bad for growth) then these conditions are reversed, and a rise of p_o relatively to x_o may help to explain slower growth. This negative sign of b is also consistent with a *positive* correlation between inflation and growth if the basic rate of inflation is low enough (less than ax_o, the rate at which real factor cost is reduced by productivity growth). But this happy state of affairs did not exist in any of our countries, even between 1960 and 1973. For some years money prices of *exports* were reduced in Japan and Italy, but this was not true of total output prices anywhere.

The Thirlwall and Barton suggestion is, presumably, that the sign of b itself changes at some critical rate of (let us say, factor price) inflation. It is positive below the critical level; this will then be consistent with a positive correlation between inflation and growth, inflation itself being positive. But if we are suddenly translated into a higher region of inflation where b is negative, our correlation becomes negative. This, however, is much too simple to be applied to our data with success. Germany's growth rate, for instance, fell with the 1973 rise of inflation rate, even though that rate remained well within the range for which the international cross-section data suggest a positive association between inflation and growth. We must get down to the question *why,* and in what conditions, inflation should affect productivity growth, either way.

In the earlier part of this chapter, we drew attention to the crucial part which the distinction between demand-pull and cost-push inflation might be expected to play in determining the effect upon growth. The most obvious way of attempting to distinguish between the two is to consider the change (if any) in the profit share of value-added, along with other relevant indicators. If acceleration in the growth of nominal income is accompanied by an increase in the profit share, there is some reason to think that faster growth of demand for final products rather than faster growth of factor prices is at work. If there is an acceleration in the growth of hourly earnings, accompanied by a fall in the profit share, wage-push seems the obvious verdict. Similarly, if import price inflation accelerates and the profit share falls, import cost-push seems to be *prima facie* indicated (the more strongly because, if prices of final products are formed by marking up total costs, a rise in import prices will tend to raise the share of profits in value-added, as opposed to final selling values).

Using these criteria, it is easy to count the frequency of year-to-year changes which appear to satisfy these criteria in, for instance, the six countries US, UK, Japan, France, Germany, and Italy. Such year-to-year episodes of demand-pull or cost-push are features of the trade cycle, so that counting them, which takes no account of their severity, is an imperfect method of evaluation when one is concerned with the medium rather than the short term. So far as expenditure-pull and wage-push are concerned, the six countries collectively show no appreciable change in the balance between the two after 1973 as compared with before (1973–4 to 1978–9 as compared with 1959–60 to 1972–3). The collective frequency of what we have identified as expenditure-pull impulses is about 1.2 or 1.3 a year, both before and after 1973, and that of wage-push impulses 1.1 or 1.2, also both before and after. There is slightly more sign of an increase in the frequency of import cost-push, but it is hardly worth noting (the frequency of rises in import prices *does* increase, but it more often fails to coincide with compression of the profit share).

If, however, one takes a less episodic view of the periods before and after 1973, the story is different. In the six big countries mentioned in the last paragraph, the period 1973–9 was certainly one of lower profit shares than the preceding fourteen years. The non-labour share of GDP fell from 26 to 22 per cent in the US, 25 to 20 per cent in the UK, 43 to 34 per cent (1974–8 only) in Japan, 34 to 29 per cent in Germany, 38 to 30 per cent in France and 43 to 33 per cent in Italy. In addition to these figures from the national social accounts, we have OECD estimates relating to the gross profit share of all non-financial enterprises in the US, UK and France, which also show falls, though less dramatic ones, and for the US, UK and Germany similar estimates for manufacturing industry, of which the same is true. All the countries experienced much higher import price inflation in the later period than in the earlier one, and most of them experienced higher average wage inflation; the exceptions being Japan, where wage inflation averaged about the same in the two periods, and Germany, where it was slightly lower after 1973 than over the fourteen years before.

According to the argument we have already set out, this would suggest a stronger average pressure of cost-push, in relation to that of demand-pull, in the second period than in the first, leading, or at least contributing to the certainly lower profit shares, which, in turn, would lead one to expect both a lower incentive to invest and lower savings (in relation to income) to be invested, and thus a lower rate of growth of productivity for a given intensity of work. This, however, is not altogether borne out by further inspection.

The chief complication, of course, especially in the UK, is the shift of the propensity to save, apparently from causes other than change in the factor distribution of income, and on a more massive scale than that change could readily have accounted for. Insofar as the shift is connected with inflation, it falls within the area of our present concern.

How, and how far, is it empirically connected with inflation? (We have already glanced at some theoretical linkages.) Casual inspection reveals both correspondences and puzzling features. In the US, UK, Japan, France and Germany the savings ratio was at a high level in 1974 or 1975, whichever marked a peak of price inflation, though in the US the ratio displayed a plateau rather than a peak, and that no higher than the levels corresponding to the much lower plateau of price inflation in 1970–1. In Germany, the main peak of thriftiness corresponds to the main peak of price inflation, which was in 1970 rather than later. It is after the 1974–5 peak that the most noticeable differences in national reactions to inflation occur. In Japan and the UK, the descent of saving from the peak is much less marked than it would have to be to correspond to the moderation of inflation; indeed, in the UK the savings ratio soon sets off again for greater heights still. In the US, on the contrary, the ratio comes down far more than one would expect in the face of a markedly upward trend in inflation. In France and Germany, subsequent movements of the two series are more nearly parallel.

Systematic empirical work on this problem has grown into a substantial industry. Perhaps the simplest approach, in principle, so far as the private sector is concerned, is that applied in an international comparative study by von Ungern-Sternberg [7]. Essentially, this amounts to relating saving, not to the sector's disposable real income as usually measured, but to a redefined version of income in which the erosion of real wealth through the effect of inflation on money-denominated holdings of public debt is taken into account. Ungern-Sternberg has shown that this approach works tolerably well with the German data for 1962–77, explaining nearly all the shift in the function as usually formulated, goes a good way towards working for the UK, and helps hardly at all with the US. Howard [4] had earlier tried a rather more conventional (and eclectic) approach to data on personal saving for the US, UK, Japan, Germany and Canada in the dozen years ending in 1976, by which he detects a significant effect of inflation through its operation on real values of liquid asset holdings, and further effects through routes which are interpreted as differing from country to country – expected inflation is presumed to act through increase of uncertainty in some countries.

On the whole, the evidence that inflationary experience in the 1970s had the effect of increasing the propensity to save (as usually defined) seems to be reasonably strong, though the way in which changes in it since the peak of 1974–5 have operated in different countries may well have been far from comprehensible in terms of a single formula. If we look at what has happened to the ratio to GDP of gross domestic fixed capital formation, we see that it has not in all cases followed the same course as the savings ratio. In France, Germany and Japan it was appreciably lower in 1974–9 than in the preceding seven years, so that there remains some *prima facie* case for inflation, through the balance of its effects on thrift and the inducement to invest in productive capacity, having contributed to reduced productivity growth by this particular route. In Italy, however, there was virtually no change in the ratio between these two periods, while in the US and the UK it was marginally higher in the later of them, so that, there, it can hardly be claimed that inflation (or whatever else) reduced productivity growth in this, the most obvious way.

Insofar as inflation has brought about this increase in the supply of savings, it has, of course, raised the warranted rate of growth of the economies in question, but it has also increased the risk that some constraint or other (whether inherent in a lower 'natural' rate of growth, or in official target growth rates, or in some other limitation) will precipitate the tendency to depression which comes from falling below the warranted rate.

Before returning to this theme, we must glance at the second reason why reference to the investment ratio (and whatever caused it to be what it is) cannot provide a satisfactory direct reason for the fall in productivity growth. In some of the main countries, we have, since 1973, had higher investment ratios than before going with slower productivity growth than before. At a more refined level, we have Denison's failure (see [2]) to account for the fall of growth in the US in terms of the measurements of factor input, the production functions, and even the empirically determined allowances for less intensive working in times of excess capacity, which have stood him in good stead for earlier years.

What we have to note, in this connection, is Friedman's suggestion, referred to earlier, that greater uncertainty about prices, going with higher inflation, somehow upsets economic calculations, not in deterring investment (the effects of that would be picked up by Denison's production function) but by making them more wasteful. Empirical verification of this seems hardly possible; we can, however, comment on one link in the chain of reasoning involved – that higher inflation goes with greater price variability.

In recent experience, at least, a link between average level of inflation and variability of inflation (standard deviation of the inflation rate) can hardly be said to have existed. Both for 1960–73 and 1974–9, the correlation between mean and standard deviation, whether across the six big countries we have considered, or across a larger sample of eleven OECD countries, is very near to zero. Perhaps it is more relevant to consider the changes from the first to the second period, country by country. There, too, however, it is by no means the case that higher mean goes with higher variability. All our countries had higher means of annual increase of GDP deflator in the second period, but the US, France and Italy showed (absolutely) smaller standard deviations. Japan, with one of the smallest increases in mean, had by far the biggest increase in standard deviation. The UK was the only country out of the eleven with a large increase in both mean and variability. If one expresses the national means and standard deviations of the later period as percentages of those in the earlier one, the correlation between them is only 0.13 ($t = 0.38$). For our Big Six, there is a correlation between the period 2–period 1 relatives of inflation rate and productivity of –0.51 ($t = -1.2$). Between the relatives of productivity growth and *standard deviation* of inflation, the correlation is only –0.28 ($t = -0.58$). We clearly have no evidence to connect lower productivity growth with greater variability of inflation. Whether it is empirically connected with greater variability of *relative* prices is a bigger question, but in the light of these facts it seems doubtful.

Let us return then to the thought that inflation has increased thriftiness, and thus the warranted rate of growth, in at least some of our countries, but that some constraint has prevented growth from actually reaching these higher rates, producing thereby a further tendency for output to fall below the equilibrium growth path. That manpower has not provided the constraint is obvious from the record of unemployment, which has increased as a proportion of the labour force in every country; an arithmetic average of the increases for the Big Six gives a doubling between 1960–73 and 1974–8 (Angus Maddison's figures [5]). That plant capacity has not set a limit is harder to demonstrate, though, in view of the maintenance of quite high investment ratios in the face of diminished growth of output and employment it seems improbable that it has done so. It seems likely that the limit has been set by effective demand, and here, lest I should be accused of trespassing outside my allotted subject, I will add, quickly, that the reason for this, in turn, seems to have been the desire of governments to contain inflation, combined with their failure to realise that increases in expansionary pressure would have been needed to maintain high levels of employment where thriftiness has increased. This line of argument carries the implication that the increased inflationary pressure, which has so alarmed governments, is a pressure from the side of costs, not (at least, directly) that of demand. In large part it springs from wage-push, which in the short, even the medium, term demonstrates its substantial independence of the general pressure of demand through innumerable inter-temporal and international differences. In part, it springs from pressure of the flexible world prices of primary products; and here, of course, the demand pressures in the industrial countries do become relevant – but that is a different story.

Finally, if it is granted that the slow-down in productivity growth since 1973 is at least largely due to the greater prevalence of depression conditions, how is it that Denison, in his study of the US experience, finds an important residual for which he is unable to account, not only in terms of factor inputs (and after allowing for the effects of environmental legislation etc, but by applying his correction for the lowered intensity of working in conditions of excess capacity? It is not easy to give a satisfying answer, but the following observations may be made. We are dealing mainly with short-term changes. US manufacturing productivity growth fell in 1973–4 in the way that is normal at the onset of recession; but this recession was a sharp one. It recovered in the following year to a level above its 1960–73 average, and remained there for two years, falling below only in 1976–7 and sinking gently further until 1979–80, when demand plunged again. Apart from the obvious impact of sharp demand recessions, therefore, the question seems to be (so far as manufacturing is concerned) why productivity growth did not achieve true boom proportions (*well* above the long-term average), or, indeed, maintain that average, after a weak boom, in the years 1975–6 to 1978–9. The interesting thing is that, throughout those years, employment was growing faster than the average rate for 1960–73. The question, therefore, is whether so many employees were taken on because US industry (apparently working below full capacity) hoped for a return to its previous golden age, which never came, or whether so many *had* to be taken on to meet even the disappointing levels of demand that existed because the capacity or the will to work had declined. In the former case, there is nothing to explain – except the paralysis of demand management by cost-push inflation, to which we have already referred. In the latter case, we go back to our drawing boards.

References
[1] Capdevielle, P. and Alvarez, D., 'International comparisons of trends in productivity and labor costs,' US Bureau of Labor Statistics, *Monthly Labor Review*, December 1981.
[2] Denison, E.F., *Accounting for slower economic growth*, The Brookings Institution, Washington D.C., 1979.

[3] Friedman, M., 'Nobel Lecture: Inflation and Unemployment,' *Journal of Political Economy*, June 1977.
[4] Howard, D.H., 'Personal saving behaviour and the rate of inflation,' *Review of Economics and Statistics*, November 1978.
[5] Maddison, A., 'Western economic performance in the 1970s: A perspective and assessment,' Banca Nazionale del Lavoro, *Quarterly Review*, September 1980.
[6] Thirlwell, A.P. and Barton, C.A., 'Inflation and growth: the international evidence,' Banca Nazionale del Lavoro, *Quarterly Review*, September 1971.
[7] Ungern-Sternberg, T. von, 'Inflation and savings: International evidence on inflation-induced income losses,' *Economic Journal*, December 1981.

Comment on Chapter 4
David A. Peel

Professor Brown has outlined a number of different mechanisms by which inflation and productivity could be related and considered some of the empirical evidence for such relationships. A recurrent theme is that the influence of inflation on productivity growth will depend on the causes of inflation, in essence whether it is demand-pull or cost-push. This type of analysis clearly presents a problem for those economists who dispute the existence of cost-push inflation and instead regard inflation as essentially caused by the excesses of the domestic or world monetary authorities under flexible and fixed exchange regimes respectively. A useful, though perhaps somewhat artificial distinction, is that between the potential influence of monetary policy in acting as an instrument of stabilisation policy, (influencing deviations of output from the natural or full-employment level) and the potential influence of monetary policy on the natural rate of output itself. It is also useful to distinguish between short- and long-run influences, where the long run is defined as a situation in which actual and expected inflation are equal. Even in an economy typified by a 'surprises only matter supply curve for output' or augmented Phillips curve, it is well known that if price expectations are not formed in an unbiased or rational manner then the level of output can be temporarily driven above the natural level by expansionary monetary policy. If the money supply is persistently accelerating over a number of years, then ex-post a positive correlation between inflation and growth will be observed (assuming that other 'real' factors have not led to a reduction in the natural growth of output which outweighs this effect).

If price expectations are formed rationally then typically anticipated changes in the mean rate of monetary expansion will have no influence on output from a stabilisation perspective though in general systematic monetary policy will influence the variance of output. (The existence of multi-period non-contingent contracts is one well known rationale for this effect.)

The empirical evidence that real output is independent of rationally formed anticipated changes in the money supply even in the short run appears quite impressive. For example, Attfield, Demery and Duck [1] have provided reduced form evidence for the UK that only innovations in money supply cause output to deviate from its trend level. Unfortunately it has been shown that this empirical work is subject to the criticism of observational equivalence (see Sargent [8] and Minford and Peel [5]). In essence, the reduced forms are also consistent with a Keynesian model of the economy in which anticipated changes in monetary policy do influence real output.

The general problem of observational equivalence appears to appertain to some of Professor Brown's analysis. One method he uses to differentiate between cost-push and demand-pull inflation involves observing the behaviour of the profit share and hourly earnings, thus he writes, 'If there is an acceleration in the growth of hourly earnings, accompanied by a fall in the profit share, wage-push seems the obvious answer'.

Suppose the behavioural wage equation in an economy has the form

$$w = p(e) + Prod + Z \qquad (1)$$

where w is the growth of earnings, $p(e)$ is the expected rate of inflation, $Prod$ is productivity growth, Z are other factors influencing wages, such as lagged real wages, or unemployment. Then the share of wages in the economy is given by

$$w - p - Prod = (p(e) - p) + Z \qquad (2)$$

where p is the actual inflation rate.

Suppose expectations are formed rationally and agents anticipate an increase in money supply, it is clearly possible for expected inflation and hence nominal wages to accelerate, but the profit share to fall, if expected inflation is greater than that which actually occurs.

At the present time the case for a non-cost-push view of nominal wage determination would appear to be most reasonably based on an empirical examination of, hopefully structural, aggregate wage equations. The recent empirical evidence for a number of different countries gives some support to a non-cost-push view and further supports the view that expectations may be formed in an essentially unbiased manner (see for example Minford and Brech, [4]).

If we ignore short-run considerations are there any channels by which monetary policy and hence inflation could influence the steady-state natural growth rate? It would appear reasonable to assume that the clearest relationship between inflation and growth will emerge when the government resorts to a policy of deficit financing in order to promote the production of capital goods. For convenience, I consider the issue within the framework developed by Mundell [7] in his seminar paper. The Mundell model takes the following form

$$Y = vK \tag{3}$$
$$M(d)/PY = Aexp\,(-\alpha p) \tag{4}$$
$$M = M(d) \tag{5}$$
$$G/Y = dK/dt/Y = mAexp(-\alpha p) \tag{6}$$

where Y is the level of real output, P is the price level. $p = 1/p.dP/dt$ is the rate of inflation, $y = 1/Y.dY/dt$ is the rate of output change, $M = M(d)$ are the demand and supply of money, $m = 1/M.dM/dt$, G is real government expenditure which is equal to investment, v is the fixed output to capital ratio, A, v are positive constants. For simplicity the fractional reserve ratio is set equal to unity though this has no salient implications for our analysis. From (3), (4), (5) and (6) we can derive the following steady state relationship ($\dot{p}=0$) between inflation and output growth

$$y = Avp/exp(\alpha p) - Av \tag{7}$$

If we restrict outselves to values of $Av<1$ which must be regarded as the typical empirical case, the relationship between inflation and growth is not monotonic. In particular, for inflation rates other than that associated with the maximum growth rate, there is both a high and low inflation rate associated with a given growth rate. Since it appears that apart from the assumption of fixed factor proportions this result will survive relaxation of other restrictive features of the model (for example zero private savings), it may have implications for empirical work. Second, Mundell has neglected a range of inflation rates under which inflationary finance appears extraordinarily attractive. This possibility deserves further attention.

We now consider the implications of replacing the assumption of a fixed capital–output ratio by a neo-classical production function exhibiting the usual properties. It turns out that in steady state that whilst output growth will obviously be independent of inflation (and equal to labour force growth), the capital–output ratio, (and hence the level of productivity) will depend in a non-linear manner on inflation. $(K/Y = (p + n)Aexp(-\alpha p)/n$ where n is labour force growth.)

We also note that the dependence of the capital–output ratio in steady state on the inflation rate is also obtained in growth models in which the proceeds of the inflation tax are not used to finance capital goods (see Burmeister and Dobbel [2], Chapter 6).

To summarise the analysis it would appear that fully anticipated inflation will almost certainly affect real variables such as output per head or the capital–output ratio in steady state though the impact will be ambiguous; further that it is possible in a variety of models that there may be a relationship with the growth rate itself.

A further channel by which inflation may influence real variables is discussed by Professor Brown. If there is a link between the average level of inflation and its variance and it is further supposed that variability upsets economic calculations, then real variables may be influenced.

Empirically at least two authors have found, *ceteris paribus*, a negative relationship in time series analysis between the *level* of real output and inflation variability (see [1] for the UK and [6] for the US).

The evidence for a link between the average level of inflation and its variability is mixed. Professor Brown, for his sample of countries, finds a correlation close to zero. Other authors, for example Logue and Willett [3], found evidence of a strong positive relationship which appeared to be non-linear; for countries with relatively low rates of inflation the correlation between the rate and variability was low; for countries with relatively high rates the correlation was stronger. In addition, the correlation was not as strong for the highly industrialised countries. Because the relationship between inflation variability and inflation represents a reduced form correlation and not a structural relationship, we should be suspicious of policy recommendations that, for instance, state that reduction of the aggregate inflation rate will reduce inflation variability with the consequent welfare and output implications. If, for instance, one-time shocks (say an oil shock) increase both the variability and the level of inflation, then reducing the average rate of inflation will not affect the variability. Further large relative price shifts, say due to a shift in energy supply, which correlate with aggregate price variability, may represent useful price signals rather than signal distorting noise. For this type of reason it would appear that this channel for inflation to have real effects should be treated with caution (see Taylor [9] for an excellent discussion of these issues).

Finally, Professor Brown discusses the important channel by which inflation could influence the savings ratio. Whist there is some disagreement as to whether it is inflation *per se* or unanticipated inflation which has an influence on real savings behaviour, it seems reasonable to assume that the interaction of anticipated inflation and the tax system will lead to distortion of saving and investment decisions which has real effects.

Conclusion

It would appear that in a monetarist model inflation and real variables may well be associated in steady state. Outside steady state, unanticipated inflation will cause further temporary real effects. From an empirical viewpoint previous work based on reduced form correlations between real variables and inflation is inadequate because it does not represent estimation of structural relationships. Moreover they do not typically allow for unanticipated inflation and consequently are not of any great value in assessing the relationship between the variables. More subtle empirical tests than have previously been carried out appear necessary. Identification problems are, however, so serious that reduced form tests are unlikely to resolve the issue. Consequently estimates of structural equations appear necessary.

References

[1] Attfield, C.L.F., Demery, D. and Duck, N.W., 'A quarterly model of unanticipated monetary growth, output and the price level in the UK 1963–1978', *Journal of Monetary Economics*, November 1981.

[2] Burmeister, E. and Dobbel, A.R., *Mathematical theories of economic growth*, Macmillan, 1970.

[3] Logue, D.E. and Willett, T.D., 'A note on the relation between the rate and variability of inflation,, *Economica*, May 1976.

[4] Minford, A.P.L. and Brech, M., 'The wage equation and rational expectations', in *Macroeconomic Analysis*, ed. Currie, D., Nobay, R., and Peel, D, Croom Helm, 1981.

[5] Minford, A.P.L. and Peel, D.A., 'The classical supply hypothesis and the observational equivalence of classical and Keynesian models', *Economics Letters*, 1979.

[6] Mullineaux, D., 'Unemployment, industrial production, and inflation uncertainty in the United States', *Review of Economics and Statistics*, May 1980.

[7] Mundell, R.A., 'Growth, stability and inflationary finance', *Journal of Political Economy,* April 1965.

[8] Sargent, T.J., 'The observational equivalence of natural and unnatural theories of macroeconomics', *Journal of Political Economy*, June 1976.

[9] Taylor, J.B., 'On the relation between the variability of inflation and the average inflation rate', in Brunner, K. and Meltzer, A.H. (eds), *The Costs and Consequences of Inflation,* Amsterdam, North-Holland, 1981, Carnegie Rochester Conference Series on Public Policy Vol. 15.

5 Capital Accumulation and Productivity Growth
J.R. Sargent*

Is the world running down? Or is it merely reverting to a more normal rate of productivity growth? The convening of this conference (and others) suggests a prevalent fear that the answer to the first question may be 'yes'. In this school of thought, the slow-down in productivity growth, which has now begun to appear as a common feature of the major industrial economies, tends to be treated as a fall from grace or a slippage from what ought to be. The disposition is to explain it in terms of failures of government policies which, by allowing too much inflation or too little demand (for example), have allowed conditions to develop in which the rate of capital accumulation cannot be sustained. Important among these conditions are the signs in several economies of a decline in the rate of profit; and this is also seen by some as vindicating prophesies made some hundred or more years ago not only by Karl Marx but also by John Stuart Mill. The purpose of this paper is to advance a different view: that the slow-down in the growth of productivity itself represents a reversion to normality in the sense of a more sustainable rate of advance. Similarly the decline in the rate of profit, although it may well rule out investment on the scale which would be needed to sustain earlier rates of productivity growth, is itself a consequence of an earlier rate of investment which was in excess of what is sustainable in the long run and was due to special stimuli whose effects have been exhausted. Thus, in my view, the answer to the first question may be 'yes', but so is the answer to the second. If this is correct, it enables the slow-down in productivity growth to be seen in a more relaxed light, analogous perhaps to the slower speed one reverts to after overtaking another car rather than the loss of power which precedes the failure of the engine.

My argument rests on the assertion that in the first of our standard periods, 1960–73, the pace of capital accumulation – the rate of growth of the capital–labour ratio – was lifted above its long-run equilibrium by a fall in the real cost of capital funds. This may be defined as the real rate of return which the owners of capital funds

* I am indebted to Mr John Capper and Mr Paul Duncan for their help in the preparation of this paper.

have to be able to expect if they are to be persuaded to commit those funds to an enterprise. It is not necessarily coincident with the real rate of interest, indeed may move differently from it, since enterprises will to a greater or lesser extent – and probably to a greater extent in the UK and US than in France, Germany and Japan – have access to the market for equity capital, whose cost will be determined by the confidence with which future profits are expected to be available after tax for shareholders. Five years ago the McCracken Report [3] recognised the possibility that through the 1950s and 1960s there was 'a fall in the real cost of capital reflecting a falling risk premium on equities and in some cases tax concessions'. Time has not allowed me (as I had hoped) to assemble evidence which might bear on this proposition in the five major economies with which we are primarily concerned and to judge how far in each of them the McCracken Report's 'possibility' can be asserted more boldly as a fact – if only of the 'stylised' variety popularised by Professor Kaldor. Nevertheless it can perhaps be asserted with enough plausibility to warrant exploring what it implies for the interpretation of recent economic history; and this is the main purpose of this Chapter. It follows that anyone convinced that no such fall in the real cost of capital occurred will not wish to read any further.

For the UK this would be difficult to deny, following the work originated by J.S. Flemming and others in the Bank of England and now reported regularly in its *Quarterly Bulletin* [1]. Their estimates, which express current profits as a percentage of the stock-market valuation of industrial and commercial companies' ordinary shares, preference shares, debentures and other debt, including their bank borrowing at its nominal value net of liquid assets held, suggest a decline in the real post-tax cost of capital from about 9 per cent in 1960 (when the series begins) to 4 per cent at the end of the decade. It seems likely that two factors which may have contributed to the fall will have also been at work in the other economies. In the first place, there has been a general disposition to ensure that tax systems were relatively favourable to investment. As a result of various *ad hoc* adjustments, T.P. Hill [2] concludes: 'The result has been that the actual allowances granted for tax purposes, although nominally based on historic costs, have, at least until recently, actually exceeded those which would have been obtained by a proper or realistic calculation of depreciation at current costs . . . . Estimates have been made for the United States . . . which show this to have been the case up to 1974, even though the United States has not been nearly so prolific as some other countries in granting various special allowances. It may be surmised that a similar situation obtained in most countries until the explosion of inflation in the early and mid 1970s.'

The various special allowances which Hill refers to were in some cases intended primarily to support regional development (for example investment in the south of Italy), but sprang from a conventional wisdom that higher investment was an essential element in higher economic growth. But apart from incentives for investment which were applied through specific government policies, there was the general and possibly more powerful incentive which strengthened during the 1950s and 1960s as a result of increased confidence that the level of aggregate demand could and would be so managed by governments as to reduce the risks of commitment by businesses to enlarged capacity. In this period doubts whether full employment could be maintained with a tolerable rate of inflation receded, and it was not until the end of it that they began to be revived as the Keynesian anti-biotics encountered the 'expectations syndrome' with which we are now familiar.

Theoretical Consequences of a Fall in the Cost of Capital
If it is a plausible assumption that a fall in the real cost of capital began in the 1950s, what effects might this be expected to have? The following analysis is appropriate where investment decisions seek to maximise profits, and starts with a Constant Elasticity of Substitution production function in which there are constant returns to scale and technical progress is Harrod-neutral. If y is output per unit of labour and k is capital per unit of labour, we have:

$$y = Me^{\lambda t}[\delta(e^{-\lambda t}k)^{-\theta} + (1-\delta)]^{-\frac{1}{\theta}} \qquad (1)$$

This equation says that the higher is the capital–labour ratio at any point of time, the higher are the average and marginal productivities of labour and the lower are the average and marginal productivities of capital. The coefficient θ reflects the elasticity of substitution of capital for labour in the productive process. The most profitable capital–labour ratio is such that the value of the marginal product of capital equates with its cost as defined above; we write this as $\bar{\rho}$ and assume it to be exogenously determined. If P is the value-added price of the product and P_k the price of capital equipment, the most profitable capital–labour ratio k is determined by the equation:

$$\frac{P}{P_k}\frac{\partial y}{\partial k} = \frac{P}{P_k}M\delta\left[\delta + (1-\delta)[e^{-\lambda t}k]^{\theta}\right]^{-\frac{1}{\theta}-1} = a\bar{\rho} \qquad (2)$$

where a is greater than unity to an extent determined by the elasticity of demand for the product and the elasticity of supply of capital goods. Imagine that, at a certain base date ($t = 0$), this condition is satisfied. Given the relative prices of the product and the equipment

Chart 5.1

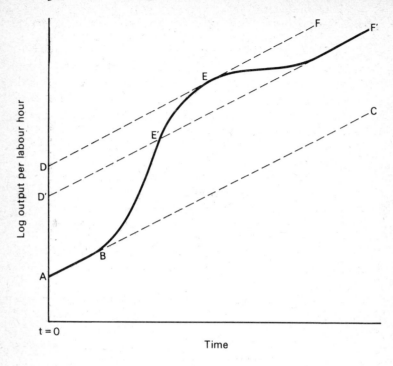

producing it, the value of k derived from (2) for $t = 0$, when entered into (1), gives the level of output per head then. But it also follows that if (2) is to continue to be satisfied over time, with $\bar{\rho}$ constant over time, k must increase over time at rate λ, and the prices of the product and capital equipment must increase over time at an equal rate. From (1) this will keep the average productivity of capital constant in real and money terms, and output per unit of labour increasing at the constant rate λ. This equilibrium path is represented by the line ABC in the chart.

But suppose that at $t = 0$ the real cost of capital had been lower, at $\bar{\rho}'$. From (2) the lower real cost of capital would have justified a higher capital–labour ratio at $t = 0$, and/or a higher price of capital equipment relative to the price of product. The changeover could be reflected wholly in the latter, if there is zero price elasticity in the supply of capital goods. Short of this, however, the response to $\bar{\rho}'$ would imply a correspondingly higher output per unit of labour, such as that denoted by point D on the chart, and a lower average and marginal productivity of capital. But to keep the lower marginal productivity of capital in line with its lower real cost would still require the capital–labour ratio to increase over time at the same rate λ, and the relativity of capital equipment to product prices to remain constant at its higher level. This equilibrium path is represented by the line DEF. (The line D'E'F' should be disregarded for the time being.) Along DEF it follows from (1) that y, k and k/y are all higher than at the same point of time on ABC. While y is proceeding along ABC, an exogenous fall in the real cost of capital will call for a transition from the lower equilibrium path ABC to a higher one such as DEF, the latter being characterised by a higher k. In the real world the transition will not be instantaneous. To clarify the stages of the adjustment, differentiate (1) with respect to time:

$$\frac{dy}{dt}\frac{1}{y} = \lambda + \frac{\partial y}{\partial k}\frac{k}{y}\left(\frac{dk}{dt}\frac{1}{k} - \lambda\right) \tag{3}$$

and assume that k is gradually modified upwards or downwards from its equilibrium growth rate, λ, according as the marginal productivity of capital exceeds or falls short of its cost:

$$\frac{dk}{dt}\frac{1}{k} = \lambda + \alpha\ \frac{\dfrac{\partial y}{\partial k} - a\bar{\rho}\dfrac{P_k}{P}}{\dfrac{\partial y}{\partial k}} \tag{4}$$

where α represents the adjustment lag. Feeding (4) into (3) we have:

$$\frac{dy}{dt}\frac{1}{y} = \lambda + \alpha\frac{k}{y}\left(\frac{\partial y}{\partial k} - a\bar{\rho}\frac{P_k}{P}\right) \tag{5}$$

Initially $\bar{\rho}$ is at its higher level and we move from point A on the chart to the right along the lower equilibrium path. The bracket on the right-hand side of (5) is zero and y grows at a rate λ. At point B the real cost of capital falls below the prevailing marginal productivity of capital. Firms therefore realise that it is profitable to use more capital per unit of labour than they currently are, and k's growth rate is lifted above λ – see (4). From (5), the rate of growth of y accelerates above λ and a movement begins along BE. But, as can be seen from (2), when k is growing faster than λ, as it now is, the marginal productivity of capital falls over time. Its fall has, of course, some way to go before it matches the fall in the real cost of capital, and in the interim can be regarded as no more than the natural response to this. The capital–output ratio will at the same time be rising, and through (5) will be an influence increasing the extent to which y's growth rate accelerates above λ. But as we proceed along BE, the bracket on the right hand side of (5) is growing smaller and will eventually be extinguished as the marginal productivity of capital falls into line with its lower real cost. When this occurs, output per head turns from BE onto EF and reverts to the rate of growth λ.

It is possible that this could fail to occur if, as the marginal productivity of capital fell, so did the current price of capital equipment in terms of the product – the P_k/P term in (5). This seems unlikely to be the case, since along BE the output needing to be absorbed by the market is everywhere higher than along BC and the demand for capital equipment is also higher. The effect of these combined influences will generally be to raise P_k/P and therefore to add to the forces which gradually rein back the accelerated growth of output per head along BE to the normal rate λ along EF. But these forces might act slowly, for example, where the higher demand for capital equipment allows economies of scale to be realised for a while in producing it, and these are passed on to the customer. Thus, the elasticity of supply in the capital goods industries could be a factor which determines the period over which different economies exhaust the benefits of a given reduction in the cost of capital and its different extent.

What happens to profitability during the process traced above? The rate of return on capital at its current replacement cost (P_k) may be written:

$$\pi = \frac{P}{P_k} \frac{y}{k} \left[1 - \frac{w}{\dfrac{\partial Y}{\partial L}} \cdot \frac{\dfrac{\partial Y}{\partial L}}{y} \right] \tag{6}$$

where w is the money wage deflated by P, the price of the product. It has been shown already that y/k begins falling away when we turn off the lower equilibrium path ABC to move along BE in response to a lower real cost of capital; and that this is likely to be associated with a relative rise in the price of capital equipment, lowering P/P_k. But what of the bracket in (6), the share of profits in value-added? Assume for the moment that w is adjusted to the marginal product of labour so that the ratio between the two remains constant. Then the share of profits will fall so long as a rise in k raises the productivity of labour more at the margin than on average, that is, raises $\partial Y/\partial L$ relative to y. But this requires us to assume that the elasticity of substitution of capital for labour in the productivity process $[1/(1 + \theta)]$ is less than unity. Apart from the possibility of an elasticity of substitution greater than unity, it may be that w proves sluggish in adapting to the new circumstances, continuing to grow at a rate not much above λ; and this would also help to sustain the rate of return on capital by raising the profit share. However, it can be shown from the comparative statics of the model that the rate of return on capital must fall in response to a fall in its cost. Intuitively, such a fall will induce enterprises to include in their investment programmes some projects whose prospective returns are below the previous cut-off point, and this will tend to lower the returns realised on the capital stock as a whole. Nevertheless the uncertainty which we have been unable to eliminate about the response of the profit share leaves it open for this to happen in different ways in different economies or in different sectors of the same one. Much the same things would be expected to happen in a model in which technical progress is completely embodied in newly-installed capital equipment of the latest 'vintage', while equipment of the older vintages retains its original productivity characteristics.

When the fall in the real cost of capital occurs at point B of the chart, it becomes profitable to instal more equipment of the latest vintage than was the case before; gross investment rises. With more new equipment added to the pre-existing stock, and therefore a greater proportion of output being produced from the newest equipment, the average productivity of labour begins to rise faster than before. But this is given a further impetus by a contraction in the scrapping margin. With more new equipment in the stock, and no less of the old, the firm will be employing more labour and producing more output, which points to some rise in money wages relative to the price of the product. But this will mean that old equipment which was just within the margin of being scrapped, will now be pushed beyond it, begin making losses, and be scrapped. Thus the average age of equipment in use will be reduced, and from this a further acceleration of the growth of output per unit of labour (though not necessarily of output) will come about. Thus begins the move along BE. But while this is happening the share of profits in total output is falling as the age for scrapping equipment falls. All vintages more modern than the oldest enjoy a positive share of profits in value-added – the higher, the more modern. But the fact of more new equipment being installed does not alter labour productivity on these other vintages; the vintage alone decides that. Thus as the money wage rises relative to the product price and is paid without discrimination to the labour working all vintages, there is a general decline in the share of profits, although it will be offset to some extent by the fact that more equipment of relatively low profitability has been expelled from the stock.

The decline in the overall share of profits leads also to a decline in the rate of return on capital, given our assumption of constant returns and Harrod-neutrality. This makes output per unit of equipment the same for each vintage, so that having more new and less old does not alter the overall capital–output ratio. But since the overall share of profits falls and the increased demand for new equipment is likely to raise the current replacement cost of capital equipment relative to the price of what it produces – as it did in the CES case – the rate of return on capital must decline. This will also apply to the rate of return on newly-installed equipment, so that investment will revert to its previous level, the decline in the average age of capital equipment will come to an end, and the growth of output per unit of labour, no longer supported by this, will return to its normal λ. The only thing that the vintage model will not do, under our assumptions, is to reproduce a rise in the capital–output ratio at constant prices. For this it is necessary to suppose either that embodied technical change is capital-using, so that increased concentration on newer vintages raises the average capital–output ratio, or that this occurs because the higher rate of installation of the newer vintages takes place at the cost of some diseconomies of scale in their operation.

The main difference which emerges between the theoretical predictions of the vintage and the CES models, under our simplifying assumptions of constant returns to scale and Harrod-neutrality, is that in response to a fall in the cost of capital the vintage model will unequivocally generate a fall in the share of profits but not (without further assumptions) in the output–capital ratio, whereas the CES model will not necessarily produce (without further assumptions) a fall in the share of profits but will unequivocally generate a fall in the output–capital ratio. It may be reasonable to argue that neither model is likely to apply realistically across the board, and that in particular industries the one is likely to be preferable to the other. This would depend upon the differential extent to which the nature of technical progress in each is such that it has to be embodied in specific new types of physical equipment or alternatively can be exploited in a more disembodied way. If this is so, we would expect when examining a mix of industries aggregated into a category such as manufacturing to find strong traces of the effects which each model on its own unequivocally predicts, namely a decline in the profit share from the one and in the output–capital ratio from the other. The product of these two components, however, which is the return on capital, is unequivocally predicted by both models.

The Facts
How far does this theoretical explanation of the productivity slowdown square with the facts – or at least with the statistics? The

Table 5.1   *Manufacturing industry*

			US	Japan	France	Germany	UK
Annual percentage rates of increase							
1.	Y	– 1960–73	4.7	13.3	7.6	5.2	3.0
		1973–9	2.0	5.0	2.9[a]	1.3[a]	−0.7
2.	L	– 1960–73	1.6	2.3	0.9	−0.2	−0.9
		1973–9	0.6	−1.5	−2.1[a]	−4.0[a]	−1.2
3.	K	– 1960–73	2.8	14.2	5.7	6.7	3.5
		1973–9	2.8	5.8	4.1[a]	2.3[a]	2.4
4.	Y/L	– 1960–73	3.1	10.9	6.8	5.5	4.0
		1973–9	1.4	6.6	5.1[a]	5.2[a]	0.5
5.	K/L	– 1960–73	1.2	11.7	4.8	7.0	4.4
		1973–9	2.2	7.4	6.3[a]	6.4[a]	3.7
6.	K/Y	– 1960–73	−1.9	0.8	−1.9	1.4	0.4
		1973–9	0.7	0.7	1.1[a]	1.1[a]	3.1
Annual averages per cent							
7.	π	– 1960–72	30.2	35.5[b]	12.8[e]	22.8	12.8
		1973–8	22.2	24.4[c]	11.0[d,e]	15.5[d]	4.5
8.	$(1-\frac{w}{y})$	– 1960–72	20.7	35.4[b]	21.4[e]	28.8	15.3
		1973–8	17.8	21.0[c]	18.5[d,e]	20.5	11.0

Sources: Lines 1–3, OECD. Lines 7–8, OECD (T. P. Hill).
Y = Value-added at constant prices.
L = Labour hours worked.
K = Gross capital stock.
π = Rate of return to fixed capital (net).
$(1-\frac{w}{y})$ = Share of net profits in net value added.

[a] 1973–8. [b] 1965–72. [c] 1973–7. [d] 1973–6. [e] Non-financial corporate and quasi-cor-
porate enterprises.
I am indebted to OECD for supplying computer printout for value-added, labour
hours, and gross capital stock at constant prices in manufacturing industry. For the
sake of consistency I have used these throughout rather than those supplied to
participants for value-added and labour hours by Mrs Ann D. Morgan. I am also
grateful to Mr T.P. Hill for some more recent data on profit shares and rates of return
than were included in his 1979 OECD study 'Profits and Rates of Return'. The capital
and value-added basis of his figures may not be identical with those of the OECD
printout.

relevant numbers are set down in the table for the two standard
periods 1960–73 and 1973–9; for 1979–81 too few are available,
particularly for the capital stock, to enable worthwhile comparisons
to be made. The figures refer to manufacturing throughout, except
that for France the profit figures are for non-financial enterprises.
    Together with the slower growth of labour productivity (line 4 of
the table) in 1973–9 (although in Germany it had barely become
perceptible), all five economies exhibit (line 7) a lower rate of return
on capital then, as would be expected from the theory deployed

above. They also exhibit (line 8) a lower share of profits in value-added, which the theory expects for at least some of the individual industries within manufacturing, where technical progress may be of the kind which needs to be embodied in new capital equipment. After this unanimity, the economies divide into two groups:

a) in Germany, Japan and the UK the capital–output ratio (line 6) is rising in both periods and the growth in the capital–labour ratio (line 5) slackens in the second. This behaviour is consistent with the theory, although in the UK it is perhaps surprising that capital accumulation did not slacken more, given the low level to which returns had fallen. Perhaps the British have been more subject to the 'money illusion' induced by historic cost accounting;

b) In France and the US the slackening of the growth of labour productivity in the second period was accompanied by an actual acceleration in the rate of growth of the capital–labour ratio. In the US this ratio appears to have increased very little in the sub-period 1960–7, but began to do so in 1967–73 and maintained the higher rate of growth in 1973–9. For France the growth of the ratio appears to have been accelerating for most of the period 1960–73. The fact that the growth of the capital–labour ratio did not slacken in the 1973–9 period in these two economies is not in itself inconsistent with the theory advanced above to explain the productivity slow-down. As can be inferred from the algebra above the rate of growth of labour productivity has three components. If the first of these, the rate of technical progress, is taken as given, a slowing-down in the growth of labour productivity may be due either to to a fall in the rate of growth of the capital–labour ratio or to a fall in the marginal productivity of capital relative to its average. The latter occurs as the economy moves along BE in the chart, provided that the elasticity of substitution is less than unity; and for a time it could act on its own to damp down the rate of growth of labour productivity, during a reaction-lag before the rate of capital accumulation was itself adjusted downwards. After a lag, of course, one would expect to observe this happening too, and the question remains why it had not yet happened in 1973–9 in France and the US. Possibly in 1960–73 these economies had a larger backlog of investment opportunities remaining to be exploited; indeed, they showed a tendency for rates of return as well as the average productivity of capital to rise during that period. In the case of France this might be attributed to catching up on the effects not only of the war but also of the period of stagnation in the 1930s when there was a long struggle to maintain the parity of the franc against gold. In the case of the US it is more surprising. It may be that some part of the rise in the capital–output ratio in 1973–9 has to be put down to measures for preserving the environment and combatting pollution enforced by the US government, whose absence or lower incidence may have allowed the ratio to decline in 1960–73; but this is outside our theory.

Since the capital–labour ratio grew more rapidly in France and the US in 1973–9 than in 1960–73, while the productivity of labour grew less rapidly, the theory suggests a sharp decline in the marginal productivity of capital. This receives support from line 6 of the table, which shows that both economies, after a decline in the capital–output ratio in the first period, joined the other three in the second period in experiencing a rise. It may be reasonable to surmise that they were en route to join the other three in a lower rate of capital accumulation also. A plot of the annual figures for the capital–labour ratio, expressed as five-year moving averages to damp down cyclical variations, suggests that a deceleration had in fact set in by the end of the 1973–9 period in the US. In France this was not obviously so, but the acceleration appeared to have ceased.

Thus I conclude that, although questions remain concerning France and the US, the behaviour of the variables in the table is not at variance with the theory which has been proposed to explain them.

Conclusion

It remains to consider what the theory implies for the future. First, is the slow-down in productivity growth likely to prove permanent or transitory? The implication of my argument is that it will be permanent, if the comparison is with the rate of productivity growth achieved in the 1960–73 period. In terms of the chart, the slow-down experienced is the one from BE, when productivity growth was accelerated above its equilibrium rate by the effects of a fall in the cost of capital, to EF, when these effects have been fully absorbed and productivity growth returns to its equilibrium rate. However, it does not follow that productivity growth will continue on the low rate of the last few years. It seems plausible to suggest that the last decade has seen a rise in the cost of capital, induced partly by the two 'oil shocks' and partly by the loss of confidence in governments' inclination and ability to manage demand in a stable way. There is certainly evidence in the UK for such a rise in the cost of capital. It would imply a downward shift in the DEF schedule to D'E'F'. The adjustment to the D'E'F' path would mean a very slow (or even negative) rate of productivity growth for a while; but eventually it should turn up along this path as equilibrium at the higher cost of capital is regained. Thus my answer to the first question is that, while productivity growth is unlikely to get back to the rate achieved in 1960–73, it may well rise permanently above the rate to which it must have descended recently.

The second question is whether anything can be done by government policy to counter the slow-down. My thesis leaves me little to say on this, since it attributes the slow-down to the completion of an adjustment to a decline in the cost of capital which was triggered at least to some extent by what governments did to stimulate capital investment. These policies have run their course, it seems, and have had the effects which theory predicted for them. If they were to be reinforced, at some budgetary cost, another period of temporary acceleration in productivity growth would be possible – as the US will no doubt find from President Reagan's programme of investment incentives – but this would be followed by another slow-down as the effects were again absorbed. In any case investment incentives are only one element in the cost of capital; and the rise in it suggested above as having occurred in the last decade must be primarily due to others. One of these could be the currently high level of real interest rates, although this is a phenomenon which has only emerged in the last two or three years. Moreover, real interest rates were respectably positive for most of the 1960s, when investment was generally high, and negative for much of the 1970s, when it weakened. This points to the dominance of the elusive factor of 'confidence'. This has been weakened not only by the trouble which Keynesian demand management ran into through inflationary expectations, but also by the failure of the monetarist experiment to prove itself any different from old-fashioned deflation. Perhaps the best that can be hoped is that we are now moving towards a consensus on what can and cannot be done to manage the economy out of which it will be possible to stabilise the confidence of investors at a higher level. At the same time there is no reason to call off the search for ways and means of improving the long-run equilibrium rate of productivity growth, or the 'technical progress' in the λ of equation (1); and this is particularly the case in the UK, where our efforts so far have been comparatively unsuccessful.

References

[1]   Flemming, J.S., Price, L.D.D., and Byers, Mrs S.A., 'The Cost of Capital, Finance and Investment', *Bank of England Quarterly Bulletin*, vol. 16, no. 2, June 1976. Revised and updated figures have been published in the June issues of the *Bulletin* in subsequent years.

[2]   Hill, T.P., *Profits and Rates of Return*, OECD, 1979, p. 13.

[3]   McCracken, P. *et al.*, *Towards Full Employment and Price Stability*, OECD, 1977, paragraph 239.

Comment on Chapter 5
Maurice Scott

Both Sargent and Glyn (see Chapter 9) in their stimulating chapters argue that rapid accumulation of capital has driven down its rate of return in many of the major OECD countries. For Sargent, this also accounts for an acceleration followed by a retardation of productivity growth. For Glyn, it is rather the subsequent fall in the rate of investment and the recession which are responsible for that. Let me take each in turn.

Sargent
During the 1950s and 1960s, there was a speeding up in the rate of accumulation (defined as the rate of growth of capital stock per unit of labour employed) in manufacturing industry in the major OECD countries. This was caused by tax changes and by the strengthening of business confidence during the long postwar boom. The rate of return which companies required their investments to earn, before tax and risk premiums are deducted, therefore fell, and they invested at a faster rate.

With his customary clarity Sargent analyses the outcome of this process using an orthodox neo-classical production function of the usual general form with constant returns to scale and Harrod-neutral technical progress. With such a function, the proportionate rate of growth of labour in *efficiency* units is the sum of its rate of growth in *natural* units (say, man-hours) and the rate of growth of efficiency per man-hour, the latter being determined exogenously and labelled Harrod-neutral technical progress. So long as the rate of growth of the capital stock is the same as the rate of growth of labour in efficiency units, there being constant returns to scale, output will grow at the same rate, the rate of return on capital will be constant and output per *natural* unit of labour (i.e. productivity) will grow at the exogenously determined rate of technical progress. If, however, for the reasons just given, the rate of investment is increased so as to make capital grow faster than this equilibrium rate for a time, this will have two effects.

First, it will make output and productivity grow faster. Secondly, since the ratio of capital to labour in efficiency units will be rising, diminishing returns to capital will set in, and so the rate of return to capital will fall. When the rate of return has fallen to its new, lower, equilibrium level justified by the new tax rates and the greater business confidence, companies will not want to see it fall any further. Steady growth should then be resumed, which means that the capital stock will once again grow only as fast as the labour force measured in efficiency units. That also means that the old, lower rate of productivity growth, equal to the Harrod-neutral rate of technical progress, will be resumed.

In this way Sargent can explain several things which have actually happened, namely, the faster rate of growth of productivity in the postwar than in the prewar years, the recent slowing down in the rate of growth of productivity, and the tendency for rates of return on capital to fall.

Most of Sargent's paper is concerned with the type of model just described, and the data he uses also relate to it. However, he points out that much the same story would be told if one were to adopt a vintage model of the clay–clay variety. There are some differences (which would have been lessened had he considered a putty–clay vintage model, I think), but they are of relatively minor consequence.

Sargent's table 5.1 does not show how K/L or productivity growth accelerated. Instead, it focusses on the subsequent deceleration of productivity growth and decline in the rate of profit. Thus the three countries which are meant to exemplify the theory, Japan, Germany and the UK, have a lower rate of growth of K/L in 1973–9 than in 1960–73, and this is accompanied (as predicted) by a lower rate of growth of productivity. At the same time, the average annual rate of return to net fixed capital is lower in 1973–8 than in 1960–72 for these three countries (and also, for that matter, for the other two countries in the table, the US and France). These data on the rate of profit are not exactly what is needed to test the theory, since for that purpose one would like to be shown that rates of return fell *during* the period 1960–73 when K/L was growing unduly fast, and that they fell less fast, or possibly rose, during 1973–9, when K/L was growing more slowly. Indeed, Glyn's chart 9.1 (which, however, refers to the whole economy of the main OECD countries taken together) shows profit rates rising until 1968, and only then sharply falling.

The more worrying feature of the table is the poor correspondence between rates of growth of K/L and of productivity, Y/L. Only Japan and Germany really fit the theory well, Japan showing a big drop in both and Germany a small drop in both. The UK shows a big drop in the rate of growth of productivity with a small drop in that of K/L, and so the former is not plausibly explained by the latter. The case of the US and France is worse, in that their rates of growth of productivity fall while K/L grows faster. Sargent attempts to explain this away within his theory by reference to equation (3), where a decline in the output elasticity of capital could offset the faster growth in K/L. However, if the share of profits in value-added can be taken as an indicator of this output elasticity (as it often is), the fall in that share shown in line 8 of table 5.1 is surely insufficient for this explanation to hold.

I do not want, however, to confine my attack on the orthodox neo-classical theory used by Sargent to this one table. There is a great deal of other empirical evidence which casts doubt on the usefulness of that theory, and there are other strong grounds for rejecting it.

So far as the empirical evidence is concerned, one can mention Denison's enormously careful and valuable studies of US growth, which have been much quoted by other contributors to this volume. Denison has done his best to account for the effect of changes in K, L and a great many other factors on the growth of output and productivity in the US. Like others using a similar approach, Denison is left with a residual, unexplained, increase in output which he attributes in the main to 'advances in knowledge' together with changes in the lag of average techniques behind best-practice techniques. Throughout the period 1948–73 Denison finds that the rate of growth in the US non-residential business sector attributable to this group of factors is approximately constant and this seems, at first sight, very satisfactory from the point of view of those favouring this approach. There are, however, two less favourable features of Denison's findings which must be pointed out.

First, if the residual is indeed a measure of the effects of technical progress why was it approximately constant from 1948 to 1973 when the ratio of R & D expenditure to national income in non-residential business approximately trebled?

Secondly, how can you have negative technical progress? This is the implication of Denison's estimates for the period after 1973, *after* he has made allowance for every factor he can, including changes in capacity utilisation. It is one which he is unable to explain.

Denison is not alone in finding apparently negative rates of technical progress using this approach. Matthews, Feinstein and Odling-Smee [1], in their very careful estimates relating to the UK, find a negative residual for the period 1913–24, and a zero residual over the forty years from 1873 to 1913. A zero over such a long period is almost as hard to believe as a negative figure. Negative residuals are also found by Ohkawa and Rosovsky [2] for the periods 1908–17 and 1917–31 for Japan – again after adjusting as carefully as they can for all measurable factors. Of course, since the residual is a residual, its behaviour can always be explained by unmeasured factors, and the question then is whether such explanations are plausible.

I have attempted elsewhere (see Scott, [3] and [4]) to attack the theoretical basis of the method adopted by Sargent and the above-quoted writers of relating capital input to growth. For lack of space I will confine myself here to one point only, namely, the use of the gross capital concept which they all employ in their production functions. If that concept is to be appropriate, it must be assumed that K is homogeneous, so that a unit change in K has the same effect on output whatever unit of the capital stock one refers to. Of course, in any aggregate empirical work one has to be satisfied with fairly crude approximations. But this assumption of homogeneity is not even a *very* crude approximation. The perpetual inventory method, which is used to construct the gross capital stock, values each item in the stock at its original cost revalued to the prices of the chosen base year by means of some price index for the relevant capital good. Each item remains in the stock, at that valuation, until the assumed date at which it is scrapped, when it disappears from the stock. The reduction in value of the stock when that occurs is then equal to the increase in value of the stock when the same amount is spent on a new good just entering the stock, but surely no one thinks that these two changes in the stock are likely to have approximately equal and offsetting effects on output? On the contrary, the good which is scrapped will leave output approximately unchanged, that being the reason why it is, indeed, being scrapped. The marginal products of the factors co-operating with that good will have risen so as to absorb all the quasi-rent earned by it, so that it will be worth nothing to its owner. Those cooperating factors can therefore produce all the output which the good and they have been producing hitherto, and they can do so without any assistance from the good. *Its* marginal product is accordingly zero, and much below that of a new item just being added to the stock whose value in the stock is the same.

It should be clear from this argument that a great deal of gross investment which in actual fact *does* increase output is not credited with doing so in the production function approach used by the authors cited and a great many others. All that part of gross investment equal to the assumed scrapping of capital goods is credited by them with having no effect on output, because it leads to no increase in K as measured. In reality, however, when a new investment occurs and some old machine is scrapped of equal value in the gross stock, output is undoubtedly increased. Small wonder, then, that there is usually a residual, unexplained, increase in output which has to be attributed to advances in knowledge. It should, however, be attributed to investment.

Defenders of the production function approach sometimes fall back on the argument that the rate of growth of the gross capital stock is often much the same as that of the theoretically better net capital stock, so that one can use the former as a proxy for the latter. However, I have a somewhat similar objection to the use of the net capital stock (see Scott [3] and [4]), although no space to describe it here.

It has always seemed counter-intuitive to me to suppose that the rate of growth of productivity in the long run is determined exogenously by the rate of technical progress. It is this iron law of technical progress which underlies Sargent's paper, but why should it be thought at all plausible? I like to define investment as the cost of changing economic arrangements, which I believe is a more illuminating way of looking at it than the conventional one of regarding it as the cost of creating capital goods. Changes in economic arrangements are made so as to increase output and efficiency, and it seems plausible to believe that the more and faster such changes are made, the more and faster will productivity grow.

Glyn

Glyn's chapter (see Chapter 9) first discusses the years up to 1973, and then goes on to consider the slow-down in productivity growth after 1973. In the first period, Glyn's main concern is to explain the fall in the 'world' rate of return on capital which his chart 9.1 shows took place after 1968, the rate of return having been gently rising according to his figures over the preceding decade or more. He attributes this fall to 'over accumulation', that is, to a speeding up in the rate of growth of the capital stock, accompanied by, if anything, a slowing down in the rate of growth of employment (chart 9.2) leading to real wages being bid up faster than the rate of growth of productivity. He also mentions the possibility that labour requirements per unit of investment were not falling as fast as before.

The only comment I will venture on this part of Glyn's paper is that, in choosing between the bidding-up hypothesis and the cost-push-labour-militancy hypothesis (which Glyn rejects) to explain the profits squeeze, it would have been useful to have considered the behaviour of unemployment. In the UK, at least, unemployment started to grow after 1966, and I (like Brown) believe that that suggests that cost-push rather than demand-pull was at work. I do not believe that the 1969–70 wage explosion is explicable in terms of expectations of inflation that exceeded actual inflation (see Comment on Chapter 4). I must agree, however, that the further wage explosion in 1973–4 could more reasonably be attributed to demand-pull, although a cost-push explanation could equally be provided.

I welcome Glyn's agreement with the view that the conventional growth accounting method 'enormously under-emphasises the role of capital accumulation'. Nevertheless, when he comes to explain the slow-down in productivity growth after 1973 he emphasises the slow-down in the growth of the capital–labour ratio, and that makes me uneasy, since it suggests that there is a production function of the traditional kind lurking at the back of his mind. Explicitly, however, he makes use of a vintage model.

Productivity has grown more slowly since 1973, according to Glyn, because the rate of growth of the capital–labour ratio has slowed down markedly (the implicit production function model), *and* (the explicit vintage model), 'At both ends of the spectrum of vintages – installation of new equipment and scrapping of old – the process of productivity growth has been slowed down'. The slow-down is thus explained, according to Glyn, by the decline in investment and also presumably by the fall in demand, since he emphasises that the true decline in the capital–labour ratio is greater than the statistics suggest because 'in a period of growing excess capacity . . . an increasing part of the capital stock counted in the estimates will not be in use'.

This explanation, while to my mind containing much of the truth, does not advance knowledge of the causes of the slow-down very far. It does not quantify the effect of lower investment on productivity growth, nor that of lower demand. Glyn himself is ambivalent about demand since he believes that the recession forces underutilised old plants to be scrapped, which tends to raise average labour productivity and since it also provides the occasion for management 'to increase labour productivity on the more efficient plants by pushing up labour intensity'.

That there are many competing explanations for the slow-down in productivity growth is very clear to anyone reading this volume. If we are to make progress in understanding it we must seek to quantify the effects of those factors which we cannot reject as negligible. The changing rate of investment is one such factor, and it is the one on which Sargent and, to some extent, Glyn, have chosen to focus their attention. While I believe it does explain *some* of the slow-down, I believe that other factors have also been important. Unfortunately, I do not think either of the chapters I have discussed enables one to say with any confidence how much of the slow-down is attributable to investment and how much to other factors.

References
[1]   Matthews, R.C.O., Feinstein, C.H. and Odling-Smee, J., *British Economic Growth 1856–1973*, Oxford University Press, 1982.
[2]   Ohkawa, K. and Rosovsky, H., *Japanese Economic Growth*, Stanford University Press, 1973.
[3]   Scott, M.F.G., 'Investment and Growth', *Oxford Economic Papers*, November 1976.
[4]   Scott, M.FG., 'The Contribution of Investment to Growth', *Scottish Journal of Political Economy*, November 1981.

6 World Shocks, Macroeconomic Response, and the Productivity Puzzle
Michael Bruno*

The output and productivity slow-down of the 1970s seems a unique phenomenon when viewed against the background of the whole of the post-Second World War period. It has been widespread and has affected virtually all industrial countries. It also seems to have been fairly widespread sectorally, although this aspect has not yet been adequately investigated.

Conventional growth accounting procedures (see, for example, [8] and [9]) decompose the slow-down in terms of quantity, quality and utilisation of labour and capital inputs, research and development effort, environmental regulations, etc. While these yield some partial explanations and may narrow down the extent of the puzzle, they leave one unsatisfied because there is a dominant characteristic of the slow-down that eludes such explanation. With a few exceptions, the beginning of the phenomenon can be dated at about 1973, when a major break occurs in the slope of the various time series. For a growth-accounting approach this is a rather disturbing feature. Changes in the research and development effort, conventional input qualities, and environmental regulations are gradual processes. They can hardly explain sharp turning points, let alone the close synchronisation of developments across countries. On the other hand, the very existence of such a watershed may provide a helpful lead for economic research. Rather than trying to chisel away the phenomenon into little boxes, one can start the analysis from the other end, so to speak. One may concentrate on the turning point itself, try to characterise the response to the worldwide shocks of the 1970s, and then ask to what extent the events themselves could help to explain

* This study was carried out at the National Bureau of Economic Research (Cambridge, Mass.), and at the Falk Institute (Jerusalem); it was supported financially by a grant from the National Science Foundation. None of these institutions bear any responsibility for its contents. I am indebted to Louis Dicks-Mireaux for help in the analysis of UK data collected by him, to Carlos Bachrach, student at the Hebrew University, for part of the computations, and to Susanne Freund for editorial assistance. I also wish to thank Jeffrey Sachs, my collaborator in earlier work, for helpful discussion of some preliminary ideas.

the apparent productivity slow-down. Such an approach may still leave some open questions but it has the advantage of a search for common causes as well as enabling one to gain insight from the differences in response among countries or sectors.

The first and obvious candidate for analysis is the sharp increase in the price of energy. This in itself may not explain much, but when viewed in the context of the general increase in the price of industrial raw materials that occurred in the 1970s, does provide a lead. For a raw material intensive activity the conventional two-factor view of the production process is only valid when the relative price of the raw material (in output units) or its unit input stays constant. When its relative price rises and it is a complementary factor of production, productivity per unit of the other factors, labour and capital, must fall. Profits must also fall, the extent of the fall depending on the extent of real wage rigidity. The profit squeeze will cause an investment slow-down, which in turn affects the accumulation of capital, thereby causing a further slow-down in labour productivity. As we shall see, the supply shifts of 1973–4 and 1979–80 go quite a long way towards explaining the slow-down in the manufacturing sector of some major industrial countries and also account for international differences. The direct link between the raw material price shock and the productivity slow-down in manufacturing (first analysed in [5]) is further explored for a cross-section of ten OECD countries, in the following section, which also contains a more disaggregated study of UK manufacturing industries.

Raw materials alone do not give a complete answer for manufacturing, let alone for non-manufacturing industries. As is well known, the oil and raw material price shocks have not only shifted aggregate supply for most industrial countries, they have also set in motion contractionary forces on the demand side. Terms of trade deterioration has reduced real income and consumption; the profit squeeze has reduced investment demand; the fear of inflation and of ensuing current account deficits has also imparted a deflationary bias to aggregate demand management in virtually all industrial countries. Finally, there is the reinforcing interaction of contracting export markets. A large part of the 1970s slow-down in output and productivity growth can be ascribed to the combined effect of these demand-side factors. This is discussed in part in the context of the manufacturing sector and more extensively in the section following, where an international comparison of the aggregate business sector is studied. A brief view of service industries is also given. It will be argued that it is most probably the interaction of depressed demand (and greater output variability) with the supply shocks that provides the main explanation for the aggregate productivity slow-down.

A major reason for the demand squeeze comes from the anti-inflation bias of macroeconomic policy in the major industrial countries. This is briefly contrasted in the conclusion to this chapter with the more expansionary policies pursued by the middle-income developing countries, whose output and productivity both continued to grow after 1973, but at the cost of higher persistent inflation and large current account deficits. While this option can probably not be pursued by all countries simultaneously, it supports the argument that productivity growth and macroeconomic response are closely linked.

Input Substitution, Demand and the Productivity Slow-down: an International Comparison of the Manufacturing Sector
A convenient starting point for empirical study is provided by comparative developments in the manufacturing sector of the industrial countries. This sector differs less from one country to another than the total business economy and is heavily dependent on purchased material inputs. Moreover, there is sufficient cross-country variation in both the extent of the slow-down in factor productivity and the magnitude of the input price shock to allow a test of the possible relationship between the two.

The approach here is to extend the conventional two-factor production framework by adding a third input, purchased materials or intermediate goods, and proceed under the simplifying assumption that gross output in manufacturing can be described in terms of a linearly homogeneous two-level function $Q = Q[V(K, L, T), N]$, where V is a real value-added index, K and L are capital and labour, N represents the composite material input, and T represents pure technical progress. An earlier paper [5] expounded the empirical conditions permitting such separability of V and N. While this assumption may not be legitimate when considering the energy input by itself, it most probably is in the case of non-energy inputs (see [3]). Given the smallness of the direct energy input in the composite N for manufacturing (of the order of 10 per cent), such an approximation may be empirically valid.

Using lower case letters for logarithms ($q = \log Q$, etc.) and dotted symbols for time derivatives, and denoting the output elasticity of intermediate goods by β and that of capital within V by ϕ we can write

$$\dot{q} = (1 - \beta)\dot{v} + \beta\dot{n} = (1 - \beta)[\lambda + \phi\dot{k} + (1 - \phi)\dot{l}] + \beta\dot{n} \quad (1)$$

where λ is the rate of technical progress in V.

Next we assume that the elasticity of substitution between V and N is constant (denoted by σ) from which it follows that

$$\dot{n} = \dot{q} - \sigma\dot{\pi}_n, \quad (2)$$

where π_n is the (log) relative price of the intermediate input. Substituting into (1) we get

$$\dot{q} - [\phi \dot{k} + (1 - \phi) l] = \lambda - \sigma (1 - \beta)^{-1} \beta \dot{\pi}_n. \tag{3}$$

The left-hand side of equation (3) represents the change in factor productivity as measured in terms of gross output relative to the weighted capital and labour input. ϕ will be constant if $V(K, L)$ is a Cobb-Douglas production function. On the right-hand side of (3) we have a conventional time-shift factor (λ) which is augmented or reduced by a material imput price term according as relative raw material prices fall or rise over time. The coefficient of $\dot{\pi}_n$ in (3) is the product of the relative share of N and V in Q $[\beta/(1 - \beta)]$ and their elasticity of substitution (σ). If we had constant proportions ($\sigma = 0$) or no change in input prices ($\dot{\pi}_n = 0$) this substitution term would be immaterial and the measurement of factor productivity would be invariant to the role of raw materials or to the choice of output measure (gross output or some GDP artefact).

In my earlier paper a similar framework was applied to four large industrial countries (the US, the UK, Germany, and Japan) and direct estimates of the parameters ($\phi, \beta, \sigma, \lambda$) were obtained from a two-equation system consisting of (3) and the associated factor price frontier. The model also allowed for some cyclical variation in factor utilisation. This and related studies [7][11] suggested an estimate of σ of the order of 0.3–0.4 for the US, the UK, and Germany, and 0.7–0.8 for Japan. While the hypothesis gives a good explanation of the relative ranking of the productivity slow-down for the four countries as well as a quantitative fit for the lowest (Germany) and highest (Japan), there is a sizeable unexplained residual for the UK and a more moderate one for the US. It could also be argued that the implied estimate of σ for Japan is somewhat high. At any rate, there seems little doubt that a fall in productivity is associated with a rise in raw material prices. The data also confirm such an effect for each of the two shocks (1973–4 and 1979–80) separately.

Table 6.1 gives the relevant average growth data for a wider sample of ten OECD countries for the periods 1955–73 and 1974–80. Column (4) shows the productivity slow-down measured under the assumption that $\phi = 0.35$ (obtained from a cross-section regression). Inspection of the figures for the drop in labour and capital inputs (columns (2) and (3)) reveals that this measure is not very sensitive to the choice of ϕ (a change of ±0.05 in ϕ changes the entries in column (4) by 0.06 on average). There is considerable variation in the estimated slow-down around the mean of 2.2 per cent (from a base of 3.9 per cent for 1955–73), the figures ranging from less than 1 per cent

Table 6.1 Selected data on average growth in manufacturing and aggregate demand, ten OECD countries: change in annual percentage rate of growth from 1955–73 to 1974–80

	(1)	(2)	(3)	(4)	(5)a	(6)	(7)
US	−3.1	−2.2	−0.9	−1.3	3.3	−0.7	−2.0
UK	−5.1	−3.3	−2.6	−2.0	6.4	−0.7	−2.1
Belgium	−5.4	−4.5	−1.4	−2.0	5.0	−1.6	−1.9
France	−4.2	−3.6	−0.1	−1.8	5.3	−0.7	−2.8
Germany	−4.8	−3.7	−4.2	−0.9	1.9	−1.6	−2.2
Italy	−3.7	−1.0	−1.8	−2.4	11.0	−1.6	−3.0
Netherlands	−4.7	−3.6	−1.4	−1.8	7.4	0.2	−2.7
Sweden	−4.9	−1.0	−2.4	−3.3	7.8	−1.2	−2.1
Canada	−4.1	−1.8	−0.8	−2.7	5.7	−3.6	−2.3
Japan	−8.5	−6.0	−3.7	−3.3	5.3	−1.5	−7.1
Mean	−4.9	−3.1	−1.9	−2.2	5.9	−1.3	−2.8

Sources: Output and manhour data from Bureau of Labor Statistics, US Department of Labor; capital stock data based on Artus [1] and updated; materials input prices based on OECD and wholesale price statistics of various countries. Public consumption from OECD, *National Income Accounts*.
Key: (1) Output, (2) Labour, (3) Capital, (4) Factor productivity, (5) Materials input prices, (6) Public consumption, (7) Domestic absorption.
a Change from 1955–72 to 1973–9.

for Germany to more than 3 per cent for Japan and Sweden.

Neither oil nor raw material prices were constant during the high growth period preceding 1972 (see [4] for a detailed study). Once the effects of the Korean boom had worked themselves out, they declined steadily at a real annual rate of 0.5–1.0 per cent from 1955 until 1971–2. The trend was reversed at the beginning of the 1970s, culminating in the price explosion of 1973–4. Raw material prices then came down again until a new shock hit both types of goods in 1979–80.

The magnitude of the total real input price shock ($\Delta \dot{\pi}_n$) is here measured by the differences in average growth from 1955–72 to 1973–9 (column (5), table 6.1). Much of the cross-country variation in $\Delta \dot{\pi}_n$, though by no means all of it, stems from differential movements of the real effective exchange rate that mitigated or accentuated the effect of the exogenous shock on domestic relative prices. It is important to stress again that even the external part of the real price increases is only in part directly due to energy prices, although extraction costs, etc., may have been indirectly affected by the energy crisis. (For more details on the large increase in primary non-fuel export prices see [10]).

A first shot at assessing the possible association between raw material prices and factor productivity growth is obtained by taking observations on average growth in each of the two sub-periods, 1955–73 and 1974–80, for the ten countries listed in table 6.1, a total of twenty observations (not detailed here), and pretending that they come from a common underlying production model. Obviously, such an approach ignores the possible inter-country differences in basic productivity growth, quite apart from possible differences in other parameters.

It is interesting to note that even this simple regression (table 6.2, line 1) yields a significant and quite plausible estimate for the input price term (−0.25). As long as basic country differences in production parameters are not correlated with the differences in raw material price changes this might give an unbiased estimate of the $\dot{\pi}_n$ term in equation (3). However, while it can be argued that the shares ϕ and β, and possibly the elasticity of substitution (σ), are similar in different countries, factor productivity (λ) almost certainly varies. Moreover, the higher the basic factor productivity growth, the more likely it is that real exchange-rate appreciation would be higher (or depreciation lower) and *ceteris paribus*, $\dot{\pi}_n$ would thus be lower. This would introduce an upward bias in the estimated effect of $\dot{\pi}_n$. Some evidence of this can be obtained when one introduces the growth of public consumption expenditure ($\dot{g}$) into the regression. Since it is correlated with real appreciation, its coefficient is overstated in the regression and that of $\dot{\pi}_n$ is substantially reduced.

One way of overcoming this statistical problem, at the cost of a severe cut in degrees of freedom, is by going to the first differences of average growth rates. If it is assumed that countries may differ in basic productivity attributes but that in themselves these attributes are time invariant, the problem is side-stepped. The resulting regression (table 6.2, line 3) shows two things. With a value of β of about 0.35 the coefficient of −0.17 suggests an average elasticity of substitution of 0.32. At the same time the significant negative intercept (−1.18) suggests a common element of the slow-down which is not captured by the raw material factor. It is interesting to note that the exclusion of Japan, an outlier, from this regression only raises the $\Delta\dot{\pi}_n$ coefficient to 0.18, but the standard error falls (from 0.094 to 0.076), and $\bar{R}^2$ rises considerably (from 0.19 to 0.37).

Regressions 5 and 6 add the deceleration in public expenditure and total domestic absorption, respectively (see columns (6) and (7) of table 6.1). These variables seem to improve the explanatory power considerably, make the intercept non-significant, and hardly change the estimate of $\Delta\dot{\pi}_n$. For a regression on ten observations this is a satisfactory result. It is important to stress that the deceleration in

Table 6.2   *Selected regressions of average factor productivity growth in manufacturing: ten OECD countries, I 1955–73 and II 1974–80*

	Constant	$(\dot{\pi}_n)_a$	$(\dot{g})_b$	$(\dot{a})_c$	$\bar{R}^2$	SE
Growth levels (I and II); 20 observations						
1	3.47 (0.43)	−0.25 (0.10)			0.21	1.56
2	0.29 (1.08)	−0.13 (0.09)	0.79 (0.25)		0.97	1.28
Growth increment (II–I); 10 observations						
3	−1.18 (0.60)	−0.17 (0.09)			0.19	0.70
4[d]	−0.96 (0.49)	−0.18 (0.08)			0.37	0.57
5	−0.76 (0.65)	−0.17 (0.08)	0.27 (0.20)		0.27	0.67
6	−0.56 (0.63)	−0.16 (0.08)		0.24 (0.13)	0.37	0.62
7[e]	0	−0.21 (0.06)		0.31 (0.11)	0.39	0.61
8[d,e]	0	−0.26 (0.04)	0.31 (0.14)		0.43	0.54

[a] Input prices, lagged one year.
[b] Public consumption.
[c] Total domestic absorption.
[d] Excluding Japan. Number of observations 9.
[e] Regression forced through the origin.

total absorption ($\Delta\dot{a}$) is virtually uncorrelated with the acceleration in raw material prices (the correlation coefficient between $\Delta\dot{a}$ and $\Delta\dot{\pi}_n$ is −0.06) so that $\Delta\dot{a}$ may be considered a truly independent factor. For a sub-sector such as manufacturing it can probably also be considered exogenous.

On the assumption that these two variables exhaust the productivity slow-down we obtain the next regression (table 6.2, line 7), which is forced through the origin. This raises the estimate of σ to 0.39 and is the preferred regression. Table 6.3 shows the estimated components of the slow-down and the errors of the regression by country. It is interesting that with this simple model the four large countries previously mentioned all come out virtually on the regression line (errors ranging between 0 and 0.1). On average, raw materials explain about 60 per cent of the slow-down, with the demand squeeze explaining the remaining 40 per cent. Two outliers for which the regression under-explains are Sweden and Canada and one extreme over-explained case is Italy.

Table 6.3 Components of productivity slow-down in manu-facturing: 1955–73 to 1974–80[a]

per cent

	Factor productivity slow-down (1)	Of which:		
		Input prices (2)	Demand slow-down (3)	Unexplained residual (4)
US	−1.34	−0.69	−0.61	−0.04
UK	−2.05	−1.34	−0.66	−0.05
Belgium	−1.96	−1.05	−0.58	−0.33
France	−1.84	−1.11	−0.87	0.14
Germany	−0.95	−0.40	−0.66	0.11
Italy	−2.37	−2.31	−0.92	0.86
Netherlands	−1.79	−1.55	−0.83	0.59
Sweden	−3.38	−1.64	−0.65	−1.09
Canada	−2.66	−1.20	−0.71	−0.75
Japan	−3.30	−1.11	−2.19	0.00
Mean	−2.16	−1.24	−0.87	(−0.05)

[a] Based on regression 6, Table 6.2.

A glance at column (7) of table 6.1 shows that Japan had by far the largest demand squeeze. With such a small sample there is a danger of accidentally attributing significance to a variable which only comes in as a result of one extreme observation. Indeed, when regression 7 is run without Japan the coefficient of $\hat{a}$ is rendered non-significant, though it retains the same estimated value. However, the alternative regression 8, using public consumption ($\Delta \dot{g}$) as a proxy for demand management, is highly significant and the estimated effect of raw material prices is even higher in this case (possibly reflecting an indirect income effect – the share of this component in the slow-down rises to 75 per cent). The earlier reservation concerning correlation between $\dot{g}$ and $\dot{\pi}_n$ does not apply in this case as the correlation coefficient for the increments $\Delta \dot{g}$ and $\Delta \dot{\pi}_n$ is virtually nil (0.055). For this regression Canada is no longer an outlier but the error for Sweden remains high. Another demand factor, exports, was also tried, but although it helps, the marginal improvement in the estimate does not justify its separate mention here. Also, its exogeneity with respect to productivity growth is probably more suspect. The relationship between demand and productivity is discussed in greater detail in the next section.

At this stage we come to another important concomitant of the shock of the 1970s. Not only has the average growth level changed but

Table 6.4   Variance of output growth in manufacturing and total GDP: coefficient of output variation

	Manufacturing		GDP	
	1955–73	1974–80	1960–73	1974–9
US	1.3	4.7	0.5	0.9
UK	1.0	2.2	0.4	1.7
Belgium	0.4	3.2	0.2	1.2
France	0.3	1.2	0.1	0.6
Germany	0.7	2.1	0.5	0.9
Italy	0.5	1.7	0.7	1.5
Netherlands	0.5	2.4	—	—
Sweden	0.4	13.4	0.4	1.3
Canada	0.6	2.4	0.3	0.7
Japan	0.5	1.0	0.3	0.1
Mean	0.6	3.4	0.4	1.0

Source: Bureau of Labor Statistics, US Department of Labor, and OECD, *National Income Accounts.*

so has its variability. Looking at the variance of output growth in manufacturing during sub-periods from 1955 to 1980 it can be shown that except in two countries, Denmark and Japan, the variance (or standard deviation) increased after 1973 even though output growth dropped substantially. The coefficient of variation, which is the ratio of the standard deviation to the mean (shown in columns (1) and (2) of table 6.4) has on average grown by a factor of five. While this ratio is, of course, largely affected by what has happened to its denominator (mean growth rate), it is nonetheless indicative of the unprecedented change that has taken place in the economic environment. At a time of severe fluctuations in output the average optimal use of inputs per unit of output is necessarily greater than in a situation of greater certainty. Average factor productivity must thus fall. Geometrically this can be illustrated by comparing the mean cost of two points on opposite branches of a U-shaped cost curve with the point of minimum-cost production (assuming this is the equivalent output level under certainty). Under uncertainty producers may opt for flatter cost curves but at the price of a higher minimum cost. Some such argument may account for an outlier like Sweden where the increase in relative variability of output growth was particularly large (mean output actually dropped in the late 1970s). It is also known that in this country reallocation of factors was hampered by government subsidies to ailing industries.

A more disaggregated view

Our view of manufacturing output as the outcome of an aggregate production process is clearly an abstraction. The estimated effect of material inputs still leaves open the question as to whether it is the outcome of analogous substitution processes within sub-sectors or the result of a change in the composition of demand in response to relative price changes. The more disaggregated a view we take, the more likely it is that the latter will dominate. A partial look inside the 'black box' is provided by considering an intermediate division of the sector into major 2-digit industries. The results of such an experiment for UK manufacturing are reported in table 6.5 and are based on an ongoing study by Louis Dicks-Mireaux. Input prices were measured for each of the major industries (from an input–output breakdown). Factor productivity growth, as defined in equation (3), using separate shares (ϕ) for each industry (see column (1), table 6.5), was regressed on share-weighted lagged input price change as well as on the growth of total GDP (a proxy for aggregate demand pressure).

Column (2) of the table gives the measured share of materials and intermediate inputs by industry. It here includes not only purchased inputs from outside manufacturing (as was the case in the earlier aggregate regressions) but also inputs that are internal to the broader manufacturing sector (30 per cent on average). The figures in italics indicate the imported part of the material input. Columns (3), (4) and (5) give the estimated coefficients (and standard errors) of the total productivity shift, λ, the elasticity of substitution, σ, and the elasticity of GDP growth, $\dot{v}$; of the two regressions in each industry, the first excludes and the second includes $\dot{v}$.

The regressions by and large confirm the results for the aggregate sector. For ten out of fourteen industries the substitution term (column (4)) is negative and in most cases highly significant. In only one industry (order 8, instrument engineering) is the coefficient significantly positive and in the remaining three (orders 7, 12, 14–15) it is zero or positive but not significant. It should be noted that in these four industries the share of the import component is very low (10 per cent or less). Except for food (order 3) the estimated elasticity of substitution ranges from 0.25 to 0.56 – the average for the ten industries is 0.39 in the first regressions and 0.27 in the second regressions. Inclusion of total GDP growth takes away some of the indirect effect of raw material prices, as we saw in the aggregate regression. At this level of disaggregation the substitution effect, or whatever phenomenon this variable measures, is obviously significant in explaining productivity slow-down by industry.

Similar results have also been obtained in an ongoing study based on Israeli data by M. Bar-Nathan of the Bank of Israel. He obtains

Table 6.5   *Factor productivity regressions for 14 UK manufacturing industries:* circa *1960 to 1980*[ab]

SIC[c]	Measured shares		Estimated parameters			$\bar{R}^2$	D.W.
	ϕ (1)	β (2)	λ (3)	σ (4)	$\dot{v}$ (5)	(6)	(7)
3	0.47	0.76	5.25 (2.51)	−0.05 (0.02)		0.13	1.88
		0.20	5.25 (0.20)	−0.04 (0.02)	0.35 (0.10)	0.42	2.09
4	0.56	0.58	2.39 (1.35)	−0.51 (0.14)		0.42	1.46
		0.47	1.64 (1.34)	−0.30 (0.17)	1.40 (0.76)	0.49	2.02
5	0.43	0.58	4.06 (0.86)	−0.37 (0.09)		0.49	0.96
		0.17	3.39 (0.76)	−0.18 (0.10)	1.23 (0.43)	0.64	1.95
6	0.20	0.66	−1.06 (1.79)	−0.54 (0.37)		0.07	1.52
		0.22	−0.85 (1.27)	−0.16 (0.28)	2.51 (0.65)	0.53	2.28
7	0.29	0.49	1.46 (1.00)	0.04 (0.27)		0.07	1.52
		0.05	1.20 (0.71)	0.51 (0.23)	1.55 (0.41)	0.46	1.54
8	0.23	0.43	3.03 (0.52)	0.04 (0.08)		0.67	2.60
		0.08	2.93 (0.50)	0.43 (0.09)	0.34 (0.24)	0.70	2.30
9	0.24	0.53	3.52 (0.91)	−0.25 (0.12)		0.17	1.39
		0.10	3.21 (0.84)	−0.10 (0.13)	0.94 (0.46)	0.32	1.13
11	0.13	0.60	−0.36 (0.90)	−0.28 (0.17)		0.15	1.62
		0.06	−0.36 (0.92)	−0.29 (0.18)	0.27 (0.38)	−0.10	1.86
12	0.25	0.57	−1.51 (1.33)	0.02 (0.22)		−0.11	1.22
		0.10	−1.74 (0.01)	0.26 (0.19)	1.28 (0.46)	0.37	2.18
13	0.29	0.50	1.86 (0.94)	−0.49 (0.17)		0.21	1.29
		0.21	1.86 (0.96)	−0.45 (0.18)	0.00 (0.01)	0.17	1.29
14–15	0.16	0.58	2.26 (1.00)	0.06 (0.19)		−0.06	1.35
		0.12	2.03 (0.84)	0.22 (0.17)	1.12 (0.42)	0.27	1.58

Table 6.5   continued

SIC[c]	Measured shares		Estimated parameters			$\bar{R}^2$	D.W.
	ϕ (1)	β (2)	λ (3)	σ (4)	$\dot{v}$ (5)	(6)	(7)
16	0.22	0.54 0.06	2.62 (1.59)	−0.56 (0.29)		0.24	1.10
			2.37 (1.26)	−0.43 (0.23)	1.18 (0.49)	0.53	0.98
17	0.22	0.52 0.29	1.83 (0.98)	−0.47 (0.16)		0.26	2.13
			1.82 (0.98)	−0.45 (0.16)	0.01 (0.01)	0.26	2.15
18	0.31	0.59 0.17	1.12 (0.78)	−0.34 (0.14)		0.19	1.84
			1.12 (0.78)	−0.34 (0.14)	0.00 (0.01)	0.17	1.86

Source: Based on detailed data compiled by Louis Dicks-Mireaux from miscellaneous CSO publications.
[a] *Figures in brackets are standard errors. Figures in italics in column (2) represent shares of imported inputs.*
[b] Initial years: 1957−3, 17, 18; 1962−4, 5; 1965−6, 7, 9, 14, 15; 1970−8, 11, 12; 1971−16.
[c] *Orders* 10 (shipbuilding) and 19 (miscellaneous) were omitted, 14 and 15 combined.

significant negative coefficients for $\dot{\pi}_n$ in ten out of seventeen major industries with all other industries showing non-significant coefficients. The estimated average σ of 0.6 is somewhat higher than in the United Kingdom, but his regressions did not include aggregate GDP, only average hours worked (as a proxy for demand).

We conclude this section with a comment on the input substitution hypothesis and the relevance of alternative theories. In this study we have treated gross capital stock as a homogeneous input over time. It may be argued that one result of a rise in energy prices may be that pre-1973 capital becomes obsolete. In this case our measure of average factor productivity would be biased. A useful alternative approach (recently started by Baily, [2]) would be to measure the change in capital stock and productivity in a way that takes this factor explicitly into account.

Which of these alternative views of the role of energy and materials in production turns out to be empirically more fruitful must await further study. Both, however, share the position that the productivity slow-down in manufacturing must somehow be related to the input price shocks of the 1970s.

Productivity Comparisons for the Aggregate Business Sector

We now turn to a more aggregative view of the total business sector. While manufacturing and its sub-sectors are heavy users of raw materials, the same cannot be said of most of the non-manufacturing sectors and yet the productivity slow-down in the economy as a whole seems, if anything, to have been more marked than in manufacturing. To what extent can any of the arguments advanced above also be applied to the broader economy?

If we consider the economy as an aggregate productive framework, this time employing labour and capital in conjunction with total imports, there would be some analogy with our previous discussion. An increase in relative import prices would cause substitution against imports, and aggregate gross output (measured in some suitable form, per unit of the two other factors) would grow more slowly. There are some important differences here, however. First of all, unlike in the case of manufacturing, there is no need to resort to a gross output measure (the analogue would presumably be total real use of resources). Both the quantity and the price of total imports are directly measurable so that one could, at least in principle, attempt to construct a real GDP index which is free of import price bias, and relate it to the inputs of labour and capital. Any remaining effect of an increase in real import prices on an unbiased factor–productivity measure could then only be the result of misallocation of factors caused by the real shock or its interaction with depressed aggregate demand or the increase in output variability, arguments that would apply equally well outside the manufacturing sector. However, this would not, strictly speaking, be the same as the input-substitution argument (part of the fall in demand is itself a reflection of a terms of trade effect on real income – see below).

In trying to search for a test of these ideas our point of departure is a recent study by Kendrick [9]. In this study the productivity slow-down from 1960–73 to 1974–9 in nine OECD countries (the ten used here excluding the Netherlands) is analysed in terms of the aggregate GDP of the business sector and its average factor (labour and capital) use. With minor modifications, columns (1) to (3) of table 6.6 replicate Kendrick's data. Column (4) shows an average factor–productivity slow-down which, on the face of it, looks more marked than in manufacturing (see column (4) of table 6.1), and is particularly high for Italy and Japan (the figures are otherwise quite similar). Kendrick applied a Denison-type growth-accounting approach to the component analysis of this change. Other than the conventional changes

Table 6.6   *Selected data on average growth in the business sector, nine OECD countries: change in annual percentage growth rate from 1960–73 to 1974–9*

	$(1)^a$	$(2)^a$	$(3)^a$	$(4)^b$	$(5)^c$	$(6)^d$
US	−1.5	0.5	−1.4	−1.3	8.0	0.09
UK	−2.4	−0.5	−0.5	−1.9	4.3	0.28
Belgium	−3.2	−1.5	−1.7	−1.6	2.1	0.58
France	−2.6	−0.9	−0.8	−1.7	3.1	0.18
Germany	−2.4	−0.9	−2.0	−1.1	4.5	0.10
Italy	−3.0	3.2	−0.9	−4.8	6.9	0.23
Sweden	−4.1	−0.8	−0.7	−3.3	5.2	0.29
Canada	−2.6	0.6	0.1	−3.0	2.6	0.26
Japan	−6.6	−0.5	−4.5	−4.7	8.4	0.12
Mean	−3.2	−0.1	−1.4	−2.6	5.0	0.24

Key: (1) GDP, (2) Labour, (3) Capital, (4) Factor productivity, (5) Relative import prices, (6) Relative import share.
[a] Kendrick's [9] estimates, based on OECD data at 1975 prices.
[b] The share of capital weighted at 0.35.
[c] The change in growth rates of import prices relative to GDP.
[d] Average ratio of imports to GDP during 1974–9.

in labour quality and technical knowledge, the main factors that account for the slow-down (see [9], p. 141, table 7) are reallocation of labour, economies of scale, capacity utilisation, and government regulations. Together these items account, in his analysis, for 1.5 points out of an average 2.4 per cent slow-down in factor productivity.

While the problem of oil and raw material prices is mentioned in Kendrick's discussion, no attempt is made to measure its contribution. Government regulations is the only item that could be associated with an increase in the cost of materials but it only amounts to 0.4 points of the 1.5 mentioned. The other three factors could be associated with the demand squeeze argument (or the interaction between the demand squeeze and the real shock).

In trying to apply our framework to the data the first point to be made relates to the problem of GDP measurement. I have shown elsewhere [5] that double deflation may cause a systematic bias in GDP growth measurement when import prices change monotonically, depending on the base-year used and on the relative size of the imported input into the sector, or economy, in question. Thus a systematic bias in the measurement of the slow-down is likely to occur if a pre-oil shock base year (for example, 1972) is used and the calculation is made for GDP of a material-intensive sub-sector like

Table 6.7 *Selected regressions of productivity growth in the business sector: nine OECD countries, I 1960–73 and 1974–9*

	Constant	$(\dot{p}_m{-}\dot{p}_v)^a$	$(\dot{g})^b$	$(\dot{a})^c$	$(\dot{p}_m{-}\dot{p}_v)\dot{a}^d$	$\bar{R}^2$	NSE
Growth levels (I and II); 18 observations							
I	2.75 (0.23)	−3.03 (0.45)				0.72	0.37
2	−0.77 (0.55)	−1.86 (0.45)	0.50 (0.13)			0.85	0.28
3[e]	−0.42 (0.51)	−0.60 (0.28)		0.78 (0.12)		0.71	0.38
4[e]	1.10 (0.50)			0.31 (0.14)	−0.64 (0.15)	0.88	0.25
Growth increment (II–I); 9 observations							
5	−0.73 (1.04)	−2.16 (1.10)				0.27	0.46
6	0.61 (0.75)	−1.90 (0.68)		0.57 (0.16)		0.72	0.28
7	0	−1.50 (0.45)		0.50 (0.14)		0.73/	0.28
8	0	−1.45 (0.49)	0.61 (0.18)			0.72/	0.29

[a] Relative import prices.
[b] Public consumption.
[c] Total domestic absorption.
[d] Interaction.
[e] Estimated by two-stage least squares with $\dot{g}$ and $(\dot{p}^*_m{-}\dot{p}^*_x)$ as instruments.

manufacturing or for a small economy with a high import content.

As an example of the possible bias consider the calculation of GDP growth slow-down for a sample of ten smaller OECD countries, not represented in table 6.6. This shows a deceleration in average GDP growth between 1960–73 and 1974–80 of 2.83 per cent when 1972 prices are used and only 2.42 per cent when 1975 base-year prices are applied, an average bias of 15 per cent. For individual countries (for example, Austria, Ireland, Norway) the relative bias is much larger. The correct procedure, using a moving weight Divisia index, shows the average slow-down to be 2.47 per cent, which is very close to the 1975-based calculation.

The recent OECD data on which Kendrick's analysis was based measure GDP at constant 1975 prices and besides these are large countries with relatively small import content. Applying a Divisia index, the Divisia index measure of GDP for the nine countries represented in table 6.6, we found only a negligible difference with respect to the 1975-based figures. (Only for Sweden and Canada is there a positive bias in the order of 0.1 per cent.) In this case we may thus safely stick to the GDP numbers, as indicated.

Let us now look at the relationship between the factor-productivity figures and the relevant supply and demand variables. The first regression in table 6.7 relates eighteen average growth-rate observations (nine countries for two periods) to the share-weighted rate of change of import prices relative to GDP prices (consistent with the quantity measure employed above). (Only the acceleration, or deceleration, of import prices is given in column (5) of table 6.6; column (6) shows the average relative M/V share for the second period.) Adding a demand variable ($\dot{g}$) in regression 2, does not remove the effect of import prices. The possibility that both reflect the effect of the demand squeeze is represented by regression 3, in which the two-stage procedure was used. The alternative view, that it is only the interaction of import prices and demand that matters, is represented by regression 4, for which the fit is slightly better (including $\dot{p}_m - \dot{p}_v$ separately in this regression adds nothing).

Regressions 5–8 present results, in terms of incremental growth for which internal correlation between the explanatory variables is much smaller. The last two regressions force a zero constant. Here it would seem again that there is a strong import price effect over and above total absorption.

Recalling the argument about the possible endogeneity and reverse causality of the relative price term these regressions were also run using the relative import–US export price ($\dot{p}^*_m - \dot{p}^*_x$), which is free of real exchange rate effects, and obtained similar, though less significant results (there is less inter-country variation in this index). It might also be objected that the sample is too small. Unfortunately, no capital stock data are available for other countries. However, little is lost by regressing labour productivity rather than factor productivity on these variables. When we extend the sample to include 29 countries (19 OECD plus 10 middle-income developing countries), the 29-observation regression of $\Delta\dot{v} - \dot{l}$ gives:

$$\Delta(\dot{v} - \dot{l}) = -0.63 - 0.31 \, \Delta(\dot{p}^*_m - \dot{p}^*_x) + 0.13 \, \Delta\dot{g} \quad (\bar{R}^2 = 0.22)$$
$$(0.48) \quad (0.14) \qquad\qquad (0.08)$$

Table 6.8 presents the breakdown by components and the residuals for regression 7. The net role of import prices is here somewhat smaller than for the manufacturing sector by itself, with the demand factor taking a larger share. Similar results are obtained for the alternative regression 8.

This discussion shows that the basic argument about the role of the supply shock and the demand response also applies with some modi-

Table 6.8   Components of productivity slow-down in the business sector: 1960–73 to 1974–9

per cent

	Factor productivity slow-down	Of which:		
		Import prices	Demand slow-down	Unexplained residual
US	−1.3	−1.0	−0.8	0.5
UK	−1.9	−1.6	−1.0	0.7
Belgium	−1.6	−1.5	−0.9	0.8
France	−1.7	−0.6	−1.4	0.2
Germany	−1.1	−0.6	−1.1	0.5
Italy	−4.8	−2.2	−1.8	−0.8
Sweden	−3.3	−2.0	−1.0	−0.3
Canada	−3.0	−0.9	−1.0	−1.1
Japan	−4.7	−1.3	−3.4	0.0
Mean	−2.6	−1.3	−1.4	0.1

fication to the aggregate private sector. By implication one would expect to find that in non-manufacturing and less material-intensive sectors (such as services) it is mainly the demand squeeze that accounts for the slow-down. Some evidence is provided by looking at such partial data as there are for the service sector in these economies. The growth of GDP per employed person ($\dot{v}_s - \dot{l}_s$) in the nine OECD countries and the two periods (data from [13]) was regressed on total domestic absorption ($\dot{a}$) and the relative price of imports, using public consumption growth and the terms of trade ($\dot{p}^*_m - \dot{p}^*_x$) as instruments. This gives

$$\dot{v}_s - l_s = -0.75 + 0.01\,(\dot{p}_m - \dot{p}_v) + 0.79\dot{a} \qquad (\bar{R}^2 = 0.70)$$
$$\quad\;\; (0.59)\;\; (0.34) \qquad\qquad (0.15)$$

The disappearance of the import price variable from this regression (it does appear highly significant in a regression in which $\dot{g}$ replaces $\dot{a}$) suggests very clearly that here it is only demand that matters directly. The latter is in turn affected by government fiscal policy as well as by the terms of trade (the elasticity with respect to each is about 1).

We now have further evidence to support the claim that the intensity of material-input use in a sector must have had something to do with the effect of the rise in material-input prices on productivity. Manufacturing industries were heavily affected, services apparently not. We can now go back to the earlier part of the discussion and ask when one aggregates across sectors, some of which were directly hit by input prices and some of which were not, how would one expect the aggregate economy to behave? On the face of it any internal relative price changes should wash out in aggregate GDP as well as in the factor input and productivity measures, provided there is full factor mobility between sectors, If, however, these assumptions do not hold for example, if factors do not reallocate freely, then a shock to any one sector may also show in the aggregate. This argument can be made more precise.

Suppose the economy consists of several sectors producing a total GNP, V, which is broken down into $V_0 = V_0(K_0, L_0)$, a reference sector in which no disturbance occurs, and $V_i = V_i(K_i, L_i, T_i)$ ($i = 1$, $2, \ldots, n$) representing the other sectors. K_i and L_i are the respective factor inputs, and T_i are exogenous shift terms (technology, material input prices and so on). Denoting relative output prices (in terms of V_0 as numeraire) by P_i, we have

$$V = V_0(K_0, L_0) + \sum P_i V_i(K_i, L_i, T_i) \qquad (4)$$

For changes we get

$$\begin{aligned} \Delta V = {} & (\delta V_0/\delta K_0)\Delta K_0 + \sum P_i(\delta V_i/\delta K_i)\Delta K_i \\ & + (\delta V_0/\delta L_0)+L_0)\Delta L_0 + \sum P_i(\delta V_i/\delta L_i)\Delta L_i \\ & \qquad\qquad + \sum (\delta V_i/\delta T_i)\Delta T_i \end{aligned} \qquad (5)$$

Denote $\sum_{i=0}^{n} K_i = K$, $\sum_{i=0}^{n} L_i = L$, $\delta V_0/\delta K_0 = R$, $\delta V_0/\delta L_0 = W$, and $RK/V = \phi$, $\Delta V/V = v$. After some manipulation we can rewrite (5) in the form

$$\begin{aligned} \dot{v} - [\phi k + (1 - \phi)\dot{l}] = {} & \sum (T_i/V)\dot{t_i} \\ & + \sum (K_i/V)\,(P_i\,\delta V_i/\delta K_i - R)\dot{k_i} \\ & + \sum (L_i/V)\,(P_i\,\delta V_i/\delta L_i - W)\dot{l_i} \end{aligned}$$

The left-hand side of equation (6) represents aggregate factor productivity as conventionally measured. The right-hand side consists of three terms. The first is the sum of the sectoral shift factors; the other two are terms involving divergences of marginal factor productivities from real factor returns multiplied by the rates of change of factors by sector.

Suppose there is a negative disturbance ($\dot{t_i} < 0$) in any one sector which is not matched by a positive disturbance in another. There are two ways in which this will not fully translate to the left-hand side of (6). Either V_i and aggregate V may be measured with T_i properly netted out; or factors always reallocate in the 'right' direction, that is, $k_i \gtreqless 0$ whenever $P_i \partial V_i / \partial K_i \gtreqless R$ (and similarly for l_i). The whole rationale of aggregate productivity measurements rests on the assumption that in the long run, and on average, marginal products of factors equalise across sectors, so that the last two terms in equation (6) disappear while V, K, and L are measured so that the only T_i disturbances that can appear are of a pure technology kind. In the situation that prevailed in the 1970s, with real shocks, depressed demand, and increased uncertainty, probably none of these conditions held. Because of capital immobility and sluggish labour adjustment there are built-in asymmetries between expanding and contracting sectors which may impart a negative bias to the two divergence terms in (6) (that is, $P_i \partial V_i / \partial K_i < R$ may more often go together with $ki \geq 0$, and similarly for labour). It may be for these reasons the import price shocks have affected aggregate productivity by more than would be expected under a fully flexible system.

Finally we may note that while the inter-country variance of labour productivity growth stayed as high in the second as in the first period in manufacturing (1.79 compared with 1.77), in the service sector it fell (from 1.36 to 1.11). For the business sector the inter-country variance fell even more (from 1.97 to 1.34). This too may be evidence that manufacturing was hit more directly by the real supply shocks which worked differentially in the industrial countries. The absolute demand squeeze, with one or two exceptions, was more uniform across countries.

Conclusion

Can one try to attach a consistent story to these international comparisons of productivity slow-down? While for some countries there may already have been signs of deceleration in productivity growth by the end of the 1960s (a point made for the US in [8], [12] and others), it seems that the dominant role was played by the commodity price shock of the early 1970s. Until then raw material and energy prices were falling in real terms. There was a turning point in 1971–2, the price rise culminating in the great shock of 1973–4. In spite of subsequent fluctuations, the earlier low levels were never recovered even for raw materials (at least not by the end of 1981). This price shock affected the material (and energy) input intensive sectors directly. As we have seen, more than half of the slow-down in manufacturing can be ascribed to this direct effect. Two secondary effects played a role on the demand side. The terms of trade effect on the income of net importers, the investment squeeze, and the induced contractionary fiscal (and monetary) measures have generally kept economic activity growing much more slowly since 1973. The major industrial countries, in particular the US, the UK, and Japan, adopted contractionary policies for fear of excessive inflation and current account deficits. The depressed domestic demand (which, in turn, interacts with export demand) has impeded the internal relative price and factor adjustment process necessitated by these supply shocks. When seen in this light, the observed productivity slow-down is thus directly linked to the choice of short-term and medium-term macroeconomic response strategy.

In this context one may refer to another structural factor that is sometimes proposed as a possible culprit – the import and export competition from the newly industrialised countries (NICs). The rapid development of the NICs is not a new phenomenon of the 1970s – it started in the 1960s and even before that – yet it was not a special issue during the rapid growth phase. Why would it cause more problems in the 1970s? The answer, which is related to our earlier discussion, seems to be that in a rapidly growing economy it is much easier to adjust to external competitive shocks because there is excess demand and factors will easily move into more productive activities with less risk of unemployment. At a time of general slack, on the other hand, the system tends to freeze into old modes of operation and fear of unemployment causes retrenchment, excessive subsidisation of ailing industries, and the like. This links up with our present topic only in the sense that it would probably be wrong to ascribe a separate role to external competition as an explanatory factor in the productivity story. Rather, it is the generally depressed internal economic conditions that tend to impede adjustment to both types of external shock and thus show up in the form of reduced productivity growth.

The NICs and the much broader group of middle-income developing countries (MICs) can be brought into the story to play another role. They provide an exception to the characterisation of OECD response which may at the same time strengthen the argument. Faced with the same exogenous input price shocks these economies, and in particular their manufacturing sectors, performed quite well in the 1970s in terms of output and general economic activity, while most OECD countries did miserably in this respect. Part of the answer, which is not directly relevant here, has to do with the emergence of an international private capital market to which many of the NICs had access and for a time could borrow heavily at zero or negative real interest rates (see [6]). The other side, more relevant to our present discussion, is that these countries have by and large been pursuing highly expansionary domestic policies. As the recent World Development Report ([14], p. 140, Table 4) shows, domestic absorption in the group of 60 middle-income countries grew at least as fast in the 1970s as in the previous decade. The cost of choosing the expansionary option was much higher inflation and larger current account deficits (which were themselves required to effect the resource transfer from OPEC). But it showed up in continued rapid growth in both output and labour productivity. (There are unfortunately no data on total factor productivity.) The data show a more expansionary response of the MICs after 1973, yet a close association between output and labour productivity in all countries. There is little doubt that the more expansionary internal policies (and smaller output variability) of the MICs have a lot to do with the difference in economic performance. Paradoxically, it is likely that the relative success of the MICs would not have been possible if the OECD countries had also followed a more expansionary policy, since competition for the OPEC surplus would have made this a much more costly option to pursue (by 1980–1 real interest rates had indeed risen). But for the present purpose this example illustrates that productivity and macroeconomic response are closely linked.

Finally, if the view of the sources of the productivity slow-down in the OECD countries advocated here is correct, it also follows that this phenomenon is only as transitory or as permanent as the macroeconomic climate of the world economy. If input price shocks continue to hit the world economy frequently, but at uncertain intervals, and if cost-induced inflationary waves are going to be followed by contractionary demand policies in the leading industrial countries, then there is no reason to consider the slow-down as transitory. If, on the other hand, the system were to find an efficient way of smoothing the fluctuations in real input prices, for example by commodity agreements, buffer stocks, or the break-up of cartels, and of better coordinating economic activity and monetary policies across national frontiers, then one of the major sources of the slow-down will be removed. The best bet probably lies with neither of the two extremes. There may be some learning and adaptation to the new environment which would allow pursuit of reasonable inflation rates without the enormous cost in unemployment that has been paid in recent years. The upshot of the present discussion is that in this case aggregate productivity growth in the industrial countries might improve along with the hoped-for improvement in overall macroeconomic performance.

References
[1] Artus, Jacques R., 'Measures of Potential Output in Manufacturing for Eight Industrial Countries, 1955–1978', *IMF Staff Papers*, XXIV, March 1977, 1–24.
[2] Baily, M.W., 'Productivity and the Services of Capital and Labour', *Brookings Papers on Economic Activity*, No. 1, 1981, pp. 1–50.

[3] Berndt, E.R., and Woods, D.O., 'Engineering and Econometric Interpretations of Energy–Capital Complementarity', *American Economic Review*, LXIX, June 1979, 342-54.

[4] Bosworth, B and Lawrence, R.Z., *Commodity Prices and the New Inflation*, Washington, D.C., The Brookings Institution, 1982.

[5] Bruno, Michael, *Raw Materials, Profits and the Productivity Slowdown*, NBER Working Paper No. 660, December 1981 (revised). (Forthcoming in *Quarterly Journal of Economics*.)

[6] Bruno, Michael, 'Petro-dollars, Real Interest Rates and the Differential Performance of ICs and MICs (preliminary draft), Jerusalem, February 1982.

[7] Bruno, Michael, and Sachs, J., 'Input Price Shocks and the Slowdown in Economic Growth: Estimates for U.K. Manufacturing', paper presented at the Conference on Unemployment, Newnham College, Cambridge, July 1981. (Forthcoming in *Review of Economic Studies*.)

[8] Denison, E.F., *Accounting for Slower Economic Growth: The United States in the 1970s*, Washington, D.C., The Brookings Institution, 1979.

[9] Kendrick, J.W., 'International Comparisons of Recent Productivity Trends', in Fellner, William (ed.), *Contemporary Economic Problems*, Washington, D.C., American Enterprise Institute, 1981.

[10] Kravis, I.B., and Lipsey, R.E., *Prices and Terms of Trade for Developed Country Exports of Manufactured Goods*, NBER Working Paper No. 774, September 1981.

[11] Lipton, D., 'Accumulation and Growth in Open Economies', unpublished Ph.D. thesis, Harvard University, October 1981.

[12] Nordhaus, W.D., 'Economic Policy in the Face of Declining Productivity Growth', *European Economic Review*, XVIII, No. 1/2, May/June 1982, 131–157.

[13] OECD, 'Productivity Trends in the OECD Area', (CPE/WP2(79), 1st revision). Paris, April 1980.

[14] World Bank, *World Development Report 1981*, Washington, D.C., August 1981.

Comment on Chapter 6
Richard Jackman

In this substantial and important chapter, Professor Bruno argues, to my mind entirely plausibly, that a phenomenon as widespread and as pervasive as the post-1973 productivity slow-down must have its roots in the economic disturbances of that time. Clearly the prime suspect is the behaviour of raw material prices which, having declined steadily in real terms from the end of the Korean War until the early 1970s, rose sharply in 1973–4 and have since fluctuated around a much higher average level than in the 1960s or early 1970s. The problem Bruno sets himself is to find a plausible mechanism linking the raw material price increase to the slow-down in productivity growth.

In the chapter two mechanisms are suggested, one concerned essentially with productivity measurement, the other with the effects of the low level of demand, which may be regarded as an indirect effect of the increase in raw material prices (since in the absence of demand deflation the raw material price increases would have led to unacceptably high inflation). These mechanisms are sketched out, evidence on the productivity slow-down for ten OECD countries is documented, and some tests of the hypotheses are provided mainly by means of international cross-section regressions.

There is a great deal of material, both analytical and empirical, in this chapter and in these comments I will only be able to focus on a few of what seem to me the more important of the issues discussed.

The Measurement of Productivity

Since the issues Bruno raises are quite complicated, it may help to set down a basic analytical framework for reference. We may assume that in the production function gross output is produced by labour and capital (value-added) and material inputs. In the case of a national economy, gross output is produced from domestic labour and capital (GDP) and from material inputs imported from other countries. In the case of a sector, such as manufacturing, gross output (industrial production) is produced from labour and capital employed in manufacturing (value-added in manufacturing) and from material inputs produced in other countries or other sectors of the domestic economy.

If the relative price of some imported input rises, and there are possibilities of substitution, the use of the input will fall and hence gross output will fall for given employment of labour and capital. If productivity is measured in terms of gross output per unit of labour (or of labour and capital) employed, this factor substitution will be recorded as a fall in productivity. If the prices of inputs are equal to their marginal products the fall in output will, for marginal changes, be equal to the reduction in the quantity of inputs purchased valued at this price. Thus the fall in gross output productivity resulting from factor substitution can in principle be calculated directly by multiplying the fall in inputs by their share in final output.

If one looks just at energy, where the sharpest price increases have occurred, the direct measure of the substitution effect turns out to be surprisingly small. (The share of energy in GDP is about 5 per cent, while the fall in its use, measured in terms of the change in the growth rate of the energy to GDP ratio, is generally taken as about 2 per cent per annum. On this basis the fall in energy input relative to GDP is 0.1 per cent per annum, and this figure provides some indication of the order of magnitude of the fall in gross output that can be attributed to lower energy usage.)

However, as Bruno has stressed in earlier papers, the post-1973 period has been characterised by increases in the relative prices of many raw materials as well as energy, and substitution away from other raw materials should also be taken into account. Unfortunately direct evidence is not readily available, but given that the relative price increase for most raw materials has been smaller than the energy price increase, it seems improbable that the substitution effect away from other raw materials would yield a very much larger figure than the substitution away from energy.

If we now turn from measures of gross output to measures of value-added, such as GDP, it is apparent that if input prices are equal to their marginal products a reduction in input usage will have no effect on the measure of value-added, or hence on productivity measured in terms of value-added.

The problem Bruno raises in this context is that in times of rising input prices, GDP statistics computed on base year prices are likely to be biased downwards. The GDP index is constructed by subtracting an index of imported inputs from an index of gross output. If the price of imported raw materials rises and consequently import volumes fall, the fall in import quantities should be valued at the marginal product (or current relative price) of the imports. If instead the fall in import volume is measured at a lower, base year price, the saving in imports will be understated. Since imports are subtracted from gross output to derive GDP, a saving in imports for given gross output adds to GDP. Thus if import savings are understated, GDP growth is also understated.

The correct procedure in these circumstances is to use a Divisia index rather than a base year index. However, an indication of the extent of the bias that might be involved can be established by comparing GDP figures measured at 1970 prices (when raw material prices were low) with GDP measured at 1975 prices. (The relative price of raw materials in 1975 was close to its average for the post-1973 period.) In the UK, the Central Statistical Office has made a very careful comparison of the effects of rebasing GDP statistics on 1975 prices (*Economic Trends*, May 1979). The measurement bias can thus be quantified: rebasing on 1975 prices reduces the growth rate of imports by about 0.4 per cent per annum over the period 1973–7. Because of various other adjustments, the bias in the growth of GDP is slightly lower (0.3 per cent per annum). The fall in oil imports in the UK has been sharper than in most other countries because of North Sea Oil, so it is probable that the measurement bias in the UK is at the upper end of the international range.

Finally, in this context it may be noted that the factor substitution effect on gross output is in a sense equivalent to setting the input price at zero, and is thus bound to exceed the effect of measurement bias. If the input price effect is important, we should expect to see a larger effect of gross output indices than on value-added indices. Yet, as Bruno points out, productivity estimates based on GDP have shown a fall very similar in magnitude to the fall in productivity based on gross output measures such as manufacturing output. Furthermore, in many countries, estimates are made of value-added in manufacturing, and these value-added indices show a very similar picture to the index of manufacturing production (see [1] for more detailed discussion).

The evidence Bruno offers for the magnitude of these productivity measurement effects is that of international cross-section regressions, relating the productivity slow-down to the increase in input prices both for manufacturing (table 6.2) and for the total business sector, that is non-government GDP (table 6.7). In fact, as Bruno points out, much of the cross-country variation in input prices derives from movements in real exchange rates, which must to some extent be regarded as endogenous, rather than from differences in the impact across countries of the world oil and raw material price shocks (which might arise, for example, from differences in industrial structure or technology). The regression results indicate a correlation across countries between the productivity slow-down and movements in the real exchange rate.

Various other explanations might be suggested for such a correlation. For example, it appears that real wages adjusted more quickly to the oil price shock in some countries than in others. Countries with slow wage adjustment will experience a longer and deeper fall in profits which may both discourage investment (and hence productivity growth) and, by lowering the return on investment, weaken the exchange rate. Or countries where trade unions have put up a strong resistance to real wage cuts in response to the oil price increase, causing disruption to economic activity, may likewise have experienced as a result both slower productivity growth and a weak exchange rate. It is because other interpretations of the regression results are possible that more direct evidence of the effect of the raw materials price shock on productivity seems to be required.

Indirect Demand Effects

Perhaps the most novel part of Bruno's paper is his suggestion that weak demand may depress productivity growth by inhibiting 'the internal relative price and factor adjustment process' required by the supply shock. While this hypothesis seems quite plausible, again Bruno provides no direct evidence of the mechanism at work.

While it seems very likely that the amount of structural change required to accommodate the increases in raw material prices since 1973 may in some sense be large relative to the required pace of structural change in the 1950s and 1960s, it would be interesting to know the appropriate way of measuring this concept. Likewise it seems plausible that weak demand will slow down economic adjustment and factor mobility but again it would be interesting to see the evidence. Japan, to take a rather conspicuous example, had 'by far the largest demand squeeze', yet it maintained a high rate of investment and it seems implausible to think that the Japanese economy was less quick to adjust than others.

It also seems likely that a reduction in factor mobility will slow down productivity growth. Rather surprisingly, this supposition is not confirmed by evidence for the seven European countries in Bruno's sample. When plotted against the change in labour mobility, based on a study by the United Nations Economic Commission for Europe, insofar as any relationship emerges, it goes the wrong way for Bruno's hypothesis (though the perverse correlation is not statistically significant).

The evidence Bruno offers for demand effects is again that of international cross-section regressions. Demand is measured by the rate of growth of domestic absorption and by the rate of growth of public consumption in tables 6.2 and 6.7. Clearly with such measures there is the risk of spurious correlation (since a fall in productivity, other things being equal, will lead to a fall in real incomes and hence a fall in desired expenditures, both public and private). But even had Bruno adopted a measure of the pressure of demand free of this difficulty (such as capacity utilisation or detrended unemployment) there could still be a problem of reverse causality.

It may help to set out this argument in the form of a simple model (adapted from [2]). If wage behaviour is described by a simple expectations augmented Phillips Curve, and prices set on a simple mark-up rule, then:

$$\dot{w} = \dot{x}^e + \alpha D + \dot{p}^e \tag{1}$$

$$and \ p = w - x \tag{2}$$

where w and p are the logarithms of wages and prices, x the logarithm of the equilibrium marginal product of labour, $\dot{p}^e$ expected inflation and D a measure of the pressure of demand. It is assumed that the constant term in the Phillips Curve which represents the 'target' level of real wage growth can be identified with the expected growth of equilibrium wages. Differentiation of (2) and substitution gives

$$D = {}^1\!/\alpha \ (\dot{x} - \dot{x}^e + \dot{p} - \dot{p}^e) \tag{3}$$

Since $\dot{p} > \dot{p}^e$ is a situation which can only be sustained, if at all, by ever accelerating inflation, the government has little choice if $\dot{x}$ falls relative to $\dot{x}^e$ but to permit, or engineer, a fall in demand. The depth of the recession depends on the productivity slow-down and on the extent to which wage bargaining is responsive to the pressure of demand.

Conclusion
The issues discussed in this paper are clearly crucial to any interpretation of the productivity slow-down. A number of our measures of productivity are likely to fall as a direct consequence of higher raw material prices, though it appears unlikely that the magnitude of this effect is sufficiently large to explain more than a small part of the slow-down that has occurred.

Perhaps more remarkable are the systematic relationships between the more important macroeconomic variables shown in the paper's regression results. There seems clear evidence that the productivity slow-down is a macroeconomic phenomenon, associated with shifts in other major macroeconomic variables and Bruno's paper is amongst the first to analyse it in these terms.

References

[1]   Grubb, D., 'Raw Materials and the Productivity Slowdown: Some Doubts', Centre for Labour Economics, L.S.E. Discussion Paper no. 133.

[2]   Layard, Richard, Grubb, D. and Jackman, R., 'Causes of the Current Stagflation', Centre for Labour Economics, L.S.E.

7 Government Intervention as a Factor in Slower Growth in Advanced Industrial Nations
Victoria Curzon Price

'Everybody knows' that there has been a decline in productivity growth in the industrial countries since 1973. Everybody also knows that there is a pretty clear and consistent rank order in the productivity growth stakes, which puts Japan, France and Germany near the top, and the UK and the US near the bottom. In fact, it is no coincidence that the earliest studies on the possible reasons for reduced productivity growth came from Britain and the US, for people have long wondered why these two economies have grown consistently more slowly than all the rest (see Denison [2] and Bacon and Eltis [1]).

Are we now to believe that the whole of the western world has caught the Anglo-American disease; that we are now *all* caught in the low-productivity, low-growth trap which seemed to characterise only Britain and the US for much of the postwar period? Or are we witnessing much the same relative differences in performance as noted in the past, masked by the fact that all countries have been subjected to a series of external 'shocks' – namely the oil price increases of 1973–4 and 1979–80? The evidence strongly suggests the latter, which implies that the Anglo-American disease has not proved contagious and that we are still left with the problem of explaining it.

Growth rates in the West have declined sharply since 1973 because of two successive oil price increases. In a recent article on 'The cost of OPEC II', Ostry, Llewellyn and Samuelson [5] identify three components of GNP loss and quantify the aggregate impact of the 1979–80 oil price increase in terms of percentage shares of OECD GNP (see table 7.1). If it is true that 5 per cent of OECD GNP was 'lost' in 1980, and almost 8 per cent in 1981, then any final net growth of GNP registered in those years would imply a most impressive growth in productivity, and not, as 'everybody knows', a decline. Like Alice, we are running hard to stay in the same place, or rather inch forward at a rate of 1 to 3 per cent per annum.

Productivity is usually understood to be output per unit of labour input. One can immediately see the statistical difficulties of trans-

Table 7.1   *Cost of OPEC II as per cent of OECD GNP*

	1980	1981
Terms of trade deterioration	1.75	1.75
GNP loss:		
OPEC-induced extra saving	3.00	4.25
OECD-induced extra saving	0.25	1.25
Total	5.00	7.75

Source: *OECD Observer*, March 1982, page 38.

lating this concept into measurable terms. What is a unit of labour? Clearly numbers of hours of labour are a more accurate denominator than numbers of people, but even hours of labour are not homogeneous – teenagers are less productive than those in their twenties and thirties; educated people are (one hopes) more productive than the illiterate and so on.

Even more problematic, what is a unit of output? There are few unambiguous answers. A kilowatt of electricity, a ton of steel, a litre of milk are all pretty homogeneous, and do not change from one period to another. But most physical outputs of modern industry are not so simple. For instance, the modern radial tyre bears little resemblance to its cousin of ten years ago. It lasts twice as long, offers 15 per cent less resistance to the road surface (but skids less) and can be driven for longer at higher speeds without heating and bursting. Yet it costs only one third more than a conventional tyre. How are all these productivity improvements to be captured in the statistics on the output of tyres per hour of human labour?

Besides accounting for such qualitative improvements, productivity changes may take more measurable forms, ranging from unit cost reductions for a constant quantity, to constant unit costs for increased quantities, depending on demand elasticities. These are best captured by assigning a real currency value to net output (that is, value-added), assuming that a suitable price deflator can be found. It might be that a sector would shrink as a result of large productivity improvements if confronted by inelastic price–income demand schedules, as indeed has been the case of agriculture. In this case the contribution of productivity improvements to growth takes the form of lower prices for food, which of course raises people's real incomes. Thus, problems of measuring labour productivity by sector on a value-added basis tend to disappear on aggregation. This is because productivity improvements, wherever they occur, and whatever shape they ultimately take, do not get lost. They have to show up somewhere in the economy either in the form of real growth of national income, or in increased leisure for the same national income, or (more typically) in a mixture of both. This is why there is such a close connection between growth in (labour) productivity and national income and why people tend to treat them as identities. However, this identity holds perfectly only if 'all other things' are held constant – in particular, international terms of trade and government policy. In periods of deteriorating terms of trade and restrictive government policy, productivity improvements are offset by real income losses and the net national income figures understate their true contribution.

I do not believe that government safety regulations, pollution control measures, paperwork and so forth are serious candidates for the role of culprits in the productivity/low growth witch hunt (Denison's research debunking this idea has been very useful in this respect), especially when two successive oil price increases quite clearly take first place. But government, by its actions and inactions, can help or hinder the process of adaptation to a higher energy cost world and in this sense can be made responsible for degrees of relative success or failure in this enterprise.

Sheer Size of Government
Public expenditure has risen in all OECD countries. Defined as all types of expenditure and transfers made by general government, including both current and capital spending and transfer payments of national, state, provincial or local governments and social security agencies, it represents the full cost of government. It is not the same as total tax receipts, which typically fall short of total expenditure by a sometimes significant margin.

According to an OECD study [4], government spending has increased its share of GDP from an OECD average of less than 30 per cent in the mid-1950s to over 40 per cent in the mid-1970s (see table 7.2). There is no point in looking for important inter-country differences in these trends, except to point out the well-known fact that both the US and Japan lie well below the OECD average. However, the low level of Japanese public expenditure should be offset by the fact that certain welfare benefits such as housing, pensions, job security and so on are supplied directly by the private sector and enter into the industrial costs without passing through government hands.

It is embarrassing for 'supply-siders' that the US and Japan stand out as having relatively small public sectors, while experiencing very different rates of productivity growth; similarly, it is awkward that the UK, France and Germany should all be within a narrow 42–45 per cent band, yet have such widely diverging growth patterns. Also, the

Table 7.2   *Total public expenditure, mid-1950s to mid-1970s*

Per cent GDP

	1955–7	1967–9	1974–9	% change in share
UK	32	38	45	+40
Germany	30	33	44	+46
France	34	39	42	+23
OECD average	28	35	42	+50
US	26	32	35	+34
Japan	17	19	25	+47

Source: Derived from *OECD Economic Outlook*, December 1981.

countries with the highest shares of government expenditure in GNP (the Netherlands, Sweden, Norway and Denmark) have experienced larger productivity gains (on a value-added basis) in the 1970s than, for instance, the UK or the US.

A novel way of looking at the size of government in relation to the rest of the economy has been developed by Bacon and Eltis [1]. The central idea is that the *marketed* sector of the economy has to produce 100 per cent of the goods and services which are consumed by all recipients of income, including those employed in the *non-marketed* sector and those not employed at all. The difference is not simply one of public and private sectors, although there is considerable overlap between the two concepts. The contribution of those sectors of government which produce non-marketed services, such as defence, health, education and public administration, are valued at factor cost, and are deducted from total GDP. The remainder, by definition, is total *marketed* output at factor cost. Total government-created claims are then set against this marketed output, and the result is the ratio of non-marketed claims to marketed output. To use a metaphor, one could say that the model relates the government-generated claims rider to the marketed sector horse and any ratio greater than one suggests that the rider is heavier than the horse. Unlike the ratio of public expenditure to GNP, which cannot exceed one, the Bacon and Eltis ratio can be any number greater than zero, which is why it tends to give a larger spread and may reveal inter-country differences hidden by the conventional approach. The authors show that this ratio has climbed in Britain from just over 40 per cent in 1961 to over 60 per cent in 1975.

Now, as Bacon and Eltis point out, if the non-marketed sector begins to claim more than the marketed sector *in fact* is prepared to part with, something has to give. Either a clandestine economy begins to flourish or people's real salaries in the marketed sector must diminish, or business profits must suffer, or some combination of the three. In practice, labour is well enough organised to shift the burden of the squeeze on to capital and, incidentally, start off a wage-price spiral reflecting the excess of claims on marketed output. Circumstantial evidence of such a process at work is to be found in trends in factor income shares.

One of the more stable relationships in advanced economies used to be the share of salaries in domestic factor incomes – so stable was it that it gave rise to a well known rough rule of thumb: two thirds to labour, one third to capital (see [3], pages 251–7). This share has shifted significantly in favour of labour in all European countries. Thus, the ratio of labour remuneration in total factor incomes rose from an average of 60 per cent in 1960 to 67 per cent in 1972 and to 71 per cent in 1980. This is not an uniquely European phenomenon, since Japan has escalated just as fast and the US, as befits the world's most capital-intensive nation, is now distributing a quarter of its national income to capital and entrepreneurship and three quarters to salaried personnel.

In fact, in periods of strong capital accumulation without significant technological change, one would expect the marginal product of capital to diminish and, if it fell fast enough, the share of capital in total income would fall with it. Has this happened in reality? Technology has been far from stable and one would expect it to offset the rising marginal product of labour, leaving the distribution of income more or less where it was before. Japan would be the possible exception, since its rate of capital accumulation has been truly phenomenal.

In any event, in Western Europe in general and in the UK in particular the absolute level of labour's share in national output and its speed of progression is totally out of keeping with underlying economic reality. We are very far from enjoying either American levels of capital investment per worker, or Japanese rates of capital accumulation. So a plausible explanation for the observed shift may be a process like the one described above, where government expansion crowds out the private sector and the resulting squeeze falls more heavily on business profits than on salaries. If this crowding out occurs precisely at a time when the private sector is undergoing a series of traumatic changes and desperately needs real resources to renew capital assets and technology, then its negative impact will not manifest itself in a gradual deceleration of growth, but in a sharp and alarming one.

Public Sector Deficits
The public sector is not only large, it also finds it impossible to

Table 7.3   *Public sector borrowing requirement as a percentage of*
          GDP

	France	Germany	Japan	UK	US
1973	2.9	1.8	5.1	6.5	1.9
1974	3.4	2.4	6.7	8.6	2.2
1975	6.2	6.3	9.5	11.2	6.8
1976	4.9	4.2	10.5	8.2	5.6
1977	4.7	3.1	10.4	4.8	4.5
1978	5.8	3.5	13.8	5.8	4.1
1979	4.3	3.1	10.6	7.7	2.6
1980	..	3.7	10.8	6.5	4.4

Source: Derived from *OECD Economic Outlook*, December 1981.

balance its books. In all developed countries governments have
become important borrowers, converting national savings into current expenditure at an ever faster rate. The alternative use to which
these savings could have been put would have been private investment. The 'crowding out' of private borrowers by the government
takes place via the price mechanism: interest rates are higher, so
fewer private investments remain viable. If one relates public sector
borrowing requirements to GDP (see table 7.3), it can be seen that
they increased steadily throughout the 1970s in all the countries
under discussion, with the exception of the UK, where they already
stood at an unusually high level in 1973. But Japan quite clearly takes
the lead in this series, its PSBR growing from 5 per cent of GDP in
1973 to almost 11 per cent in 1980. However, if one wants to get a
feeling for the extent of the 'crowding out' phenomenon, the important ratio to bear in mind is the size of the PSBR in relation to
available savings. In Japan, a PSBR of 11 per cent currently confronts
a gross national savings rate of over 30 per cent leaving a full 20 per
cent of GDP available for private investment. In the UK a much
lower PSBR of 6.5 per cent is taken from a much smaller pool of
national savings amounting to 19 per cent of GDP.

   Figures for all five countries over the last eight years are presented
in table 7.4, which shows that the proportion of GDP available for
private investment *after* the government has exercised its pre-emp-
tive rights has fallen in most countries since 1973. The UK on the
other hand has been through a cycle: in 1974–6 the PSBR rose to
unusually high levels and left very small amounts available to the
private sector for investment (only 4.2 per cent of GDP in 1975). The
record since has been somewhat better, although we have still to
return to 1973 levels. On average over the past eight years, only 11

Table 7.4 *Per cent GNP available for private investment*

	Japan	Germany	France	US	UK
1973	34.1	24.8	23.1	18.8	14.6
1974	29.6	22.7	21.1	17.1	8.3
1975	22.7	15.3	16.8	10.7	4.2
1976	22.1	18.5	18.1	12.3	8.4
1977	21.5	19.6	18.0	14.2	14.1
1978	18.5	19.9	16.9	15.5	13.8
1979	20.6	20.7	18.5	17.3	12.6
1980	19.9	19.4	..	13.9	12.7
Average					
1973–80	24.0	20.0	19.0	15.0	11.0

Source: Derived from *OECD Economic Outlook*, December 1981.

per cent of GDP was available for private investment in the UK, as opposed to 15 per cent in the US, 19 per cent in France, 20 per cent in Germany and 24 per cent in Japan. If one considers that one is talking about gross investment and that the mere renewal and upkeep of capital assets absorbs between 10 to 15 per cent of GDP, then it is no mystery why the UK and the US should have been growing more slowly than France, Germany and Japan.

It is important to note that the 'crowding out' hypothesis implies not only that private investment will fall, but that *total* investment (that is, private plus public investment) will fall too, since the state does not merely borrow to finance capital expenditure but, increasingly, to cover current commitments. There is strong evidence that total non-residential investment did in fact fall substantially below trend in all major developed countries, including Japan, during the 1970s. Calculations by the Bank of International Settlements show, for instance, that while real fixed investment in Britain had risen at a rate of 5.8 per cent per annum from 1955–73, it did not grow at all from 1973–8, and actually turned negative in 1975–6. In Japan, the long term trend growth rate of 15.5 per cent per annum fell to a mere 6 per cent, while Germany, like Britain, suffered three years of 'negative growth' in 1974–5.

This evidence begs a further question: why have gross savings rates tended to decline in most countries in the 1970s? Also, why do some countries systematically save more than others? If one takes the view of Maurice Scott, that investment is central to the process of growth, then answers to questions such as these would help to explain long term, systematic differences in growth rates. But this takes us too far from the subject of this paper.

The Problem of Allocation

Not only have governments laid claim to a growing share of marketed output; not only have they pre-empted a significant proportion of the public's savings and diverted them from investment to current consumption; they have also interfered with the process of allocating resources in what remains of the productive sectors of the economy.

It is by now commonplace to bemoan the large sums put at the disposal of loss-making firms, the opportunity cost of which are the investments which would have been made by profitable ones. Indeed, the taxpayer's patience is wearing thin and it is unlikely that we shall repeat the mistake of giving large visible subsidies to firms like British Leyland or the British Steel Corporation.

But what of the huge *implicit* cross-subsidisation game which is being played throughout Europe and which cannot but have the long-run effect of reducing growth and efficiency? I refer, of course, to protection. The largest and oldest sector to be shielded from the normal process of competition is agriculture. The explicit subsidies (taking the form of expenditure on surplus production in order to enforce a guaranteed price) are already far from negligible (some $15 billion in the EEC in 1980–1). But the implicit subsidy, contained in the higher price of food and which takes the form of a direct transfer from consumers to producers, is very much higher. If we assume that prices in the EEC are double those on world markets, then half of the 4.5 per cent of EEC GDP produced by agriculture – $60 billion in 1980 – is in fact a transfer rather than real output.

Similarly, we currently shield our textile and clothing sectors, which account for 3 per cent of EEC output. Price differences between the EEC and many third world countries are of the order of 5:1 or even more. If one takes a conservative 3:1 ratio, then 2 out of the 3 per cent of GDP 'produced' in the textile and clothing sector is in fact a transfer from consumers to producers of clothing – another $56 billion worth.

Turning to steel we have a potentially far more serious problem. Thanks to a mixture of protection by means of variable levies, 'orderly' cuts in productive capacity, cartelisation and a system of fines for ungentlemanly price-cutters, steel prices in the EEC have risen by between 40 and 60 per cent. Primary steel production does not contribute more than 1.5 per cent to EEC GDP, but part of this is now clearly a transfer rather than real output – say 0.5 per cent of GDP or $14 billion. But this is not the only indirect cost. Food and clothing are final current consumption goods and the only victims of the cross-subsidisation game are consumers, some of whom may be well enough organised to recoup their losses through union action. But steel is an intermediate product. It accounts for over 10 per cent of the cost of an automobile. To the extent that steel-using industries are in the traded goods sector, this policy inflicts a loss of competitiveness on them and they must either lose ground or seek protection in turn. We have already seen the beginning of this dynamic process at work in the automobile sector, which since May 1981 has been protected from the full onslaught of Japanese competition, even in Germany. The transport equipment sector has therefore been able to raise its prices above what they would have been in the absence of the orderly marketing agreements. By how much? 5, 10 per cent? If the latter, it would be equivalent to an implicit transfer from consumers to producers of automobiles of about 0.3 per cent of EEC GNP, or $11 billion.

These figures have no pretence to be more than very rough guesses. The purpose in presenting them at all is simply to point out that protectionist policies imply large transfers. In the terminology developed by Bacon and Eltis, part of the apparently marketed output should in fact be placed in the non-marketed sector, and the picture is that much the worse as a result. If we tot it all up it comes to a grand total of some $140 billion, or 5 per cent of EEC GDP. This may not sound like much, but these misallocations are all situated in the traded goods sector, which is our only mainstay for the future. If we consider in addition that large parts of the non-traded goods sector would tend quite naturally towards overmanning and inefficiency, then one reaches the conclusion that the misallocation of productive resources is a large and growing phenomenon.

Another important but unquantifiable cause of misallocation is to be found in regional policies, pursued relentlessly over a generation or more in most European countries. In order to raise incomes in low-income areas, governments have combined the carrot and the stick to force new investment out to the economic periphery. While the results are pointed to with pride (though not always – Corby was the result of enlightened regional policy) no one ever spares a thought for the investments which would have taken place in their absence. That they would have occurred *and* been much more productive seems to me to be obvious.

If incomes are low in delightful rural areas and sleepy provincial towns, and high in beastly congested cities it is worth asking why before trying to correct this gross inequity. The answer is simple – the marginal product of people tends to be low in sparsely populated, remote areas because they generate few if any positive externalities; conversely, their marginal product tends to be high in crowded, congested cities, where they can work together with any number of specialists, suppliers, customers, communications systems, bankers, insurers, consultants, the lot. Investments which are lured away from this primeval economic soup cannot prosper and grow, as a great many firms have discovered to their cost and surprise. On a macro-economic scale, the policy of trying to raise incomes in low productivity areas via regional investment grants has proved a costly failure: regional incomes remain low and indeed the numbers of poor regions are growing. The danger now is that formerly congested and thriving cities may have been turned into concrete deserts – in our attempt to make poor regions rich, we have made rich regions poor. It would have been far more sensible to allow investments to gravitate to where their marginal product was highest, and tackle the problem of regional income disparities by sending a cheque through the post (unless, on reflection, one thought that a low income and a quiet life were more than a match for the high income rat-race, especially if people were free to choose between the two).

The full extent of output lost as a result of regional investment policies cannot be easily quantified. However, since *per capita* incomes in thriving congested cities tend to be 50–100 per cent higher than in outlying regions, it must be assumed that regional investments are between half and a third less efficient.

If we add total subsidies (running currently at 3.7 per cent of EEC GDP), indirect subsidies due to protection (at least 5 per cent of EEC GDP as suggested earlier), lost output due to regional policies, and lost output due to the crowding out of investment by public expenditure, not to speak of inefficiencies due to inflation, one is forced to conclude that government policies are responsible for more real income transfers, and possibly more real income losses, than the oil price increase.

Conclusion

The main thesis in the above analysis is that government policy (sheer size, but also direction) is largely responsible for differences in growth rates. These differences were apparent well before the oil price shocks of the 1970s, but the latter brought them sharply into focus since they inflicted large real income and asset losses, and set off a series of long-term structural changes. Only those countries which set aside a substantial proportion of national income for private investment needed to meet the challenge of long-term structural change, were able to confront the problems of the 1970s without actual loss of income. The UK was in a privileged position in that it had indigenous oil resources of its own. But its manufacturing and traded goods sectors have suffered as much, if not more, than those of its main trading partners.

If the analysis is correct, it follows that Japan's strength lies not only in some inscrutable love of saving, but also in its ability to inhibit the growth of government. It also implies that our own weaknesses are self-inflicted – and therefore can, in due course, be corrected. If, on the other hand, we choose not to correct them, then we must conclude that as a society we prefer other things to wealth creation.

References
[1] Bacon, R., and Eltis, W., *Britain's Economic Problem: Too Few Producers*, London, Macmillan, 1976, 2nd edition, 1978.
[2] Denison, E.F., *Accounting for Slower Economic Growth*, Washington, Brookings Institute, 1979.
[3] OECD, *The Growth of Output 1960–1980*, Paris, December 1970.
[4] *OECD Bulletin*, 'Public expenditure trends', February 1978.
[5] Ostry, S., Llewellyn, J. and Samuelson, L., 'The cost of OPEC II', *OECD Bulletin*, March 1982, pages 37 and 39.

Comment on Chapter 7
W.A. Eltis

Dr Curzon Price has considered the influence of both government macroeconomic and microeconomic policies on productivity growth and these will be discussed in turn. Three aspects of macroeconomic policies may have been important. It may be that countries with high ratios of taxation and government expenditure (appropriately measured), or those with high government borrowing in relation to private sector saving, or those with a high share of wages in the national income, have found it especially difficult to raise productivity. Her paper is mainly concerned with the slow-down of British productivity growth, which is particularly notable because at the time when the slow-down began Britain's absolute level of productivity compared so unfavourably with that elsewhere. Her data do not indicate that Britain suffered from a larger public sector, or from faster growth of public expenditure than in France and West Germany, but her evidence does suggest that Britain has had a lower savings ratio in relation to government borrowing, and a higher and increasing share of wages.

There is one aspect of the growth of Britain's roughly average public expenditure ratio which still merits attention. Robert Bacon and I estimate that in Britain the ratio of government financed purchases to net marketed output increased from 39.8 per cent in 1973 to 42.8 per cent in 1979 ([2] updated), which is in fact a slightly

Table 7.8   *The growth of British non-market claims in relation to marketed output*

	1973	1979	
Real net marketed output	100	105.1	
Non-market financed expenditures	39.8	45.0	$\left\{\begin{array}{l}42.8\% \text{ of}\\105.1\end{array}\right.$
Remains for market sector	60.2	60.1	

Source: [2], updated to 1979 using *National Income and Expenditure*, 1981.

smaller increase than that in the conventionally measured public expenditure ratio. Dr Curzon Price quotes our much higher figure of around 60 per cent [1] for the ratio of pre-tax government claims to marketed output, but this is too high because, among several reasons which are set out in detail in [2], it includes the full pre-tax incomes of government workers and not the far smaller sums they actually spend. In her vivid phrase, the British government rider is still therefore substantially smaller than the market sector horse. We do not have comparable estimates for France and Germany, because our method of estimation requires some data from the published British National Income Accounts for which equivalents are not available in *IMF Government Finance Statistics*, etc.

Robert Bacon and I would nevertheless wish to argue that when the slow growth of British output is taken into account, as in table 7.8, the modest increase in the British non-market claims ratio, of 3 percentage points from 1973 to 1979, produced exceptional strains because it pre-empted the entire growth in output. Net marketed output grew only 5.1 per cent from 1973 to 1979 and this entire extra 5.1 per cent had to go to extra non-market expenditures to enable their share to rise from 39.8 per cent to 42.8 per cent of marketed output. France and Germany enjoyed far more growth of output from 1973 to 1979 which meant that they could raise their public expenditure ratios by a few percentage points and also allow market sector producers to invest and consume more. The British market sector in contrast had to produce and allocate resources in zero-sum conditions where workers could only gain to the extent that companies as a whole lost real resources, and individual companies only gained to the extent that others fell back. These zero-sum conditions clearly played a part in furthering the unusual degree of conflict between different groups of workers and between workers and companies which prevailed in Britain. We wrote at length [1] about the effects of the near zero-sum conditions in an earlier period in Britain (including its tendency to raise the natural rate of unemployment). However, the sole reason why the 3 percentage point increase in the non-market expenditure ratio, which was in no way unusual internationally, produced these zero-sum conditions in Britain was because productivity advanced so slowly that net marketed output increased only 5.1 per cent in six years, and why this occurred is precisely what we are attempting to explain. Britain's internationally average public expenditure ratio cannot have been a first cause of its extraordinary productivity slow-down.

Dr Curzon Price's suggestion that Britain's low saving net of government borrowing was a primary explanation of the slow-down in productivity growth is important and interesting, especially when its further tendency to reduce the ability of the economy to adjust to external shocks and in particular the oil price increase is taken into account. Averaging out her data over the seven years from 1973 to 1979, Germany's gross private saving of 23.7 per cent of GDP provided a surplus of 20.3 per cent of GDP over government borrowing: France's saving of 23.2 per cent provided a surplus of 18.6 per cent while Britain's gross private saving of 18.7 per cent of GDP provided a surplus of only 11.1 per cent over government borrowing. The surplus of private saving over government borrowing should equal private investment plus the current account balance of payments surplus. If Britain had only around half as much saving net of government borrowing as France and Germany, it should have had only about half as much investment, leaving aside the complications due to international investment and borrowing. If capital consumption is deducted from the gross savings data, and if this was similar in France, Germany and Britain, then the discrepancy was still larger than the gross savings data indicates. Here is a very considerable possible difference between Britain and the continental economies which achieved so much more productivity growth.

A difficulty with this line of argument is that British private sector net investment was indeed low in the 1973–9 cycle when it averaged 4.8 per cent of GDP, but it was almost as low at 5.3 per cent of GDP in the two previous cycles of 1965–9 and 1969–73 when productivity rose exceptionally rapidly by British standards, and budget deficits averaged only 2 or 3 per cent of GDP. Dr Curzon Price has therefore pointed to an international difference which was important throughout the post-Second World War period, namely low British investment in relation to France's and Germany's, but British private sector investment did not fall particularly in the cycle in which productivity growth collapsed. It may be that, because of the oil price shock and the necessary changes in Britain's economic structure that this called for, Britain's 'permanently' low investment ratio was an especial handicap in the 1970s. It must be noted, however, that the much larger public sector borrowing requirement in the 1973–9 cycle was not associated with a significant fall in private sector investment, and it was indeed accompanied by a large rise in the personal savings ratio with the result that there was no significant net squeeze on the finance available to the private sector. Keynesians do not in any case acknowledge that *ex ante* savings determine the resources available for investment when the economy is below full employment. They believe that an investment upsurge will itself generate the savings necessary to finance it. All are now familiar with the strengths and weaknesses in this line of argument.

The high public sector borrowing requirement in the 1970s may of course have raised inflation through the well-known monetarist mechanisms and a faster growth in the money supply; the oil price shock and union militancy, which may have been partly associated with the considerations set out in table 7.8 may have combined to produce far more rapid inflation than in earlier cycles, or in other comparable economies. After 1975, British governments undoubtedly reacted to this faster inflation by seeking to implement new 'monetarist' policies which have had the effect (among others) of greatly reducing the rate of growth of effective demand. The slower growth of demand may then have had a considerable effect on productivity growth in manufacturing via the well-known Verdoorn relationships which cannot be wholly negligible. The most important effects of the high public sector borrowing requirement on productivity may well prove to be this indirect effect via their tendency to raise nominal inflation rates which governments then sought to correct through real demand reductions.

Dr Curzon Price's third macroeconomic link betwen government policy and productivity growth is Britain's unusually high share of wages in the national income, which worker frustration due to lack of growth in net of tax incomes may have helped to bring about. It is exceedingly plausible that research and development expenditure has been squeezed as a result of the consequently low share of profits, and that this has had adverse effects on productivity growth. It would be most interesting to see data on whether there was actually less research and development spending in the 1970s than in the 1960s. It may well be that the financial squeeze had the expected effect on expenditures in this case, but it did not significantly reduce private investment as a whole – it did of course reduce investment in manufacturing. Data on private sector research and development spending might equally fail to reveal a significant fall.

It may be that the main explanation of the fall in the rate of productivity growth is microeconomic and not macroeconomic, and Dr Curzon Price draws our attention to several microeconomic distortions due to government interventions which, while present in the 1960s, arguably became still more acute in the 1970s. In the most stimulating paper she contributed to the Conference on 'Western Economies in Transition' which the Hudson Institute organised in 1979, she argued that because of various government-induced distortions to markets, investment in Italy and Britain produced virtually no growth in output after 1973. In this respect the behaviour of British manufacturing investment and output in 1973–9 is especially puzzling. Manufacturing output actually fell 4 per cent in Britain from the 1973 cyclical peak to the 1979 cyclical peak. Investment was low in these six years but British industry still invested 4.1 per cent of its value-added net of capital consumption, and 9 per cent gross of capital consumption. Why did British industry invest almost one tenth of its output in order to move backwards? The investment might in theory have been labour displacing, but that does not appear to have been the case. If capital had been substituted for labour at an exceptional rate, which could explain why there was continuing net investment despite the fall in output, then productivity should have risen exceptionally. We are, however, attempting to explain why labour productivity scarcely rose at all in British manufacturing industry from 1973 to 1979. If investment was not exceptionally labour displacing in this period, why did it persist? Three possible explanations come to mind.

First, British managements may have become significantly less skilled at finding the correct balance between capital and labour, so that they invested in new plant that had no significant effect on either output or labour productivity. Much of British industry had to become more competitive in the 1970s, both internally and in relation to foreign competitors, so it is a little unlikely that British managements as a whole became less skilled at microeconomic decision taking than they had been in the 1960s.

The second possible explanation is the one that Dr Curzon Price emphasised in 1979, and she now adds the effect of tariff protection and import restriction to her previous catalogue of productivity reducing state interventions in Britain. The governments of 1973–9 may have so distorted decision taking in industry that companies were induced to invest purposelessly. Nationalisation removed market tests from Leyland and Rolls Royce in the 1970s. Investment incentives were as strong as ever, especially in development areas, and it has been shown that these can easily make productivity reducing investments potentially profitable [4]. Loss making activities were subsidised in a growing fraction of the private sector. The overall effect of these distortions to market resource allocation is obviously impossible to quantify, but it may be that it was especially significant in the 1973–9 cycle when trade union support for job preservation subsidies strongly influenced what governments actually did, and when the newly created National Enterprise Board was willing to throw money into the private sector to support projects labelled 'investment.'

A third and new explanation is one that can be developed from Dr Curzon Price's chapter. It may be that the price indices used to deflate the nominal value of manufacturing output to establish its real value have taken quality improvements insufficiently into account. To take her example of a radial tyre, if this was 30 per cent more expensive than a conventional tyre, did the CSO register this as a 30 per cent increase in the price of tyres (where firms switched from producing conventional to radial tyres), or a zero rise in price and a 30 per cent increase in real quality and therefore output? Whatever figure it chose between these would be arbitrary for the reasons she states, since quality change has several dimensions, and even if each could be measured (and most cannot) the effect of the total gain from the combination of quality changes would still be impossible to pin down. What if the quality improvements achieved by British manufacturers were understated by just 2 per cent per annum from 1973 to 1979? In that case British manufacturing output will actually have risen by 12 per cent more than the CSO estimated in these six years, that is, 'output' will have risen 8 per cent instead of falling 4 per cent. Most important of all so far as the present enquiry is concerned, labour productivity in British industry will have been rising at 2.7 per cent per annum instead of by the mere 0.7 per cent per annum which is officially assumed. Investing 4 per cent of manufacturing output net of capital consumption, and 9 per cent gross of this in order to raise output 1.3 per cent per annum and productivity 2.7 per cent per annum, would make perfectly good economic sense. So, is it possible that official British data have overstated price inflation in British industry in the 1970s, and understated the growth of output and productivity correspondingly; and did this error first become significant in the early 1970s? This could have occurred if manufacturing growth in the 1950s and 1960s was predominantly quantitative so that it could be measured straightforwardly, becoming then far more qualitative in the 1970s. Exports consisted increasingly of electronic and capital goods where the functions, which articles are designed to fulfil, are paramount, and progress takes the form of producing increasingly effective manufactured products. The possibility that the CSO has failed to pick up all the quality improvements which British industry has achieved deserves examination.

One reason why it may not be absurd to suspect that quality improvements have been underestimated in the 1970s is the remarkably satisfactory growth of British exports of manufactures in the face of significant increases in the real exchange rate of sterling towards the end of the decade. The IMF index of normalised relative British unit labour costs rose from 89.0 in 1973 to 113.0 in 1979 and 138.9 in 1980. Britain's share of world markets for exports of manufactures rose at the same time from 9.4 per cent of the world market in 1973 to 9.7 per cent in 1979 and 10.3 per cent in 1980. If the 'quality' and 'effectiveness' of British exports was rising faster than most assume, and export prices correspondingly less, this unexpectedly strong export performance would be readily explicable.

It can be concluded that insofar as there has been a productivity slow-down which requires explanation, and insofar as British governments were responsible for this, attention should be focused on their micro-interventions in the economy. It is difficult to sustain a case that macro-intervention, however misconceived, reduced the rate of growth of *productivity* to a far greater extent in the 1970s than in the 1960s. However, it is not easy to explain why British industry invested throughout the decade in order to produce less; nor why it increased its exports so much more than any model predicted. This throws doubt on the accuracy of the productivity data which gives such a depressing account of British industry in the 1970s.

References
[1] Bacon, Robert and Eltis, Walter, *Britain's Economic Problem: Too Few Producers*, 2nd edn, London, Macmillan, 1978.
[2] Bacon, Robert and Eltis, Walter, 'The Measurement of the Growth of the Non-Market Sector and its Influence: A Reply to Hadjimatheou and Skouras', *Economic Journal*, June 1979, pp. 402–15.
[3] Leveson, I. and Wheeler, J.W. (eds), *Western Economies in Transition: Structural Change and Adjustment Policies in Industrial Countries*, Croom Helm, 1980.
[4] National Economic Development Council, *Investment Appraisal*, HMSO, 1965.

8 How Much of the Slow-down was Catch-up?
Robin Marris *

The Objectives of this Chapter

To what extent can the slow-down of the medium-term trend of *per capita* product that undoubtedly occurred in the 'developed market economies' after 1973 be attributed to forces that were already at work, and to what extent to a change in the state of the world? Or, to put the question in the language of applied economics, suppose we had a cross-sectional econometric model that had done a reasonable job of explaining growth rates before 1973, and applied it with unchanged coefficients to the observed values of its own predetermined variables after 1973, how much of the slow-down – both of individual countries and in aggregate – would be accounted for by changes in these observed variables and how much would remain to be explained by known or unknown forces that were not included in the original model?

This chapter is particularly concerned with the first part of the question. Inevitably, however, the general approach that has been adopted was based on some preconceived notions of possible causes of the changed state of the world since 1973. Thus, following the prevailing conventional wisdom, we assume that there may have been supply-side forces and demand-side forces from the energy crisis, as well, possibly, as other supply- or demand-side forces unrelated to energy that could have arisen coincidentally during the period.

Structural Change in Economic Models

If a model conceived and successfully tested against one body of data appears to break down when applied with unchanged coefficients to another body of data it is customary to speak of a change in 'structure'. The concept of structural change in economic models has two alternative connotations that are sometimes implicitly confused. To

* I am extremely grateful to Mr Gerry Kennally and to other colleagues in the Social Science Research Council programme in quantitative and comparative macroeconomics at the Department of Economics, Birkbeck College, London University, for invaluable assistance and advice at all stages of this project.

the non-econometrician a change in structure might imply a change in kind – different explanatory variables and/or different equations. To the econometrician, generally speaking, the concept of structural change is limited to the case of a change in the true values of the coefficients of a constant set of equations.

In the absence of a generally accepted jargon for distinguishing between these two concepts of structural change, this article uses the expressions 'Q-change' and 'K-change'. The former refers to the effects of quantitative change in the coefficients of an otherwise unchanged model, the latter to the broader concept or 'change in kind'. Finally, the set of changes predicted by the original model using new observed values of the predetermined variables with the old coefficients will be referred to as 'P-change'.

In principle, therefore, it should be possible to partition the total slow-down, both of individual countries and of the sample as a whole, into the effects of P-change, Q-change and K-change respectively. In practice it has unfortunately proved impossible to distinguish the quantitative effects of Q- and K-change over the 'hinge' of the year 1973, for the reason that if we estimate the original model on post-1973 data we find standard errors that are so large that we can make no useful inferences.

The foregoing ideas are tested on cross-section data relating to the developed market economies over the past twenty years. All the testing is based on cross-section analysis and no concepts or problems associated with time-series analysis come into play. We define country variables in one of three ways: (i) levels at the beginning of a time period, (ii) average levels over the duration of a time period, or (iii) exponential growth rates calculated from the end points of a time period. Throughout the analysis the essential target is the explanation or prediction of the exponential growth rate of real domestic product (calculated with terms of trade held constant) per head of population. Given this general approach we now discuss further the countries, the time periods and the variables.

The countries
The principle for selecting the country sample was to include any country that is today a member of OECD, which in 1965 had real GDP *per capita* (measured as described below) no lower than that of Italy. The result is a constant sample of nineteen countries which includes Japan but excludes the southern European OECD members – Portugal, Spain, Jugoslavia, Greece and Turkey; it also excludes the Republic of Ireland. In 1965 the ratio between the poorest country in the sample, Italy, and the richest country, the US, was 1:2.1 Today, the ratio between the same two countries is 1:1.8.

The time periods

Two time periods only are chosen for comparison, 1965–73 and 1973–9. The 'hinge' (a term suggested by Professor Robin Matthews) is set at 1973, not only on account of the fourfold rise in the OPEC oil price which occurred in November of that year, but also on account of the widespread belief, supported by a variety of evidence, that it was in fact an important turning point. The first time period is selected as the last period before the hinge that is of reasonable length and begins in a year of reasonably buoyant conjuncture. The second period ends in 1979 partly because when this research began some country statistics for later years were not yet available but also for the better reason that there is a case for avoiding end points in years such as 1980 or 1981 when government-induced demand-side effects were evidently stronger than had been typical of earlier years of the post-1973 era.

The variables

There are altogether five variables, namely: *LRDPP*: the natural log of real gross domestic product per head of population in international dollars at constant 1975 prices. For eleven countries, Austria, Belgium, Denmark, France, Italy, Germany, the Netherlands, Japan, Luxembourg, the UK and the US, these data are based on data published in Kravis, Heston and Summers [5]. For the remaining eight countries the real product figures are estimates of the same concept using estimation methods similar to those described in Summers, Kravis and Heston [7]. 'International dollars' represent a fixed set of price-weights for converting national currencies into US dollars at purchasing-power, rather than nominal exchange rates.

The Kravis data relate to the year 1975. For other years, for all countries, the figures are extrapolated from this benchmark year by means of the real growth rates implied in national constant-price GDP data. Since these data are weighted at national prices there is an inconsistency of weighting with the international prices which is not thought likely, however, to significantly bias the results of the present study. In principle the national growth rates are calculated in such a way as to hold constant the external terms of trade (increased production, but not increased price, of oil for example could increase a national figure, although where sharp increases in both production and price occur simultaneously conceptual problems may significantly blur this distinction). Unless otherwise stated, *LRDPP* relates to the first year of the indicated time period.

INV (investment rate): gross domestic investment at 1975 international prices divided by real domestic product at the same prices.

The effect of this method is to eliminate variations in national investment ratios due to variations in the comparative price of investment goods. Methods of estimating this adjustment for countries or years outside the benchmark are described in Summers, Kravis and Heston [7]. *INV* is the average value over the stated time period.

EXP (exports growth): the exponential growth rate of the nominal value of total commodity exports converted into dollars at nominal exchange rates, less the US inflation rate (see below) in the indicated period.

INF (inflation rate): the exponential growth rate of the domestic GDP deflator (defined as the excess of the nominal growth rate over the real growth rate as defined below), less the corresponding unweighted average inflation rate for all nineteen countries in the same period.

GRDPP (growth rate of real domestic product per head of population): *LRDPP* at the beginning of period minus *LRDPP* at end of period, divided by number of years in period.

Method of analysis
Using the above data and no other we now proceed as follows. We first set up a 'maintained hypothesis', that is a model that we initially regard as appropriate for explaining economic growth among advanced industrialised countries in the period 1965–73. We then estimate this model by the usual methods and inspect the results. Then we modify the model in the light of the results and re-estimate: the new model is called 'the selected model'.

By comparing actual with predicted *GRDPP*s in the period 1965–73 we may study the performance of individual countries. In preparation for the study of 'slow-down' we also calculate weighted and unweighted averages of the actual and predicted growth rates, as well as of the residuals, for this period.

By applying the coefficients of the selected model estimated from the 1965–73 to the actual values of the exogenous variables of the same model in the period 1973–9 we can estimate both 'predicted slow-down' (see above) and the residual slow-down attributable to the combined effects of Q-change and K-change. We shall then develop various methods for further analysing these results, finally discussing conclusions.

General Description of the Model
The maintained hypothesis is described in Chart 8.1. It is a recursive

Chart 8.1   *The 'maintained' hypothesis and the selected model*

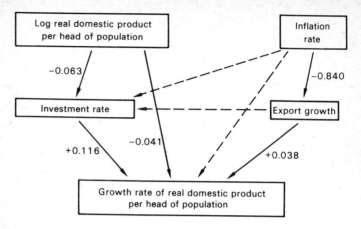

Note: Lines show relationships in the 'maintained' hypothesis. Dashed lines refer to relationships where coefficients were wrongly-signed or not significant. Solid lines show the relationships in the selected model; the figures beside them are the values of their partial coefficients.

model with two exogenous variables (*LRDPP* and *INF*), two intermediate endogenous variables (*INV* and *EXP*) and one final endogenous variable, *GRDPP*.

The general idea is that these nineteen countries were substantially affected by 'catch-up' effects, due to the existence of technology gaps between the most advanced and the less advanced among them (see [1] and [3]). The size of this gap is negatively proxied by *LRDPP*. The larger it is the greater the incentive to invest (top left arrow in the chart) and the larger also will be the productivity of such investment as is actually carried out (centre downward arrow in the chart). The investment relationship is completed by the lower left arrow, which represents the idea that for a given technology gap, the more investment the more growth.

The rationale of the relationships on the right-hand side of the chart is based on treating *INF*, rightly or wrongly, as exogenous (if for no other reason than that we do not know how to model it endogenously) and then investigating its effect, if any, on real phenomena. If a country experiences above average domestic inflation it may experience greater difficulty than other countries in maintaining the dollar competitiveness and hence the dollar purchasing power of its exports. Inflation may also, perhaps, have adverse direct effects on *INV* and *GDRPP*. Thus, in effect, there is an unobserved model, or *deus ex machina*, block-recursive to the present model, which generates inflation and influences the observed model but is not influenced by it.

Finally, the lower right arrow represents the widespread belief that real exports have a positive direct effect on *GRDPP*, even when *INV* and *LRDPP* are held constant. This is 'export-led growth'. The phenomenon is usually hypothesised to relate mainly to manufacturing exports but, as in this paper we are attempting to explain total domestic product, it was felt better to employ a correspondingly broad concept of exports.

Comparison with Previous Models

The model differs from that of previous authors (see [3] and [1]) who have worked with the 'catch-up' idea in being recursive (in effect the previous models were partial reduced forms of the present model); in using real, rather than nominal GDP data; and in attempting to take some account of the possible exogenous effects of inflation. These differences should not be exaggerated: essentially this model is a continuation of the previous tradition in the area. Probably the most important difference is the practical one of a significant reduction in errors in variables by using the Kravis data.

As compared with the work of Denison and of Jorgenson, the present model differs conceptually in being inherently dynamic (it is a differential equation in which the level of *per capita* real product materially influences its own rate of change), whereas the models of these workers are basically founded on a static production function which is then differentiated to obtain the effects of change. In Denison and Jorgenson type models the production function explains output in terms of inputs representing material capital and education-adjusted labour force. In the present model, because of our interest in the catch-up effect (which produces a non-linear technology-trend term in the Denison/Jorgenson context) we concentrate attention directly on the growth rate per head, as, in effect, the essential phenomenon to be explained. Nor do we adjust for the educational quality of the labour force.

Another way in which this model differs from other models, especially for example those associated with the work of Denison, lies in making no attempt to go behind the concept of total output per head of total population. In reality the change in this variable can be properly divided into a number of separate parts, such as the change in the participation rate, the change in the unemployment rate, the change in average annual working hours and the change in output per man-hour. It is also affected by large scale structural shifts such as shifts from industry to services. In the US, for example, our data show a gross slow-down of *GRDPP* between our two time periods of no more than one percentage point, whereas the NIESR tables show that output per person-hour in US manufacturing industry slowed down by about twice as much. It is known that the greater part of this difference was due to an increase in the participation rate associated with a massive increase in the proportion of married women working.

The problem is we do not have a quantitatively testable theory of the participation rate; we do not know how much it is to be regarded as exogenous or endogenous. In the US case all we know is that despite a secular increase in reported unemployment rates, in the period 1965–79 the economy supported a large increase in the proportion of the total population who were able to find productive employment. Thus we concentrate attention on the final outcome, *GRDPP*, attempting to explain this in terms of variables, such as beginning-period *LRDPP,* which are unquestionably predetermined.

Results of Model Selection and Estimation
The chart gives the signs and significance levels of the partial coefficients of the maintained hypothesis. These results are based on OLS estimation of three regression equations each one containing, as independent variables, the effects representing all the arrows pointing into a given box, the latter indicating the dependent variable. The three regression equations were as follows:

$$INV = \text{CONSTANT} + LRDPP + INF + EXP \qquad (1)$$
$$\text{Adj. } \bar{R}^2 = -0.03$$

$$EXP = \text{CONSTANT} + INF \qquad (2)$$
$$\text{Adj. } \bar{R}^2 = 0.14$$

$$GRDPP = \text{CONSTANT} + INV + LRDPP + EXP + INF \qquad (3)$$
$$\text{Adj. } \bar{R}^2 = 0.60$$

The low value of the adjusted $\bar{R}^2$ in the first equation is due to the initial inclusion of variables which proved in the event to be non-signficant. When *INF* and *EXP* are removed the $\bar{R}^2$ becomes 0.14. When *INF* is removed from equation (3) the adjusted $\bar{R}^2$ becomes 0.65.

The Selected Model
The chart also shows the model selected after removing all relationships where either the estimated coefficient proved to display the wrong sign or, although displaying the right sign it was not significant at the 10 per cent level on a one-tailed test. These rather lenient

hurdles are based on the notion that basically we are already convinced that the relationships in question exist; we are mainly concerned with obtaining the best estimates of them from the data of the period in question, namely 1965–73. The partial coefficients set by the arrows now represent modified equations as follows:

$$INV = \text{CONSTANT} + LRDPP \tag{1a}$$

$$EXP = \text{CONSTANT} + INF \tag{2a}$$

$$GRDPP = \text{CONSTANT} + INV + LRDPP + EXP \tag{3a}$$

(For $\bar{R}^2$s see previous paragraph.)

Comparative Performance in 1965–73

In order to calculate the selected model's predictions of individual countries' growth rates in the base period, we first calculate the total effects of the two exogenous variables, $LRDPP$ and INF, on $GRDPP$. They represent the sums of the direct effects (e.g. of $LRDPP$ down the central arrow onto $GRDPP$) and the indirect effects via intermediate endogenous variables (e.g. the product of -0.063 and $+0.116$ for the indirect effect of $LRDPP$). The total effects, applied to the exogenous variables and appropriately combined with relevant constants, provide the desired predicted values of $GRDPP$.

Table 8.1 gives the weighted and unweighted all-country means of the observed values of the variables in both time periods.

Table 8.1   Average values of variables

	1965–73	1973–9
Unweighted averages		
Log real GDP %	8.387	8.698
Investment rate	0.285	0.284
Inflation rate	0.077	0.111
Exports growth	0.065	0.041
Growth rate real GDP %	0.039	0.016
Weighted averages		
Log real GDP %	8.362	8.703
Investment rate	0.270	0.247
Inflation rate	0.061	0.095
Exports growth	0.067	0.061
Growth rate real GDP %	0.042	0.020

Table 8.2   *1965–73 Predicted and actual growth rates and analysis of deviations: average annual rates, per cent*

	Predicted growth rate	Actual growth rate	Deviation attributable to:			
			Invest-ment	Exports	Residual	Total
Australia	2.9	3.6	+0.2	−0.2	+0.7	+0.7
Austria	4.8	4.9	−0.1	−0.2	+0.3	+0.0
Belgium	4.4	4.6	−0.5	−0.1	+0.8	+0.2
Canada	3.0	3.8	−0.4	−0.1	+1.3	+0.8
Denmark	3.6	3.5	+0.1	−0.2	+0.1	−0.0
Finland	4.3	4.8	+0.5	−0.1	+0.1	+0.5
France	4.1	4.5	+0.2	−0.1	+0.3	+0.4
Germany FR	3.6	3.7	+0.7	−0.2	−0.4	+0.1
Iceland	3.1	3.2	−0.3	+0.1	+0.4	+0.1
Italy	5.9	4.3	−0.6	−0.1	−0.8	−1.5
Japan	6.6	9.0	+0.6	−0.1	+1.9	+2.4
Luxembourg	3.2	3.9	−0.2	+0.9	+0.0	+0.7
Netherlands	4.1	3.9	+0.2	−0.2	−0.3	−0.2
New Zealand	3.9	1.9	−0.2	−0.2	−1.6	−2.0
Norway	2.9	3.8	+0.5	−0.2	+0.6	+0.9
Sweden	2.0	2.4	+0.4	−0.2	+0.2	+0.4
Switzerland	2.8	3.0	+0.8	−0.2	−0.3	+0.2
UK	4.2	2.4	−0.8	−0.2	−0.8	−1.8
US	2.3	2.7	−0.7	−0.2	+1.3	+0.4
Average	3.8	3.9	0	−0.1	+0.2	+0.1
Weighted average	3.9	4.2	−0.2	−0.1	+0.6	+0.3

Note: The predicted values are based on the total effects of investment and inflation and the deviations attributed to investment and exports are calculated in the manner represented in Chart 8.1. The residual deviation is the total deviation less these effects.

   Table 8.2 gives the predicted and actual values of *GRDPP* for each country for 1965–73. The final column of the table gives the deviation of actual from predicted values and is a rough measure of residual country performance. At the bottom of the table weighted and un-weighted averages of the predicted values and deviations are also given: the failure of the unweighted predicted value to precisely equal the actual value is due to rounding error.

   Given the method of calculating the predicted values, the figures in table 8.2 are not subject to the constraint that the total variance (second column) is equal to the sum of the explained variances (first column) and the unexplained variance (third column). Therefore the usual $\bar{R}^2$ is not necessarily the best measure of goodness of fit. The standard error of prediction (third column) was 0.7, that is just under three-quarters of one percentage point on the growth rate. This seems reasonably small. A more down to earth measure of the predictive quality of the model may be obtained by counting the number of countries which displayed a prediction error of one percentage point or more. Out of the nineteen countries there are only four such, three with negative deviations, Italy, New Zealand and the UK, and one with a rather large positive deviation, needless to say, Japan.

The UK case looks subjectively worse than that of Italy. Italy actually grew at a faster rate than the unweighted average of the whole sample, that is, she grew at 4.3 per cent. But because Italy was a poor country, her predicted growth rate was substantially above the average, 5.9 per cent, so there was a shortfall of 1.5 points. By contrast the UK, although predicted to grow only a little faster than the average, produced an almost record shortfall of 1.8 points.

Further Analysis of the Residuals

One advantage of the recursive model is that it enables us to look behind the individual country deviations and to partition these into those parts that were due to deviations in the intermediate endogenous variables and the remaining part that was fully unexplained. This analysis is carried out in table 8.2.

The UK, it will be noticed, had both a substantial negative investment-effect deviation and a substantial negative residual deviation. It also had a small amount of negative export-effect deviation. Since the UK inflation rate was in fact above average, this means that UK exports did even worse than would have been predicted by her poor inflation record. Thus the conventional view that in the sphere of economic growth this country could not get anything right, at least in the period 1965–73, seems confirmed.

It will also be noticed that Japan had both a positive investment deviation effect and a positive residual deviation. Such observations stimulate a fear that the model may have been in some way misspecified leading to correlation between significant residuals.

This fear may be investigated in a general way by regressing the residual deviation simultaneously on the investment deviation effect and the exports deviation effect. The results were reassuring. The regression produced an $\bar{R}^2$ of virtually zero and neither t value greater than 0.5. This was frankly a better result than had been expected and suggests that the model may in fact have succeeded in isolating the effects of catch-up and investment effects from other disturbances.

Estimate of the Slow-down

The procedure by which we propose to estimate the slow-down has

Table 8.3   *1973–9 Predicted and actual growth rates and analysis of deviations: average annual rates, per cent*

	Predicted growth rate	Actual growth rate	Deviation attributable to:			
			Invest-ment	Exports	Residual	Total
Australia	1.5	1.3	+0.1	−0.1	−0.2	−0.2
Austria	3.0	3.1	−0.0	−0.2	+0.2	+0.0
Belgium	2.6	2.1	−0.3	−0.2	+0.0	−0.5
Canada	1.5	2.2	+0.4	−0.0	+0.3	+0.7
Denmark	2.3	1.6	−0.3	−0.2	−0.2	−0.7
Finland	2.3	2.1	+1.4	+0.0	−1.7	−0.2
France	2.6	2.4	+0.3	+0.0	−0.5	−0.2
Germany FR	2.3	2.4	+0.3	−0.3	+0.1	+0.1
Iceland	1.4	1.5	+1.4	+0.7	−2.0	+0.1
Italy	3.7	1.9	−0.5	+0.3	−1.6	−1.9
Japan	3.1	2.8	+0.7	−0.1	−0.8	−0.2
Luxembourg	1.6	−0.5	+0.6	−0.4	−2.3	−2.1
Netherlands	2.6	1.5	−0.3	−0.3	−0.4	−0.1
New Zealand	3.2	−0.8	+0.5	−0.1	−4.4	−4.0
Norway	1.7	3.8	+1.5	−0.1	+0.6	+2.1
Sweden	1.1	1.2	+0.5	−0.1	−0.2	+0.2
Switzerland	1.8	−0.5	−0.2	−0.4	−1.8	−2.3
UK	3.1	1.2	−0.8	+0.1	−1.2	−1.9
US	1.3	1.7	−0.8	−0.0	+1.3	+0.4
Average	2.2	1.6	+0.2	−0.1	−0.8	−0.6
Weighted average	2.3	2.0	−0.2	−0.1	−0.0	−0.3

Note: The predicted values are based on the total effects of investment and inflation and the deviations attributed to investment and exports are calculated in the manner represented in Chart 8.1. The residual deviation is the total deviation less these effects. In this table coefficients estimated from 1965–73 data are applied to actual values of appropriate independent variables in 1973–9.

already been generally explained. Table 8.3 represents the figures that would correspond to table 8.1 when we apply the total-effect coefficients of the selected model estimated from 1965–73 to the data of the exogenous variables (*LRDPP* and *INF*) for the period 1973–9. Thus the total deviations given in this table, which represent the sum of Q-change and K-change, but not of P-change, will not sum to zero. Their weighted and unweighted averages, given at the bottom, are a first measure of the slow-down.

The results are rather surprising. They are most conveniently summarised in table 8.4 where all figures are given in the form of changes between the two time periods. The greater part of the slow-down was predicted!

Table 8.4   *Estimate of the slow-down in* GRDPP *1965–73 to 1973–9*
Percentage points

	Unweighted average	Weighted average
Predicted	1.6	1.6
Actual	2.3	2.2
Residual	0.7	0.6

This was due, of course, to the catch-up effect. The nineteen countries were on average 35 per cent richer in 1973 than in 1965 and their previous behaviour implied that this fact alone would be sufficient cause of a substantial slow-down, of the order of 1.5 percentage points. Only just over half of one percentage point of the actual slow-down was left to be explained by residual factors, ie by change in the state of the world, that is to Q-change and K-change.

The reader may ask where the potential effects of faster world inflation of the second period come into the story. The answer is that such effects were excluded by definition. The model related to comparative inflation, so that no change in average inflation can affect its results. Of course this does not mean we are assuming that the world inflation of the 1970s may not, directly or indirectly, have been a major cause of residual slow-down – that is may not have been a significant source of K-change – but there is no way that a cross-section model based on one period could estimate the effects of a change in the mean value of a variable whose only effect in the selected model emerged as an effect on comparative export performance.

The foregoing analysis of the gross slow-down must inevitably provoke further questions. How does the slow-down partition into investment, exports and residual effect? This question is addressed in table 8.3. The results show significantly that the aggregate unpredicted slow-down was not mainly explained by unpredicted shortfalls in investment and exports.

The analysis of individual countries' *comparative* slow-down performance is carried out in table 8.5, where there suddenly emerges some news! The comparative slow-down residual deviation for the UK is quite significantly positive (+0.6). By contrast Japan's comparative residual slow-down performance was quite the opposite (−1.7). Another strong positive performance in this respect comes from the US, which country, despite the burden of faltering manufacturing productivity referred to above, comes out with a comparative residual deviation in table 8.5 equal to a whole percentage point.

Table 8.5   *Comparative changes 1965–73 to 1973–9; predicted and actual growth rates analysis of deviations*

| | Attributable to: | | Residual | Total |
	Investment	Exports		
Australia	−0.4	−0.1	+0.1	−0.1
Austria	−0.2	−0.2	+0.9	+0.7
Belgium	−0.1	−0.2	+0.2	+0.0
Canada	+0.6	−0.1	−0.1	+0.6
Denmark	−0.6	−0.2	+0.7	+0.1
Finland	+0.8	+0.0	−0.9	−0.0
France	−0.1	+0.0	+0.1	+0.1
Germany FR	−0.6	−0.3	+1.5	+0.8
Iceland	+1.5	+0.7	−1.4	+0.7
Italy	−0.2	+0.2	+0.2	+0.4
Japan	−0.2	−0.2	−1.7	−1.9
Luxembourg	+0.6	−0.5	−1.3	−2.1
Netherlands	−0.8	−0.3	+0.8	−0.1
New Zealand	+0.5	−0.1	−1.9	−1.3
Norway	+0.8	−0.1	+1.0	+1.9
Sweden	−0.1	−0.2	+0.6	+0.5
Switzerland	−1.2	−0.4	−0.4	−1.8
UK	−0.2	+0.1	+0.6	+0.6
US	−0.3	−0.1	+1.0	+0.8

Note: The figures in this table represent inter-period changes normalised by unweighted averages of inter-period changes

It is attractive to consider the hypothesis that a large part of the residual deviation in table 8.5 can be explained by oil and natural gas, an idea that is immediately somewhat dampened by the observation that Germany had a strong positive comparative performance, having been, perhaps surprisingly to some, a more or less average residual performer in 1965–73. For what it is worth, we therefore made the following calculation. Define a 'fortunate' country as one which by the end of the period was not a net importer of more than a third of its oil requirements or which had reached a similar position by virtue of natural gas. There were five such countries, namely the UK, the US, the Netherlands, Norway and Canada. They had an unweighted average positive residual deviation in table 8.5 of 0.66. The corresponding figure for the remaining fourteen countries was −0.24. On a two-tailed test, however, this difference of means was not even marginally significant, so that on this test the hypothesis that the two groups of countries came from the same population with respect to residual slow-down performance cannot be rejected.

Conclusions

The total slow-down among the advanced industrialised countries averaged 2.2 percentage points a year. Of this about two-thirds was predicted by earlier behaviour (essentially the playing out of the catching-up phenomenon) and one-third was left to be explained by a change in the state of the world. However, given that the system appears to have been on a flattening path, from which it then deviated moderately but rather abruptly downward, the appearance of a sharp 'hinge' in the actual data was inevitable. It was the effect of kinking downward an already downward bending path.

The comparative performance of individual countries (in the sense of residual deviation) in the period 1965–73, conforms to expectations. The comparative 'slow-down' performance, however, produces some apparent surprises: both the UK and the US emerge on this count as positive performers. So, however, does Germany.

Postscript: reply to discussion

Charles Feinstein makes, among others, two powerful points; one is that I have not established that my results are free from bias due either to simultaneity or to omitted variables; and the other that the specification of the 'catch-up' effect contains a theoretical defect leading to an overestimate of the 'predicted' slow-down. In discussion a further substantive point arose, namely that a cross-section catch-up model is effective in explaining differences in the growth rates of individual countries, but not for explaining a change in the mean growth rate: hence, it was argued, the slow-down was rather general and did not, according to table 8.5, vary greatly between countries.

Simultaneity

I accept that this is an obvious concern. *Ex post*, I did carry out the unrigorous but, I think, quite forceful test for recursiveness described at the end of the section above, entitled 'further analysis of residuals'; this test was not criticised in the discussion. *Ex post*, the main reason that the model is exposed to this criticism is that both the two most obvious feed-back loops, that is from the growth rate of output per head to inflation on the one hand (hypothesised to be negative) and to investment on the other (hypothesised to be positive), if incorporated in the model, leave it underidentified unless additional identifying variables can be found. In the case of the inflation loop, the theory that suggests that countries with low growth of output per head are more likely to suffer wage inflation is not, unfortunately, associated with an established additional variable. In the case of the investment loop, the theory suggests an effect that could be expected to work through the real, risk-adjusted, marginal return on private investment. Here, my problem is lack of a sufficient number of internationally comparable observations. I believe, however, that there is rather strong evidence, from the pattern of first-order correlation coefficients, that bias from either of the sources, in the model as at present formulated, is moderate if not small. This particularly applies to the case of inflation, where the first-order correlation between the variable in question and every other variable except exports is virtually zero.

Omitted variables
We did not include in the maintained hypothesis variables which we already knew to be non-significant in all directions (that is to say, in the language of chart 8.1, variables which, if included, would have radiated dashed lines only); one such was the proportion of the population engaged in agriculture. With the exception of the educational quality of the labour force, already discussed above, I have not received, nor found in the literature, suggestions for other exogenous variables. My confidence on this point is reinforced by the rather strong performance of the model in explaining growth rates in the 1965–73 period. I conceded that the post 1973 period is another matter.

Specification of the catch-up effect
This point, as such, is generally valid. In previous work [6] I found the most effective specification to be one in which the dependent variable was the *per capita* growth rate of a country *relative* to the US growth rate and the explanatory variable was X/Y, where X is the US *per capita* real income level at the beginning of the period over which the growth rates were defined, and Y the corresponding figure for the country in question. This was applied to data for seventeen countries relating to four five-year periods between 1953 and 1973, making in all 68 pooled observations. Without any additional explanatory variables, this equation produced a cross-section $\bar{R}^2$ of 0.28, (*cf* 0.60 in equation 3 above) and the sum of its constant and its coefficient were not significantly different from unity, supporting a hypothesis that the non-US countries were following a non-linear path that would approach, but never overtake, the US path.

This last described model, however, as indicated, related to pooled observations within which the normalising variable, namely the US growth rate, could and did vary. Consequently the normalisation had an effect. By contrast, when we are considering a single period, such as 1965–73, no normalisation of this type can affect the results. Furthermore, if we normalise by the US we are deprived of the opportunity to predict for the US, a major handicap in the slow-down analysis. For these reasons I deliberately chose the present arrangement.

I concede, however, that having done so I have created a logical problem that could be considered as awkward as the problem I was trying to avoid. Between 1965–73 and 1973–9, the US in fact slowed down by one percentage point, that is, by precisely the amount the model in its present form predicted she would slow down. Had I used the old specification, the US would have disappeared from the tables but the US growth rate in 1973 would have had to have been included, along with investment and so on, in the variables required to obtain an estimate of the slow-down: the 'old' model, as such, would have predicted only *comparative* slow-downs. At the end of the day my table 8.4 above would have been exactly the same, but the interpretation would have been different: one whole point of the 'predicted' slow-down for the average non-US country would have been the US slow-down! To put the point more shortly, in the formulation I use in this chapter I am ascribing the whole of the US slow-down itself to some kind of catch-up effect. This I concede is questionable.

In the early post-Second World War period it was reasonable to suppose that what had happened was that in the first half of the present century individual countries had fallen behind the US technology level in varying degree and that, in the absence of a strong international transfer mechanism, had then failed to catch up, that is had merely maintained their relative positions. After the Second World War, the advent of freer international trade, better communications and international companies changed the situation in a once-and-for-all manner, leading to a catch-up phenomenon which could best be specified by postulating the US as the unique, most advanced country. By 1965, however, there were clearly countries or industries where the US was no longer the technology leader, and the catch-up phenomenon must therefore have been diffused. In such circumstances it is not unreasonable to attribute some 'catch-up' behaviour to the US, a proposition which is reinforced by the present model's successful prediction of the US slow-down. However, one must agree, the model notwithstanding, that my procedure has the somewhat extreme implication that no part of the US slow-down remains to be explained by any factor *other* than catch-up! If one were to split the difference between the one extreme (no US slow-down due to catch-up) and the other, one would reach the conclusion that of the total slow-down in growth of output per head in the OECD world, one percentage point (rather than one and a half percentage points as suggested above) was due to catch-up and therefore necessarily permanent. If all the other effects discussed at this conference are impermanent, or at least capable of reversal by appropriate policies, one might expect that the maximum OECD growth rate of output per head, if and when the present convulsion is finally ended, could be of the order of 3 per cent a year. If some of the other effects are also permanent, the figure would be accordingly less.

Cross-section and prediction

This point can always be made against any prediction based on cross-section analysis: the catch-up phenomenon has been modelled above as a differential equation and yet is estimated from stationary observations. The fact remains that it appears that, had the convulsion of 1973–9 not occurred, the 1965–73 model, as estimated above, would probably have done a good job of forecasting the subsequent period. The mean residual, therefore, appears to be a strong candidate for an estimate of the unforecast slow-down. I would also claim that it is not true that the criticism of my logic on this point is supported by the results of table 8.5. In fact, the standard error of the residual deviation (which is the relevant column, I think) is no less than 0.80.

References

[1]   Cornwall, J., *Modern Capitalism, Its Growth and Transformation*, Martin Robertson, London, 1977.

[2]   Denison, E., *Why Growth Rates Differ*, Brookings Institution, Washington DC, 1967.

[3]   Gomulka, S., *Inventive Activity, Diffusion and the Stages of Economic Growth*, Aarhus, Institute of Economics, 1971.

[4]   Jorgenson, D., Christensen, L. and Cummings, D., 'Relative productivity levels 1947–1973: an international comparison', Harvard Institute of Economic Research, discussion paper no. 773, June, 1980.

[5]   Kravis, L., Heston, A. and Summers, R., *World Product and Income: An International Comparison of Real Gross Product*, Johns Hopkins for World Bank, Baltimore, 1982.

[6]   Marris, R., 'Some New Results on Catch-up', University of Maryland Department of Economics Working Paper, 79–6, College Park, Maryland, 1979.

[7]   Summers, R., Kravis, I. and Heston, A., 'International comparison of real product and its composition: 1950–77', *Review of Income and Wealth*, March, 1981.

Comment on Chapter 8
Charles Feinstein *

Robin Marris has given us a characteristically lucid and stimulating chapter. His approach is distinguished by its economy – only four explanatory variables are invoked – and by its use of a cross-section analysis to explain changes over time. Both these features provide significant benefits but, as always, there is a price to be paid. In what follows I shall take for granted the merits of the paper and concentrate on the few points at which it seemed to me to give rise to some doubts.

His basic model applies a cross-section analysis to a sample of nineteen OECD countries. The cross-section relates initially to the period 1965–73, with data measuring either levels at the beginning of that period or averages and growth rates over the period. The coefficients obtained from that period are then applied to the corresponding cross-section data for the period 1973–9, and the predicted results compared with the actual experience in the second period.

The model has two exogenous variables and two intermediate endogenous variables. The dependent variable is the rate of growth of real GDP per head of population ($GRDPP$). The first, and most important, exogenous variable is the level of GDP per head of population at the beginning of the period ($LRDPP$). This is intended to capture the notion of a 'technology gap', as suggested by Gomulka [2] [3], Cornwall [1] and others. The basic hypothesis is that once countries have passed a certain threshold level, those which are furthest from the technological frontier (most closely approached by the most advanced countries) will have the greatest opportunities for catching up. This will be reflected in higher investment ratios and higher rates of growth relative to those of countries nearer the frontier. Over time all countries will converge to the (slower) growth rate determined by the exogenous rate of technical progress in the leading countries. Any inter-country differences in productivity levels which then remain will be the result of institutional and social features. A simple formulation of this approach would thus be $\hat{Q}_i = \lambda(T^* - T_i) + u_i$ where $\hat{Q}_i$ = the rate of growth of output per manhour in country i, $(T^* - T_i)$ = the 'technology gap' proxied by the difference

---

* I am most grateful to John Hutton for helpful discussions of the issues considered in this comment.

in the level of *per capita* GDP between the leading country and country i, and u_i = a stochastic disturbance term. This is not quite the same as the form in which the hypothesis is applied by Marris, but the underlying logic is the same. In his version the gap is indicated simply by the initial levels of *per capita* GDP in each country, so that the distance from the leading country (λT^*) is implicit in the constant term, and it would have been interesting to know what steady state value of T^* is given by his model. The role of the average investment ratio (INV), as one of the two intermediate endogenous variables in the model, is implicit in the above approach.

The second exogenous variable is the relative inflation rate over the period (INF). This is itself entirely unexplained. It is assumed to affect adversely the rate of growth of exports (EXP) (the other intermediate variable) and possibly also the investment ratio, and thus to be negatively associated with the rate of growth of output per head.

On the basis of this model Marris finds that almost 70 per cent of the actual slow-down in growth of output per head in 1973–9 is predicted by the experience of 1965–73: the actual fall between the two periods for the nineteen countries as a whole averaged 2.3 percentage points as compared with a predicted fall of 1.6 points. How persuasive is this demonstration that the greater part of the slow-down was the effect of countries closing the technology gap? The author's own view is indicated by his statement, 'basically we are already convinced that the relationships in question exist; we are mainly concerned with obtaining the best estimates of them from the data of the period in question'.

Those who take a more sceptical view might justify their doubts on a number of grounds, including the following.

(i)   The model is said to be recursive but no evidence is offered to show that the relationships can reasonably be specified in this way. It is not difficult to think of hypotheses which would suggest that it might not be. The rate of growth of GDP per head might influence the rate of investment on the basis of an accelerator model; and the rate of inflation on the basis of a target real wage approach. A sceptical reader might thus ask to see the results of tests which would show whether or not such more general relationships are rejected by the data.

(ii)   The cross-section procedure automatically excludes from consideration potentially important factors responsible for changes in the mean value of the variables over time. To take a classical example: it is comparable to a model which explains the regression in heights towards a mean value from generation to generation, but omits the effect of nutrition and other factors in changing that mean value. Marris might reply that his results show that the effects of the catching up and inflation hypotheses which his model is designed to test account for the greater part of the observed decline, and leave only a relatively small residual. However, that is a *net* residual and could be the outcome of positive and negative effects, some of which might be at least as important as those explicitly modelled.

(iii)   As an elaboration of this it seems relevant to note that the form in which the technological gap is specified in the paper implies that growth rates must steadily converge over time towards zero: the more advanced technology is diffused, the less scope there is for further growth by diffusion. A further implication of this formulation is that average growth rates should have been higher in the early post-war period, say 1951–60, than they were from 1960–73. This is not true for the sample as a whole, and the individual countries for which growth rates were markedly lower in the earlier period include Italy, Japan and Finland, which were among the least advanced at the beginning of the 1950s.

(iv)   The model obtains its attractive economy at the cost of excluding such factors as the variation in the timing of the slow-down in different countries; the distinction in the dependent variable between output per head and output per manhour and thus the possible differential effects of changes in participation rates, unemployment and hours worked; the transition from fixed exchange rates in the early period to floating rates in the later period and the possible effects of this on the relationship between inflation, exports and growth; and the significance of structural changes within each economy, in particular the much-discussed shift between manufacturing and other sectors.

Professor Marris is, of course, aware of all these points and passing reference is made to most of them in this chapter. The point at issue is simply the importance which should be attached to them in qualification of his very interesting findings, and as a means of reducing his estimate of the effect of 'catch-up' to a more plausible level.

References
[1]   Cornwall, J., *Modern Capitalism: Its Growth and Transformation*, Martin Robertson, 1977.
[2]   Gomulka, S., *Inventive Activity, Diffusion and the Stages of Economic Growth*, Aarhus, Institute of Economics, 1971.
[3]   Gomulka, S., 'Britain's Slow Industrial Growth. Increasing Inefficiency versus Slow Rate of Technical Change', in Beckerman, W. (ed.), *Slow Growth in Britain*, Oxford University Press, 1979.

9   The Productivity Slow-down: a Marxist View
Andrew Glyn *

At first sight the slower growth of productivity since 1973 seems one of the lesser problems faced by the advanced capitalist countries. Would not faster productivity growth have led simply to a faster growth of unemployment? Experience in British manufacturing industry over the last year, with a nearly parallel fall in employment and rise in productivity, seems to support this view.

Yet, despite the exploding body of literature dealing with the implications for unemployment of accelerating productivity growth, since 1973 rising unemployment has of course been associated with a far slower rate of productivity increase. The slow growth of output represents a gigantic loss of potential production. If the biggest seven OECD countries had grown as fast between 1973 and 1981 as they did over the years 1960–73, their output in 1981 would have been nearly 23 per cent higher. The equivalent of the GDP of France and Germany combined was lost in 1981 alone by this shortfall in production. The slower growth of GDP since 1973 is practically all accounted for by the slow-down in productivity growth (1.4 per cent a year between 1973 and 1981 compared to 3.7 per cent between 1960 and 1973). Employment growth only slowed to 0.9 per cent from 1.3 per cent a year. The historic justification for capitalism in terms of its ability to develop the productive forces is tarnished to say the least. That is, of course, provided the stagnation of the 1970s can be explained, in terms of the dynamic of capitalism as a system, and the 'shocks' and 'policy errors' it induces, rather than by sunspots or stupidity.

Marxists and Productivity
The very fact that I am supposed to be giving 'a Marxist explanation', whereas the other papers deal with particular factors, suggests that I should produce an entirely different set of considerations. This I cannot do; indeed, why should I? Many of the recent concerns of mainstream economists (for example, the relation of capital accumulation to profits, variations in labour intensity) have always been at the heart of the approach of Marxists.

* My thanks to Philip Armstrong, Wendy Carlin and John Harrison for their comments and to Gillian Holliday for help with the computations.

A Marxist explanation of the growth of labour productivity centres on two factors. First is the accumulation of means of production. For Marx the primary determinant of the level of labour productivity was the 'technical composition of capital', the mass of means of production each worker operates, that is the capital–labour ratio. Marxists view technical progress as primarily incorporated in new means of production. A 'vintage' approach embodies very well Marx's analysis of capital accumulation, as the mechanism by which competition is fought out. From this perspective the neoclassical growth accounting school, by attempting to isolate technical progress from investment, enormously under-emphasises the role of capital accumulation. Faced with the long-run relative constancy of the capital–output ratio in different countries, despite varying rates of growth of the capital–labour ratio, they have to postulate diverse rates of technical progress which allowed a faster or slower rate of accumulation. Marxists would view the causation as being primarily in the other direction; diverse rates of accumulation have brought with them different rates of productivity growth.

But a more fundamental difference is that Marxists regard production as a social as well as a technical process. Work is extracted from workers under certain hierarchical relations of production. The balance of power and thus the intensity of labour can alter, leading to a change in productivity as conventionally measured. Indeed technology itself, and the workplace organisation of the work, are directed to maintaining and increasing labour intensity. The fact that labour intensity is practically impossible to measure, especially on a macroeconomic scale, does not justify ignoring it.

In the rest of this paper I want to focus first on the course of capital accumulation in the advanced capitalist countries, and in particular its link to profitability and productivity. The most important question is whether the seeds of the slow-down after 1973 are visible in the turbulent period from the mid-1960s. Secondly, I want to discuss management's attempts to reorganise work in response to the productivity slow-down.

Accumulation and Profits

The boom years
The latter part of the 1960s saw the beginning of the break-up of the long boom which began in the 1950s. In order to capture the essential features of the boom in summary form I have constructed figures for the rate of profit and the rate of accumulation for the biggest six advanced capitalist countries combined (see Glyn [12]). Charts 9.1 and 9.2 show that in the 1950s and early 1960s the rate of profit in the

Chart 9.1   *Business profitability: major advanced capitalist countries*

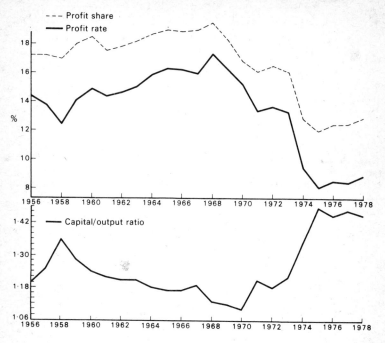

Sources: As table 9.1.

business sector as a whole rose gently; with the rate of accumulation (growth rate of the gross capital stock) tending to increase a little as well.

This constancy, or slight upward trend, in the rate of profit can be decomposed into the behaviour of the profit share and output–capital ratio; the profit share was constant or rising slightly, the output–capital ratio flat. The behaviour of the profit share implies that the real cost of employing labour (the wage gross of all taxes and social security contributions, deflated by the output price index) was rising at the same rate, or slightly slower than the growth of productivity.

This rise in the real cost of employing labour (the product wage) played two crucial roles in sustaining the boom. Obviously it allowed real wages and workers' consumption to rise, thus providing an essential component of expanded demand. Second, and just as important, it ensured that labour would be available for the new means of production by making the old means of production un-profitable and thus forcing their scrapping. The 'labour-repelling' aspect of accumulation described by Marx works in this way; by

Chart 9.2 Growth rates in major advanced capitalist countries

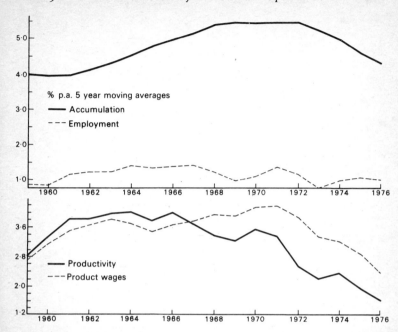

Sources: As table 9.2.

dragging up the product wage the viability of backward enterprises and plants is destroyed. Without such a mechanism for channelling workers, accumulation would have run out of steam for lack of labour. Whilst employment growth was around 1 per cent a year with a life of means of production of, say, twenty years, something like 5 per cent of the labour force would be released each year by the scrapping of old equipment.

The constant output–capital ratio in turn reflects a rise in labour productivity as fast as the rise in the capital–labour ratio. The tendency for capital accumulation to drive down the profit rate was offset by a sufficient devaluation of capital.

Over-accumulation and the late 1960s
As is well known, profit rates began to decline in the late 1960s. According to our calculation (table 9.1) for the average of the major advanced capitalist countries, the rate of profit overall falls by about one quarter for the business sector as a whole between 1968 and 1973, and one third for manufacturing. For the business sector well over

Table 9.1   *Components of declines in profitability: 1960s to 1973*

	Business			Manufacturing		
	Peak[a]	1973	1973 as % of peak	Peak	1973	1973 as % of peak
	Profit rates per cent[b]					
ACC[c]	16.9	12.5	0.74	27.1	18.9	0.70
US	14.9	9.2	0.62	36.4	21.9	0.60
EED[d]	17.9	12.1	0.68	17.4	10.5	0.60
Japan	45.7	27.7	0.60	46.8	28.0	0.60
	Profit shares per cent[b]					
ACC[c]	19.6	16.2	0.83	22.3	18.5	0.83
US	15.4	11.4	0.74	22.2	16.4	0.74
EEC[d]	25.5	19.3	0.76	21.8	15.3	0.70
Japan	32.3	21.9	0.68	39.4	29.3	0.74
	Capital–output ratio[e]					
ACC[c]	1.16	1.30	0.89	0.82	0.98	0.84
US	1.03	1.24	0.83	0.61	0.75	0.81
EEC[d]	1.42	1.60	0.89	1.25	1.46	0.86
Japan	0.71	0.79	0.90	0.84	1.04	0.81

Source: Glyn, Andrew, 1982, 'Data on profitability, capital accumulation and state spending advanced capitalist countries 1952–78' printout.
[a] The year from which the decline in profitability is measured is the peak for the country or block, that is: ACC – business 1968, manufacturing 1966, US – 1966, Europe – 1960, Japan – business 1970, manufacturing – 1969.
[b] Net of capital consumption.
[c] Canada, Japan, US, France, Germany, Italy, UK. Figures for business exclude Italy.
[d] France, Germany, Italy, UK. Figures for business exclude Italy.
[e] Net capital stock divided by net output at current prices.

half the decline in profitability is accounted for by a declining profit share, but a falling output–capital ratio still plays a significant role; for manufacturing the two are equally important.

The profit squeeze
Of these two components, falling profit share and falling output–capital ratio, the first – the notorious profit squeeze – has received more attention. It is important to know whether it reflected a slower growth of productivity or faster growth of living standards, or an increase in tax taken by the government.

Table 9.2 is addressed to this question. It shows that, for the advanced capitalist countries as a whole, the profit squeeze reflected an acceleration in the growth of take-home pay. Average labour productivity growth did slow down a bit, but this did not imply a slower growth of consumption for there was a fall in the growth of

Table 9.2 *Productivity, real wages and profit squeeze: annual average change per cent*

	Product-ivity	External terms of trade	'Internal terms of trade'	Tax	'Warrant-ed' post-tax real wage	Actual post-tax real wage	Share of wages
	(1)	(2)	(3)	(4)	(5)	(6)	(6)–(5)
ACC[a]							
1960–68	3.9	0	0.2	−0.4	3.7	3.5	−0.2
68–73	3.4	0	0.6	−0.4	3.6	4.4	0.8
73–75	−0.2	−0.6	0.5	−0.4	−0.7	2.0	2.7
75–78	2.8	−0.1	−0.1	−0.5	2.1	1.8	−0.3
EEC[b]							
1960–68	3.9	0.1	0.2	−1.0	3.2	3.7	0.5
68–73	4.2	0	0.8	−0.3	4.7	5.4	0.7
73–75	1.0	−0.7	0.5	−1.3	−0.5	2.8	3.3
75–78	3.4	0.1	−0.2	−1.0	2.3	1.3	−1.0
US							
1960–66	3.1	0	0.2	−0.1	3.2	2.5	−0.7
66–73	1.2	0	0.5	−0.6	1.1	1.7	0.6
73–75	−1.3	−0.5	0.5	0.4	−0.9	0.7	1.6
75–78	1.4	−0.2	0.4	−0.9	0.7	0.1	−0.6
Japan							
1960–70	9.7	0	−0.6	0	9.1	9.5	0.4
70–73	7.0	−0.2	0	−0.7	6.1	11.0	4.9
73–75	0.9	−1.4	−0.2	−1.0	−1.7	2.9	4.6
75–78	4.7	0.3	−1.8	−0.3	2.9	3.8	0.9

Sources: As table 9.1 plus OECD *National Accounts* 1952–78, Vols I and II, *Economic Outlook*, December 1981, Reference Statistics.
(1) GDP per person employed.
(2) External terms of trade measures effect of relative rise of import prices on purchasing power of domestic incomes.
(3) Internal terms of trade measures effect of rise of consumer prices relative to prices of total output on purchasing power of domestic incomes.
(4) Tax measures effect of burden of tax (direct and indirect) on take-home incomes.
(5) Warranted post-tax wages is increase which will leave share of profits constant given productivity, terms of trade effects and tax, i.e. the sum of columns (1) to (4).
[a] Canada, US, Japan, France, Germany and UK.
[b] UK, France and Germany.

the price of consumer goods compared to the rest of production. Taxation took a slightly higher share of incomes each year, but the tax take rose no faster than in the earlier part of the boom. Whilst the room for increased living standards hardly changed, actual post-tax real wage and salary incomes are estimated to have accelerated by a full percentage point a year, and a good deal more than that in Europe.

It would be tempting to attribute the profit squeeze in a causal sense to this faster growth in take-home pay, with the well known development of worker militancy being the underlying cause. Marxists have been no less ready than others to argue that workers can bargain in real terms. But if the increased militancy is not to be dissipated in faster inflation there must be some factor restraining the employers' ability to raise prices.

Lack of demand is one possible candidate, emphasised by Bob Rowthorn in particular. But surely it is not a plausible explanation for the late 1960s and early 1970s. A reduced degree of monopoly, following Kalecki, but emphasising international rather than national competition has also been suggested (Glyn and Sutcliffe [9]). The equalisation of productivity levels amongst the advanced countries and the increasing trade and foreign investment flows are consistent with this view. But one would have expected this pressure to be reflected more sharply in the exposed manufacturing sector than for business as a whole. This is arguably the case for the EEC countries, but not for the rest.

The profit squeeze, certainly in the EEC and Japan, reflects labour shortage. Over-accumulation of capital in relation to the labour supply leads to a faster bidding up of product wages, that is, money wages in relation to output prices. This ensures accelerated scrapping, a faster transfer of labour to the new means of production to make up the balance not provided by additions to the labour force. Whilst excessive demands *by* labour can be absorbed, for a time at least, by accelerating inflation, excess demand *for* labour is only eliminated by rising real wages. This is not to say that the rise in real wages must be a smooth process, or that it cannot be frustrated by excess demand for commodities driving inflation up, but it at least constitutes a strong tendency.

Over-accumulation must reflect a combination of three factors: (a) an accelerating tempo of accumulation; (b) a decreasing growth rate of the labour force; and (c) a decreasing growth of capital–labour ratio in new means of production (so that a given rate of accumulation represents an accelerating pace of demand for additional labour).

The data do not allow a very precise disentangling of these possibilities. For the advanced capitalist countries as a whole the rate of accumulation reached its peak around 1966–7 and was sustained right up to 1973. Total civil employment (shown in chart 9.2) barely slowed down; nor did the supply of wage labourers, since the number of wage and salary earners rose by 2 per cent a year between 1960 and 1967, and 1.9 per cent a year between 1967 and 1973. So, looking at the balance between the overall rate of accumulation and the growth of the proletariat, it was accumulation that reached its peak, rather than the growth rate of employment that declined.

Finally there is the intriguing possibility that the newly accumulated means of production were more labour intensive, that is, involving a more slowly increasing capital–labour ratio. This could be a sectoral effect (a twisting of the pattern of accumulation towards sectors with a lower capital–labour ratio). But if productivity gains achievable by increasing the capital–labour ratio were diminishing as EEC and Japanese productivity levels began to approach American standards, then capital intensification may have been slowing. Lags in the response of new technology to the labour shortage would be consistent with this story.

In Japan, for which we have carried out a detailed analysis, the period 1967–73 saw the pattern of accumulation twisted towards sectors of low technical composition (capital–labour ratio). This increased the demand for labour implied by the accumulation rate (as compared with a balanced pattern of growth) by around $\frac{1}{2}$–1 per cent a year – not a huge amount, but not entirely negligible all the same.

It is impossible to obtain independent evidence for the hypothesis of a decline in the rate of mechanisation within sectors (as expressed in the growth of the capital–labour ratio on new equipment). It is striking, however, that the rate of productivity growth did *not* accelerate in the late 1960s and early 1970s. A higher rate of accumulation and faster growth of product wages 'should' have led to a *faster* process of scrapping and thus an *acceleration* of productivity growth as the average age of means of production *in use* was reduced.

For the major advanced capitalist countries as a group, productivity growth slowed down slightly in the early 1970s, despite an increase in the growth of the measured capital–labour ratio and an acceleration of the growth rate of product wages. In manufacturing the pattern was the same (table 9.3). In Europe the early 1970s were not very different from the 1960s in respect of accumulation, productivity or profitability trends, though the faster growth of product wages in manufacturing must have speeded up rationalisation. In the US productivity growth in manufacturing did not rise despite accelerated growth of the capital–labour ratio, whilst for the economy as a whole productivity growth slumped. So in relation to capital accumulation the slow-down in productivity includes manufacturing (see Baily [1] and Nosworthy *et al.* [19]). The really striking case is Japan, where a substantial acceleration in the measured growth of capital–labour ratio and of product wages coincided with a slowing down of overall productivity growth. Manufacturing productivity growth (per hour) also fell. This is the strongest indication

Table 9.3   *Productivity, the capital–labour ratio and product wages: annual average change per cent*

	ACC[a]	US	Japan	EEC[a]
		Business		
Productivity per worker				
1960–9	3.8	2.4	9.6	4.0
69–73	3.4	1.4	7.8	4.2
73–8	1.6	0.3	3.1	2.5
78–81	1.2	0	3.6	2.3
Capital–labour ratio				
1960–9	3.4	1.8	9.5	4.8
69–73	4.1	2.0	12.7	5.0
73–8	3.3	1.1	7.9	4.5
		Manufacturing		
Productivity (per hour)				
1960–9	6.2	3.2	10.6	5.6
69–73	5.4	3.2	8.6	5.1
73–8	3.6	1.6	6.1	3.8
78–81	3.2	1.3	5.4	2.7
Capital–labour ratio				
1960–9	3.2	0.5	10.3	5.4
69–73	5.1	2.8	12.7	5.2
73–8	4.4	1.2	8.8	4.7
Product wages				
1960–9	6.2	3.1	11.6	6.0
69–73	6.3	3.5	12.6	6.9
73–8	4.2	1.6	8.3	4.8

Sources: As table 9.1 plus Capdevielle and Alvarez [4].
[a] For definitions see table 9.1.

that accumulation may not have been yielding such substantial productivity gains.

There is no lack of alternative explanations of course; one is that the failure of productivity growth to rise was associated with increased worker resistance to further increases in the speed and intensity of the labour process. Such an explanation fits in well with the wage explosions of the same period.

Rising organic composition at last?

The falling output–capital ratio at the end of the 1960s seems at first sight to be an example of Marx's rising organic composition of capital in the course of accumulation. Admittedly Marx's own formulation compares capital in the form of materials and machinery (constant capital) to the outlay of wages (variable capital). But modern discussions of the 'law of the tendency of the rate of profit to fall' (for example Van Parys), have emphasised that it is rather the ratio of the value of constant capital to the value of output which better captures the limits to profitability set by increasing mechanisation. The capital –output ratio is an indicator in price terms of this value (labour–time) ratio and can be expected to move broadly parallel with it.

Even if this interpretation is adopted, the conclusion that rising organic composition is a causal factor in the falling rate of profit has to be framed very carefully. What can be said is that, given the rise in the technical composition of capital (capital–labour ratio), if the productivity of labour had risen faster, and in particular if it had risen as fast as technical composition, then the output–capital ratio would not have fallen. This would have bolstered the rate of profit. So again, there is the suggestion that productivity was not increasing as fast as it 'should have' done if mechanisation had continued to have the same impact on productivity, as earlier in the 1960s. Accumulation continued at the same or an accelerated rate overall, but the possibilities for profitably increasing mechanisation at the same pace seem to have slowed down. The effect was a declining profit share as scrapping increased (the slower rise in mechanisation intensifying the demand for labour) and a falling output–capital ratio as the accumulation yielded smaller productivity gains. The fundamental idea behind Marx's law of the tendency of the rate of profit to fall, that accumulation yields insufficient productivity gains to maintain profitability, could be said to apply; though in a very modified form for it was the labour shortage and rising real wages that lay at the heart of the process.

The fall in the output–capital ratio may, however, be more or less of a mirage, reflecting only accelerated scrapping, for the capital stock statistics are based on conventional, and fixed, assumptions about asset lives. If the faster rate of increase in product wages really did lead to a shortening of the length of life of equipment, then the measured growth rate of the capital stock will exaggerate the growth of the stock of means of production in use. What should show as increased capital consumption and a fall in the profit share appears as a fall in the output–capital ratio. If all the fall in the measured output–capital ratio is really due to this effect it would not signify anything about the speed of mechanisation.

This whole discussion has been highly aggregative. Taking the US, Japan and the EEC as the major blocks, tables 9.1 and 9.2 present the relevant data. The outstanding feature is that, beginning at different times, 1960 in Europe, 1966 in the US, 1970 in Japan, profit rates fell substantially by 1973. In fact the falls are of uncannily similar amounts – in the case of manufacturing to 60 per cent of the original level for each of the three blocks. The decomposition into profit share and output–capital ratios are also rather similar; in all cases the profit squeeze being considerably more important than the fall in the output–capital ratio.

It should not be inferred that identical processes were at work. In particular much, though not all, of the decline in profitability in the US is directly attributable to the decline in capacity utilisation after 1966 (see Grimm [4]). But it is to Europe and Japan that the analysis of over-accumulation is most applicable. Rapid accumulation relative to employment is clearest in Japan, where the decline in profitability was concentrated into three years after 1970. The growth rate in capital stock per hour worked in the non-agricultural business sector in Japan was nearly 12 per cent a year between 1967 and 1973 (as compared with around 2 per cent a year between 1955 and 1961).

Post 1973

1973–5 represents the transition from the feverish final period of the boom to the stagnation of the 1970s. The decline in profitability between 1973 and 1975 appears to be greater than can be explained simply by the fall in capacity utilisation (at any rate as measured in a crude way by the GNP gap). The stagnation of productivity compounded by the deterioration of the terms of trade (though this effect is not so marked except for Japan – see table 9.3), required a faster fall in the actual growth of take-home pay than could be achieved. The severity of the recession, colliding with the remnants of militant wage bargaining, seems adequate to explain the additional squeeze. In this sense the fall in profitability may in part reflect an overhang from the preceding over-accumulation; real wages had perhaps been held back below the growth rate indicated by the intensity of demand for labour by the accelerating inflation. The reversal of government policies towards restriction in 1974–5 permitted some catching-up of the real wage. The decline in the rate of profit during 1973–5, whilst obviously compounded by the oil shock, must be seen as the development of the previous trend.

Stagnation

The stagnation of the later 1970s and early 1980s is most clearly reflected in the fall in the rate of accumulation – from around $5\frac{1}{2}$ per cent in 1973–4 to $3\frac{3}{4}$ per cent in 1977–8 and perhaps $2\frac{1}{2}$-3 per cent in 1981–2; in manufacturing the decline has been steeper. Both the excess capacity and the decline in profitability have no doubt played a role; it is impossible and rather meaningless to try and separate out their individual effects.

The decrease in productivity growth since 1973 has been very marked, but is hardly surprising in relation to the excess capacity and the slow-down in accumulation (the figures for the growth of the capital–labour ratio seriously underestimate the real slow-down in a period of growing excess capacity as an increasing part of the capital stock counted in the estimates will not be in use). In addition the slowing down of the growth rate of product wages by some $1\frac{1}{2}$ per cent a year for business, and $2\frac{1}{2}$ per cent in manufacturing, played a role in delaying the scrapping of old equipment. At both ends of the spectrum of vintages – installation of new equipment and scrapping of old – the process of productivity growth has been slowed down; in addition, if we believe the circumstantial evidence for a decline in the labour productivity gains on new equipment in the early 1970s, such a process might well have continued, exacerbated by a further slowing of R and D and so forth.

The slow-down in productivity was matched by declines in the rate of growth of take-home pay. In the mid-1970s at least the profit share increased a little. It was surely a testimony to the impact of rising unemployment on workers' bargaining positions that this halving of the growth rate of real take-home pay was accomplished without accelerating inflation, but the impact of the stagnation is not entirely in the direction of stifling productivity growth.

The recession itself forces the scrapping of underutilised old plants, which would be profitable (at the existing product wage) if only demand were higher; the transfer of production to lower cost (or just more utilised) plants will increase average productivity, or at any rate reduce the drag on productivity of underutilisation of plants (see Glyn [11]). Moreover, the pressure grows from management to increase labour productivity on the more efficient plants by pushing up labour intensity. The relative strengths of capital and labour have a decisive influence here. It is very striking that in both Italy and the UK manufacturing productivity growth plummeted after 1973, but has grown faster again since 1979. The employers' offensive in both countries is rather well-known. In Germany and France, by contrast, declines in manufacturing productivity growth comparing 1969–73 and 1973–8 were negligible; since then, however, the momentum has slipped. Only in Japan has the rate of manufacturing productivity growth been maintained throughout the whole period since 1973 at a high rate, though much slower than that of the 1960s. A full study of these diverse developments has yet to be undertaken. But it is already possible to observe one rather widespread reaction on the part of management to the problems posed by stagnating productivity.

Crisis in the Organisation of Work

The central problem faced by management throughout the history of capitalism is how to make workers work. This is brilliantly conceptualised in Marx's insistence that what capitalists buy is *labour-power*, workers' capacity to work. The *labour* itself is forced out of workers, not in the market-place but on the factory floor. Marx's own analysis of modern industry (see [18], ch. 15) underlined the crucial significance of the fact that machinery could remove control over the rhythm of work from the labourer. The essence of Taylor's scientific management was, Braverman explains, the separation of the execution of work from its conception. So even in industries where the worker still controlled the machine rather than *vice versa* (metal machining was the classic example analysed by Taylor), this control was to be reduced to mechanically following a set of instructions within a time span scientifically determined as feasible. Taylorist deskilling plus mechanical control of workspeeds came together in the continuous flow production line, aptly described as the Fordist system of work organisation (see Coriat's analysis [6] and Gartman's [8] fascinating historical description).

Workers were induced to submit to Taylorist and Fordist work conditions by lack of alternative jobs, or where labour markets were tight, by premium rates of pay (Taylor's piecework bonuses, Ford's five dollars a day). But to imagine that henceforth output would be limited only by the physical possibilities of workers and machines was a fallacy. Taylor's work norms were always subject to haggling by shop stewards, thus losing their objective status. This was paralleled on the production line by bargaining over line speeds and manning levels. Organised opposition of workers weakened what Richard Edwards calls hierarchical control – based on the arbitrary power of foremen and line managers – and the technical control of work 'founded in the physical and technological aspects of production'. Individual opposition, expressed in absenteeism, a high proportion of defects and rapid labour turnover, further limited the efficiency of this system of work organisation.

The crisis of Fordism became increasingly severe as reserves of labour dried up at the end of the 1960s in both the US and, more especially, Europe. It was signalled in a famous article in *Fortune* magazine in 1970, *Blue Collar Blues*, was highlighted by the notorious revolt at General Motors' Lordstown plant in 1972 and took its most extreme form in the struggle of the Fiat workers in the late 1960s and early 1970s. Management's response was most developed in Sweden, where labour market conditions were especially tight and workers' expectations rather high. The new Volvo plant at Kalmar was based on what seemed like a revolutionary new system of work organisation replacing the production line with work groups. Conferences to explain it were organised (see [13]). Then in the mid-1970s the issue disappeared from view.

The explanation seems obvious enough. Management used the

discipline of mass unemployment to break down union opposition to their technical control (through line speeds) and hierarchical control (of shop-floor discipline). British Leyland is a classic example. *The Sunday Times* (March 21, 1982) described the 'miracle' at Longbridge where 'a marriage of men and machines has dramatically improved the productivity of BL'. This is how one Longbridge worker, transferred to five different departments in one year, and having done ten different jobs in that department in three months, described the 'miracle': 'In the past management couldn't shift you without the agreement of the union; now it's done without consultation . . . it means you never get to know any of the blokes, it breaks up any unity . . . In the old days the target was set by timing the operator, now the target is based on the 'gross potential' of the machine, that means they set the machine as fast as possible, the only limit being quality, and you have to keep up with it. They give you targets you can't reach. The gaffer comes to check your counter every hour; blokes have been suspended for failing to have an adequate explanation of why they haven't reached their target'. (*Militant*, April 23, 1982)

As well as speeding up individual work processes a central part of the drive towards greater intensity of labour is to increase labour flexibility, that is, the range of tasks the worker is called upon to undertake. Ford, for example, is bringing in a plan for production workers to carry out quality control, rectification of faults and maintenance of machinery; skilled workers are to give up demarcation lines (*Management Today*, May 1982).

It is precisely this labour flexibility which big non-union firms in the US value so highly (see [21]), and which earns Japanese firms so much envy for the pliability of their unions. Not only does this flexibility allow demanning of current production processes; possibly more importantly it clears the way for introducing new technologies in the most profitable way.

Now flexibility is difficult to organise on a very large scale. More scope for labour flexibility is provided by the division of work into chunks carried out by a group of workers – in which each worker performs a number of tasks. An enthusiast explains: 'As a manager I love that. If you look at fork lifts in traditional plants they never have more than 20 to 25 hours of running time on the clock at the end of the week. So what are the operators doing in the other 15 hours? Here we don't have that', (*Fortune*, July 27, 1981). Two developments have widened the potential for reorganisation of labour into work groups.

The traditional assembly line is too inflexible when it comes to complicated model mixes. Slight variations in the pattern of production may require considerable reorganisation and rebalancing of the production line. Where assembly is carried out by parallel work groups, adjustments can be made to the schedules of one or two of them without affecting the rest.

Extra fixed capital costs are incurred as individual pieces of machinery may not be able to be used with such intensity by the teams (Hopwood mentions typical increases of 10–30 per cent), and stocks of materials are increased. But these costs are typically offset by reductions in labour costs resulting from the extra flexibility with which the labour is used. As well as complexity of model mixes, the increasing use of computer controlled machinery in manufacturing processes, calling for workers to 'baby-sit equipment' as *Business Week* puts it, also seems to have increased the possibilities for profitable introduction of work groups.

A typical example of reorganisation into groups is reported from Chevrolet's gear plant in Detroit – 'While a worker might have stood in one place all day tightening bolts on a rear brake assembly, he is now responsible with other team members for the production and quality of an entire brake system' (*Fortune*, July 27, 1981). This reorganisation is part of GM's Quality of Work Life Program whose 'salient feature from the managerial point of view', writes Michael Piore, is 'flexible job assignments'.

So work groups seem to be increasingly feasible for organising technically efficient production within which labour flexibility is maximised. Wages are often increased to pay for upgrading or to buy the labour flexibility – increases of 10–20 per cent are mentioned as typical by Hopwood. But direct labour requirements are frequently drastically cut (10–40 per cent) and overtime reduced. Supervision costs are slashed (25–50 per cent) and reductions reported in scrap, wastage and reject rates and in inventories of goods waiting to be checked. Hopwood says that reports of such schemes indicate productivity improvements in half the cases, cost improvements in one third and improvements in quality, labour turnover and absenteeism in about one fifth each. Such detailed studies as are available, he says, confirm the 'economic potentiality of work reorganisation programmes'. They represent a new, less splintered division of labour, implemented in conditions in which trade unions are in a weak position to resist resulting job losses. The central point is that each worker performs more work. The fact that it is more varied is a by-product. But do they represent a new system of labour control?

Richard Edwards distinguishes three elements of a system of labour control. These are the *direction* of work, what needs to be done and how quickly; the *evaluation* of work, to correct defects and identify those responsible for inadequate work; and *discipline*, the mechanism used to enforce compliance with work standards.

In all these respects, work groups appear to involve some degree of movement away from the hierarchical (arbitrary authority of the foreman) and technical (determination of work pace through machine speeds) systems of control. As far as *direction* of the work is concerned work groups may have considerable flexibility in allocating work tasks amongst members, in deciding the pattern of work during a day, and so forth. The crucial point, however, is that this autonomy is entirely within the work norms and targets set by the management. Granting workers such self-direction in detailed matters appears to cost management little or nothing and may save on supervisory costs. The groups typically carry out the function of *evaluation* by checking the work itself for quality; workers operating below par will be obvious to the rest of the group who may be obliged to make up the difference themselves through rectification, for example. The saving in costs of supervision and rectification are clear. As for *discipline*, workers performing below par at work, or frequently absent, will be under pressure from other group members, especially when bonuses are organised on a group basis. In one small, non-union plant, *Business Week* (11 May, 1981) reported that team members 'even initiate discharges if necessary'. Encouraging team members to acquire a range of skills, on which pay structures and perhaps promotions are based, also helps to bind the worker to the individual firm especially when the range of skills is firm-specific. The benefits to employers of organising worker self-discipline are obvious; it may be not only more effective but it is also free. It seems likely that a substantial part of the 'economic potentiality of work reorganisation programmes' comes precisely from its more effective system of labour control. Workers perform more work, and (ideally speaking) they themselves ensure that this continues.

In cases where work groups cover whole departments, with a definable cost structure, attempts are sometimes made to represent them as separate businesses which set their own goals 'and whose members are responsible to each other for the success of the business', as one GM executive put it (quoted by Batt and Weinberg[2]). This is of course pure ideology. Basing bonuses on team output no more makes a business out of the team than piecework makes workers self-employed. But there is an important way in which the market is used to ensure that work groups do perform the function of work evaluation effectively. Faults which do get through can be readily traced to the group concerned. Having switched from assembly line to team assembly, the expensive ranges of Raleigh bicycles are now sent out bearing the name of the skilled craftsman in charge of the team. By personalising the product, the market is brought into the factory as a direct discipline on the individual groups of workers. Changing the organisation of clerical work so that one worker has responsibility for individual customers' accounts, instead of performing detail operations, has the same intent (see Pignon and Querzola [20]).

As well as reorganising the structure of work through work teams, a vogue has recently emerged for a new form of worker-management participation – Quality Circles. Small groups of workers meet to discuss, analyse and solve detailed production problems. Apparently 750 US companies and government bodies (*Fortune*) and 100 firms in Britain (*Personnel Management*) had set up Quality Circles by 1981; improvements in lay-out and design of equipment, design of products and modification to tasks and working practices have been widely reported. A more comprehensive scheme of employee involvement in the reorganisation of one GM plant was reported by the management as being 'entirely positive' from the point of view of costs. There is a certain irony in management, whose philosophy has been to 'deskill our workforce' (in the words of one American executive) suddenly discovering 'this huge resource of knowledge and skill which resides in every workforce' (as a management consultant, admittedly with an interest in the matter, put it). However, as an American trade unionist pointed out, Quality Circles give 'workers no real transfer of power over their work environment'. *Management Today's* correspondent, in response to this comment, noted (March 1982) that', it is precisely this feature which explains the noisy QC bandwagon'. One enthusiastic manager told *Fortune*, 'The workers know that if I feel there's no payback to the company in the solution they arrive at, there will be a definite no. I'm not here to give away the store or run a country club' (27 July, 1981). The wholly negative response of the management of Lucas Aerospace to the Combine Committee's alternative plan for the company, involving the substitution of socially useful for military production, is instructive. Even in cases where there *would* be a payback to the company, management would have no truck with suggestions which transgressed the absolute prerogative of management to determine all essential elements of corporate strategy.

Business Week and *Fortune* have recently (Summer 1981) featured major articles heralding 'smarter work' involving 'participative options and a new industrial relations system' with the object of ending 'the adversarial relationship' between labour and capital. Both have traced the development of Quality Circles and work teams as deriving from the human relations school of industrial management. But there seems no reason to attribute any significant part of the productivity gains which result from these initiatives to the positive effects of employee involvement, rather than the pressure exerted through fear of plant closures and through more effective labour control.

The famous Hawthorne experiments in the 1920s into the determinants of labour productivity are regarded as the founding step of the 'human relations school'. Macarov ([17], p67), however, quotes a recent re-evaluation of these experiments which concluded that 79 per cent of the improvement was due to managerial discipline, 14 per cent to the onset and continuation of the depression and hardly anything to the human relations factors of feeling important and partici ating in decisions. seems very likely that a post-mortem on current developments in work organisation will come to similar conclusions.

It is also essential to bear in mind the context of the Japanese experience which is so frequently taken as a model (Ford's programme for labour flexibility i. called 'After Japan'). Whilst making due allowance for cultural u ad..ion, an essential component of the Japanese success in manufacturing was the systematic destruction of the independent trade union movement and its replacement by wholly pro-management unions; these function as an adjunct of the industrial relations department to stifle any workers' opposition (see Halliday [15] and Glyn [10]). Whatever the setbacks suffered by the labour movement in Europe and the US over the years since 1973 it has not been smashed. When the economic situation improves a little, or even stops deteriorating at the present breakneck pace, the pressure against rationalisation, whether by old-fashioned speed-up, or by work groups or through Quality Circles, will mount. Work groups of course involve a further risk for management; they naturally lead to demands for an extension of the field of control.

Fortune makes a significant comment on how management has reacted to the crisis by, above all, focussing attention . . . 'on how goods and services are *actually produced* – a basic concern that has been sloughed aside to an astonishing degree by a generation of executives pre-occupied with finance, marketing, strategic redeployment . . . (15 June, 1981). The conditions for profitable accumulation could possibly be re-established, through the implementation of new technologies and methods of work organisation. It is quite a different proposition to suppose that they could be sustained once the reserve army of labour began to shrink.

References
[1] Baily, M., 'Productivity and the Services of Labour and Capital', *Brookings Papers on Economic Activity* 1, 1981.
[2] Batt, W.L. and Weinberg, E., 'Labour Management Co-operation Today', *Harvard Business Review*, January–February, 1978.

[3]   Braverman, Harry, *Labour and Monopoly Capital*, New York, 1972.
[4]   Capdevielle, P. and Alvarez, D., 'International Comparisons of Trends in Productivity and Labour Costs', *Monthly Labour Review*, December, 1981.
[5]   Cooper, C.L. and Mumford E. (eds.) *The Quality of Working Life in Western and Eastern Europe*, London, 1979.
[6]   Coriat, B., 'The Restructuring of the Assembly Line', *Capital and Class*, no. 11, Summer, 1980.
[7]   Edwards, R., *Contested Terrain*, London, 1979.
[8]   Gartman, D., 'Origins of the Assembly Line and Capitalist Control of Work at Fords', in Zimbalist.A.(ed.), *Case Studies in the Labour Process*, New York, 1979.
[9]   Glyn, A. and Sutcliffe, R., *British Capitalism, Workers and the Profit Squeeze*, London, 1972.
[10] Glyn, A., 'Profitability and Capital Accumulation in Japan 1945–61', 1981.
[11] Glyn, A., 'Wages and Unemployment', mimeo, 1982.
[12] Glyn, A., 'Data on Profitability, Capital Accumulation and State Spending Advanced Capitalist Countries 1952–78', printout, 1982.
[13] Gregory, D. (ed.) *Work Organisation*, London, 1978.
[14] Grimm, B.T. 'Domestic Non-financial Corporate Profits', *Survey of Current Business*, January 1982.
[15] Halliday, J., *A Political History of Japanese Capitalism*, New York, 1974.
[16] Hopwood, A., 'Towards an economic assessment of new forms of work organisation' in Cooper and Mumford (eds.)
[17] Macarov, D., *Worker Productivity*, Beverly Hills, 1982.
[18] Marx, K. *Capital*, Volume 1.
[19] Nosworthy, J.R. Harper, M.J., Kunze, K. 'The Slowdown in Productivity Growth' *Brookings Papers on Economic Activity*, 2, 1979.
[20] Pignon, D. Querzola, J. 'Dictatorship and Democracy in Production' in *The Division of Labour*, A. Gorz (ed.), Brighton, 1976.
[21] Piore, M., 'American Labour and the Industrial Crisis' *Challenge*, March/April, 1982.
[22] Rollei, M., 'Taylorism and the Italian Unions' in Cooper and Mumford (eds.)
[23] Rowthorn, R., *Capitalism, Conflict and Inflation*, London, 1980.
[24] Van Parys, P., 'The Falling Rate of Profit Theory of Crisis', *Review of Radical Political Economics*, Spring, 1980.

Comment on Chapter 9 *
I *G.C. Wenban-Smith*

My comments are based partly on detailed statistics, and partly on a sample survey I recently carried out on behalf of the National Institute. They suggest that Andrew Glyn's remarks on 'the employers'

---

* Andrew Glyn's paper differed from others in this volume, first in devoting a substantial amount of attention (in its latter pages) to the period 1979–81, and secondly in its theoretical approach. Two comments were therefore invited.

Table 9.4 *Output, employment and productivity growth in UK manufacturing industry: 1968–73, 1973–9 and 1979–81: annual average percentage changes*

	Output	Employment	Productivity
1968 II – 73 II	2.9	−1.1	4.0
1973 II – 79 II	−0.7	−1.6	0.9
1979 II – 81 IV	−6.9	−7.4	0.6
1979 II – 80 IV	−11.1	−6.8	−4.7
1980 IV – 81 IV	−0.1	−8.3	9.0

Table 9.5 *Annual growth rates – Output, employment and productivity, UK manufacturing industries, 1979 II –1981 IV: annual average percentage changes*

	Output		Employment		Productivity	
	1979 II − 80 IV	1980 IV − 81 IV	1979 II − 80 IV	1980 IV − 81 IV	1979 II − 80 IV	1980 IV − 81 IV
Food, drink, tobacco	−0.7	−2.2	−2.4	−5.9	1.7	3.9
Coal and petroleum products, chemicals	−9.8	3.3	−3.8	−6.4	−6.2	10.4
Metal manufacture, metal goods n.e.s.	−22.2	6.4	−10.1	−11.6	−13.5	20.4
Mechanical eng.	−11.0	−3.2	−7.4	−10.8	−4.0	8.6
Instr. and elect. eng.	−3.7	1.3	−5.3	−8.4	1.7	10.6
Shipbuilding, vehicles	−12.7	−0.4	−6.0	−10.2	−7.1	10.9
Textiles, leather, clothing	−17.8	−2.1	−10.7	−6.5	−7.9	4.8
Other manufacturing	−10.7	−3.2	−6.3	−6.0	−4.8	3.0
All manufacturing	−11.0	−0.2	−6.8	−8.3	−4.6	8.8

offensive' and recent net investment do not tell the whole story.

The growth rates of output, employment and productivity in UK manufacturing industry for the three periods (a) 1968–73, (b) 1973–9 and (c) 1979–81 are summarised in table 9.4. It can be seen that between periods (a) and (b) manufacturing industry as a whole experienced a sharp reduction in output growth. This reduction also occurred in every SIC Order level industry. Employment fell relatively less, with the result that in every industry productivity growth fell. An examination of these changes at Minimum List Heading industry level (115 industries) found a significant correlation between the slow-down in productivity growth and the reduction in output growth, but failed to detect any other significant relation [2].

Although output growth declined further after 1979 in every industry, in contrast to the previous period productivity growth improved in some industries, such as food, drink and tobacco and electrical engineering. Deterioration in other industries, however, led to a further slowing of the manufacturing productivity growth rate as a whole. A subdivision of the last period at the fourth quarter of 1980 exposes the productivity 'boom' (bottom of table 9.4 and table 9.5) and reveals that the experiences of different industries varied considerably; food, drink and tobacco, for example, maintained a steady improvement over the two and a half years, whereas the turn-round in metal industries productivity growth was +34 percentage points – this was a change in the right direction, it is true, but it is hardly to be expected that anything like this rate will be maintained.

Evidence from sample surveys suggests that companies have in recent years been investing almost solely to increase efficiency and/or to replace old machines and that there is now considerable spare capacity in those plants which have survived the recession. Nearly all companies responding to a recent National Institute survey [3] reported increased capital deepening; cost increases had speeded up the adaptation of production methods to incorporate more up-to-date technology. An additional effect of the cost increases of fuel and raw materials had been to enforce more efficient overall operation; no company reported that labour productivity had fallen because of lower energy use or reduced raw material inputs (in apparent contrast to the substitution effect implied by neoclassical economics and calculated by Professor Bruno [1]). The consequence of these changes was that an increase in output today could be met by most companies with a much smaller increase in employment than would have been the case ten years earlier, before the latest wave of investment and reorganisation of work methods had taken place. It seems from the survey as though manufacturing industry does not anticipate contributing much to solving the immediate unemployment problem.

As for future prospects, it seems likely that 'the employers' offensive' was a delayed response to the events of the mid- and late-1970s and that the labour productivity gains which were realised had been made possible by past investment in plant and machinery. Few of the companies surveyed expected that future productivity growth would be as high as in 1981, especially without a revival in output, and it is hardly to be expected that even a general expansion of demand would assist those which are basically uncompetitive in costs or quality. On the other hand, the survey did not provide evidence to suggest that the pre-1973 underlying rate of labour productivity growth had changed.

References
[1] Bruno, M., several papers including chapter 6 of this volume.
[2] Wenban-Smith, G.C., 'A study of the movements of productivity in individual industries in the United Kingdom, 1968–1979', *National Institute Economic Review*, no. 97, August 1981.
[3] Wenban-Smith, G.C., 'Factors influencing productivity growth – report of a survey', *National Institute Economic Review*, No. 101, August 1982.

Comment on Chapter 9
II *S.J. Prais*

I welcome Mr Glyn's paper for the opportunity it provides for looking at our problem from a broader, longer-term and very different point of view; even if, at times, a 'through the looking-glass' point of view.

While welcoming the opportunity, I must at the outset also say why I have not found it easy to prepare this comment. First, the conceptual apparatus and language is strange; but, it might be said, so is that of the many other sectaries of economists today who each lives in an almost private world of discourse. We have become accustomed to a new Babel in which one person barely 'understands the speech of another'. The curse of misunderstanding led to the collapse of that Tower and, as we are told, of the Civilisation which gave birth to it. The avoidance of misunderstanding, and the advance of understanding, always require of us an effort, which we must not shirk – not least in scientific matters. Is it scientifically accurate, or in any way useful, to describe our economic system as one in which, as Mr Glyn puts it, 'labour is forced out of workers on the factory floor'? What happens, one wonders, on the factory floor in Communist countries? And in which countries are workers able to organise themselves in trade unions and, when dissatisfied, strike against their employers or against Society as a whole? I give this as an example of the questions that passed through one reader's mind while trying to understand this paper. Nevertheless, I believe we must be grateful to Mr Glyn for drawing attention to what are, I agree, very important aspects of our problem.

The second difficulty I have had to face is a more general one. If economists had been agreed on which factors had been responsible for the growth in output per head in the past century or even, say, in the two decades until 1973, we might reasonably ask them to say which of those factors has changed (or which new factors have intervened), and what could be done about it. But what have we learnt from the past? Researchers have tried to evaluate the quantitative contribution to economic growth of changes in the capital stock, education and technology, the scale and specialisation of production, and much else; but at the end of the day a large residual remains. Not only that, but much doubt attaches to the estimated contributions of the specified factors. Education may serve as an example. The introduction of compulsory schooling, and the progressive raising of the school leaving age over the past century, make it attractive to take the number of years of full-time schooling per head of population as a simple quantitative measure of education; but in comparing productivity levels and their recent rates of change in advanced countries, little relation can be found with this measure of education.

The reason perhaps is, as a paper by Anne Daly suggests [1], that from the point of view of the productivity of advanced economies we need today to be less concerned with the quantity of education than with its content and quality: how much of it is vocationally-oriented, and how much of it is designed to get the pupil to prescribed *standards* – rather than provide him with inchoate generalised *'learning experiences'*. Some signs of a return to reality can be descried in a recent British House of Commons Committee report on secondary schooling. With all the joy to be gained from rediscovering the wheel, it commends a move amongst British educationists towards what is now called 'criterion referencing': this is nothing more than the earlier system of graded tests based on prescribed standards of achievement [2]. The German system of day-a-week vocational education for 16–19 year olds, with tests in theory and practice at the end of the course, may total only 0.6 years per person; but I have no doubt that it is more effective in raising productivity than the full extra final year spent in full-time compulsory schooling in Britain (there is also an extra initial year in Britain, making a total of two years extra compulsory full-time schooling compared with Germany!).

Difficulties of measurement of this kind, combined with long lags in response, seem so far to have inhibited the success of 'growth-accounting' based on aggregate economic inputs. We are therefore driven back to more general, if more debatable, assessments of the long-term consequences of economic and social developments. Mr Glyn's paper has drawn attention to the declining rate of profit, the growth in capital intensity, and changing employer–employee relations; and, if I have understood correctly, we are to infer that changes in growth rates are related to these factors. Interestingly enough, in a seminar held two years ago on the theme of declining industrial profits, elements of a similar argument were put forward from a very different point of view by Professor Maynard, previously Deputy Chief Economic Adviser to HM Treasury. The seminar was held under the auspices of HM Government, and the proceedings were published by HMSO in a book (see [3]). The book-cover spoke, on the one hand, of those who believed the decline 'heralded the collapse of the capitalist system'; on the other hand, it noted that 'the papers of these distinguished economists . . . offered no agreed interpretation of evidence, or view on effects and cure'. That, presumably, was meant to reassure us (perhaps similar comfort will in due course be drawn from the present book).

Professor Maynard was quite explicit. The rise in trade union bargaining power, and the acquiesence of government policy, have led to a rise in the share of wages and a decline in profits; investment would have fallen, but was maintained by excessive tax allowances on both fixed assets and stocks. In that way the rise in unemployment was deferred. The anticipated labour-saving effects of modern machinery were not reaped because of restrictive labour practices. Advances in productivity were increasingly limited by the rise in union power. Essentially, it seems to me, there is agreement between this view and that of the paper before us.

But why is it that the slow-down has become apparent particularly in the past decade? The right of employees to join together to strike, and to cause inconvenience and damage, is now accepted in all 'Western' countries as a matter of elementary justice, and incorporated as a basic human right in international conventions; at the beginning of the century it was regarded as an unlawful conspiracy in respect of which the Courts could award damages. While there has been a complete *volte face* on the legal position, to which precise dates can be attached, yet there have been long lags, varying from country to country, between the granting of greater powers to trade unions, and the full-bodied exercise of those powers. Similarly, contracts of employment are now legally restricted such that no one who sees to employing another for a limited period dare do so without worrying as to the long-term obligations imposed by law. The contract cannot be terminated without the employer having 'good reasons', and he must be prepared to argue them before a tribunal. The full effects of the changes brought about by the Acts of 1971 and

1975 on the ability of management to manage – and equally on the willingness to become an employer – are likely to take many years before they are fully manifest. Mr Glyn has rightly noted the important effect of changes in 'the economic situation' (that is, the rate of unemployment) on the rate at which unions exercise their powers. Timing may depend too much on unpredictable accidents of political history, and it may be more important to concern ourselves with the long-term trend – as I think Mr Glyn implies – than with the precise timing.

I should finally like to offer some remarks on the economic basis of the changes in 'work organisation' to which the second half of Mr Glyn's chapter is devoted. The remarkable feature of the rise of American manufacturing was the extent to which it was able to push the division of labour, while relying on European immigrants of whom only a minority were craftsmen – and a majority of whom were more familiar with life on a farm than in a mechanised factory. The task of the manager was to divide the work into as many simple, 'short cycle', operations as possible; the great size and uniformity of the American market did the rest. That recipe for efficiency was of course also applied in other countries as they industrialised, that is, as the workforce moved from agriculture into industry. But we must remember that the optimal pattern of labour division depends on the capability of the labour force – not only on the *average* capability, but also on the *dispersion* of capabilities – and on the nature of available techniques. Since both the capability of the workforce and techniques have changed, it is to be expected that the optimal division of responsibilities should also change. Routine simple 'mechanical' operations no longer require a human operator, but can be handled by an automated machine: the 'operator' now does much of what a chargehand used to do – he checks that all is working well, he takes away the finished goods, and occasionally loads a fresh batch of raw materials. Hence we see a variety of moves towards the sharing of responsibility for the quality of work, as Mr Glyn has noted.

It is worth spending a moment here to elaborate on the broad nature of those technical changes, and their bearing on wage differentials; in turn, that will help to make clearer the increased difficulties now faced by firms in raising productivity, and it bears also on the generally greater problem today of achieving full employment. The point can be made most simply by notionally dividing recent technical progress into a phase of mechanisation followed by (but in reality partly overlapping with) a phase of automation. When a process is mechanised, work previously done by skilled craftsmen by hand is done by a machine: a few skilled workers are required to make tools which are then operated by a great many unskilled workers. The demand for unskilled workers in this phase increases more than for skilled workers; consequently, the relative wages of unskilled workers rises (supporting the tendency towards egalitarianism).

All this is familiar; the contrasting economic consequences of the subsequent phase of automation are perhaps less familiar. In this phase the routine work of the unskilled operator is eliminated; the demand for unskilled workers thus tends to fall, while demand increases for those highly skilled in modern techniques and also for those with a broad range of intermediate skills (broader, it must be said, than those of traditional British craftsmen who have mostly been given narrow 'on-the-job' training). In this phase the relative wages of the unskilled need to fall again; but that tendency is inhibited by the general inflexibility of wages, and by the large unions of unskilled workers who had become accustomed to previous trends favouring a narrowing of differentials.

If we are looking for a further reason for the slowing of productivity growth, it seems plausible – I doubt whether we can put it more strongly – that technical progress in the 1970s was characterised by a preponderance of advances in automation rather than in mechanisation, with all the difficulties in the release and re-absorption of unskilled labour that this implies.

There are clear long-term implications for training policy. But, as economists, we must also note that optimum use of the *existing* stock of skills requires that relative wage rates reflect relative scarcities. If differentials are too low, employers will prefer to employ experienced persons, and leave inexperienced and unskilled youngsters without jobs. Equally youngsters will see little point in undertaking training, if skill differentials do not provide adequate incentives.

In brief, I believe serious practical problems remain to be solved in work-organisation and in the balance of work-responsibilities if industry is to make the best use of the present-day mix of skills in the labour force and of modern automated machinery. This has to be done in a context in which relative wages and job demarcation lines are more or less inflexible, depending on the particular time and place. I do not believe that the recent slowing of productivity growth is to be explained entirely by the nature of technical developments and the lag in matching skills; but I believe that they form very important parts of the story.

References

[1] Daly, Anne, 'The contribution of education to economic growth in Britain: a note on the evidence', in *National Institute Economic Review*, no. 101, August, 1982

[2] *The Secondary School Curriculum and Examinations*, House of Commons Education, Science and Arts Committee, *Report*, 1981–82, Vol. 1, p.lvi.

[3] W.E. Martin (ed.), *The Economics of the Profits Crisis* (HMSO 1981); Chapter 6 (pp. 197–218) is by Professor G.W. Maynard on 'Factors affecting profitability and employment in UK manufacturing industry 1960–78'.

Index